Electric Power in Brazil:
Entrepreneurship in the Public Sector

Electric Power in Brazil:
Entrepreneurship in the Public Sector

Judith Tendler

Harvard University Press
Cambridge, Massachusetts
1968

3 38.761
T291

To my father

There was a time, during the past two decades of intensive concern with economic development, when an economist was most likely to establish a reputation by discovering a new vicious circle, by describing how economies are apt to get caught in low-level equilibrium traps, or by showing how rich and poor countries (or regions) are fated to drift ever farther apart as a result of various processes of cumulative causation. These constructs made a vital, though dismal, contribution to our understanding: they revealed the seriousness and complexity of the development problem.

The new insights gave rise at first to a call for radical remedial measures. Underdevelopment having been diagnosed as something so multifaceted, tangled, and deep-rooted, it was often concluded that the situation called for revolution, massive redistribution of wealth and power from the rich to the poor countries, or at least coordinated attack on pervasive backwardness through highly competent central planning.

But what if none of these *dei ex machina* are available to take matters properly in hand? What if the fortress of underdevelopment, just because it is so formidable, can not be conquered by frontal assault? In that unfortunately quite common case, we need to know much more about ways in which the fortress can be surrounded, weakened by infiltration or subversion, and eventually taken by similar indirect tactics and processes. And I suggest that the major contribution to our knowledge of economic development must now come from detailed studies of such processes.

Statements about research priorities are often gratuitous; fortunately the one I have just put forward finds a full-fledged illustration in Judith Tendler's study. Its starting point, the Brazilian economy in the immediate postwar period, has all the earmarks of a low-level equilibrium trap. On the one hand, inflationary finance fueled an industrial boom. On the other, with powerful political pressures compelling a lag of regulated power rates behind the general price level, inflation impaired the profitability and hence the growth of the foreign-owned electric power industry. Electric power expansion, however, was essential to sustain the industrial boom. In these circumstances one might have predicted that the boom would be short-lived *unless* either rates could somehow be properly adjusted or the industry could be nationalized. Actually, Brazil achieved a prolonged industrial upswing without resorting to either of these "frontal assault" solutions; how this became possible is told in the following pages with a fine eye for the elusive yet critical details of socio-economic change.

The book does more, however, than document *one* particular escape from *one* of the dilemmas that time and again face countries setting out on the path to development and modernization. It offers, if not a general theory of such escapes, at least a strong hint about their typical structure. By scrutinizing the *technologies* of hydro and thermal power, as well as of generation and distribution, Miss Tendler has come up with a variety of differential characteristics of those technologies that explain a great deal about the surprising breaking of the power bottleneck in Brazil, about the curious, prolonged coexistence of private and public power, and about the unexpected and striking success of Brazil's first state ventures in power generation.

Technology (and more generally, environment) is thus cast in a novel role. Theories that show society to be wholly shaped or at least strongly influenced by climate or by the tools and "media" which man himself has fashioned are familiar through the current of social thought leading from Montesquieu via Marx to such contemporaries as Wittfogel and McLuhan. By opposing temperate to tropical climate, the feudal to the capitalist mode of production, rainfall to irrigation agriculture, or finally, the typographic to the electric age, these "macro-technological" theories cut history and the human experience in general into huge slices. As a result, everything is movement and even upheaval when a transition occurs from one slice to the other, but the room for maneuver and change is minimal during the very long stretches of historical time that lie between such transitions. The uncomfortable impression that these theories confine human freedom may therefore be due, not to their stress on the undeniable influence of technology on human and social choice, but to the excessively grand and few dichotomies that they establish between significant technological configurations.

The scene becomes far more lively and variegated once one recognizes that the number of such configurations is limited only by the ability of social scientists to detect them. To give just a few examples, it can be shown that the growing of coffee for export, the use of hydropower for energy and the development of railroad transportation exert wholly different sets of influences on social events from the growing of sugar cane, the use of thermal power, and the proliferation of trucks. The more configurations we manage to discover, the more frequently will we perceive societies in the process of effecting transitions. As a result of such a "microtechnological" approach, the study of technological influences will become predominantly the study of social change rather than of social immobility.

Along these lines, the present work shows how a specific technology permits a society to acquire new abilities and attitudes that were believed to be wholly beyond its grasp, how it lays out new options, and how it can provide positive-sum solutions to group conflict. Rather than as a force restricting human freedom technology appears here as a *liberator* from rigid models and stark dilemmas—a thread of Ariadne by which developing countries may find a way out of the labyrinth of vicious circles, low-level traps, and cumulative causations.

As Miss Tendler explains how the technology of hydropower generation performed these roles in conjunction with geography and other environmental factors at a certain stage of Brazil's development, she also demonstrates that the Brazilian solution was unique and can not easily be applied or reproduced elsewhere. But by revealing to us the many openings for economic and political change that hydropower generation brought with it in Brazil, she makes us suspect that similarly change-promoting configurations of technology must from time to time become available in other sectors and in other countries. For this reason, her study has a dual merit: in tracing the career of electric power from bottleneck to leading sector, it enhances our understanding of recent economic growth in Brazil; and it changes our general vision of the development scene by making us attentive to opportunities for progress that are embedded in apparently trivial properties of technology.

Another virtue of this book should not go unnoticed. From its first page the reader finds himself plunged into the *total* economic, social, political, and human reality of Brazil. In the course of writing what was originally her doctoral dissertation in economics, Miss Tendler was most assuredly not aware that she was in effect practicing "interdisciplinary" research. The best work of this type, so it has been said, is that which goes on within one skull; I am now tempted to add that such work is apparently further improved if it is carried on unconsciously therein.

Acknowledgments

This book grew out of a doctoral dissertation in economics. The research was carried out during 1964 and 1965, in the cities of Rio de Janeiro and São Paulo. I am most grateful to the Foreign Area Fellowship Program for its support of the research and writing of my dissertation. The program is not responsible for my information or ideas.

I would be greatly indebted to Professor Albert O. Hirschman even if he had not been the sponsor of my dissertation. Reading his work, long before I knew either him or Brazil, taught me to look where I would never have looked before for insight into a country's development. His *Strategy of Economic Development* is a preventive against the economic researcher's variety of "culture shock." Upon first encountering the frenzy of development, the researcher almost naturally backs away from his subject, seeing everything as unrelieved chaos and disorganization. A prior reading of *The Strategy* impels him into the midst of these events with the feeling that, if he is patient enough, he will find a rich complexity of both success and failure, efficiency alongside incompetence, order cohabiting with disorder.

I would like to thank Professor Donald Dewey for giving the manuscript considerable attention. His familiarity with the institutional aspects of my subject in other countries, and his willingness to discuss them with me, were important in helping me to think out my own material.

Those to whom I am most indebted are the Brazilians—and

those Americans associated with the Brazilian power sector
through international lending institutions. Because electric
power is politically explosive in Brazil, and because many of
the developments described here are still unfolding, I will not
attempt to name any of them—although most would probably
not object. It was the Brazilians who patiently led me to the
heart of their development process. They treated me with the
greatest consideration and respect. And, as anyone who has
done research in Brazil will report, they graced the task of a
year's dissertation research with charm and constant surprise.

JUDITH TENDLER

Rio de Janeiro
April 1968

Contents

Tables

Figures

Abbreviations

AID	United States Agency for International Development, Rio Mission
AMFORP	American & Foreign Power Company
BNDE	Banco Nacional de Desenvolvimento Econômico
CANAMBRA	Canada-America-Brazil: consortium of Montreal Engineering, Gibbs & Hill, G. E. Crippen Associates
CEEE	Conselho Estadual de Energia Elétrica (São Paulo)
CELUSA	Centrais Elétricas de Urubupungá, S.A.
CEMIG	Centrais Elétricas de Minas Gerais, S.A.
CESP	Centrais Elétricas de São Paulo, S.A.
CHERP	Companhia Hidrelétrica do Rio Pardo, S.A.
CHESF	Companhia Hidrelétrica do São Francisco, S.A.
CHEVAP	Companhia Hidrelétrica do Vale do Paraíba, S.A.
CNAEE	Conselho Nacional de Águas e Energia Elétrica
DAEE	Departamento de Águas e Energia Elétrica (São Paulo)
ELETROBRÁS	Centrais Elétricas Brasileiras, S.A.
FFE	Fundo Federal de Eletrificação
Furnas	Central Elétrica de Furnas, S.A.
Light	São Paulo Light and Rio Light, wholly-owned subsidiaries of the Toronto parent company, Brazilian Traction, Light and Power
USELPA	Usinas Elétricas do Paranapanema, S.A.

Electric Power in Brazil:
Entrepreneurship in the Public Sector

Introduction

The Paraíba River of south-central Brazil rises near the city of São Paulo, flows northeastward toward Rio de Janeiro, and then empties into the Atlantic a certain distance beyond that city. For years it has been the subject of multipurpose plans for control of floods and reconstruction of its eroded valley. It has even come to be called "the most studied river in Brazil" —partly in irony over the fact that none of the development schemes has ever been realized. In commenting disparagingly on this difficulty of action, an enthusiast of Paraíba planning described the sort of fate that commonly befalls state initiative in developing countries: "Almost all the problems of our country have been studied, aired, and incorporated into various plans. The plans, in turn, have been debated and brought up to date again and again. Yet in spite of all this activity, our problems live on. One begins to feel that there is a kind of inertia, a complex of resistances, a series of factors that hamper and trammel, and erect barriers in the path of our attempts to grapple with development." [1]

One of these much debated problems of Brazil was the shortage of adequate power facilities in the most industrialized region of the country. The power problems of metropolitan Rio and São Paulo were tackled in the same milieu and under the same conditions that doomed such undertakings as the one

1. Plínio Queirós, "A utilização dos recursos hidráulicos do Vale do Paraíba," *Revista do Clube de Engenharia* (July 1955), p. 49. All translations are my own, unless otherwise noted.

envisaged for the Paraíba Valley. The power problem, however, did not "live on." The state's achievement in that sector was noteworthy and merits detailed examination.[2]

The Canadian-owned Brazilian Traction, Light and Power Company is the most important power utility in Brazil and the sole distributor for the Rio-São Paulo metropolitan area, center of the country's postwar boom in economic growth. Throughout the postwar period the utility's service grew increasingly inadequate, and in the late 1950's its expansion program came to a halt. The company's principal problem was the impossibility of securing protection against inflation for the price of its product. The intractability of the rate problem, and the consequent insufficiency of supply, were largely the result of the foreign ownership of the company. "The Light," as it is called in Brazil, was the classic case of a foreign company with monopoly privileges to supply a public service. Its actions were often construed as predatory by the public and the host government, and rate increases were met with great popular resistance.

Throughout this period, however, power production demonstrated a rate of growth that was high by any standards. The increase resulted in part from an important transformation taking place in the Rio-São Paulo power supply. The government, through various federal or state companies, had started to construct its own generating plants. When the rate stalemate was finally broken in late 1964, therefore, the power problem of the region was well on its way to being solved. The expansion in power facilities that the rate increase was supposed to call forth was in fact already occurring.

Why was the power situation improving rather than worsening during a period of rate stalemate? How was the foreign utility able to continue functioning through so many years of rate inadequacy and of intense hostility between it and the

2. I use the terms "state" and "state enterprise" to include government action in the power sector at both the state and federal levels. The text makes clear the level at which each particular state power company was sponsored.

host country? What explains the agility with which the state moved into a completely new activity? What facilitated the coexistence of private and state enterprise in an industry so often marked by conflict between the private and public sector?

A constellation of circumstances accounts for the success of the Brazilian government's first venture into power, and the ability of two antagonistic sectors to coexist for a time with a degree of stability—and even to benefit from each other—as suppliers of the same market. Within that constellation I choose to emphasize here the organizational transformation of the industry. The state went into generation construction, and the vertically-integrated foreign utility began to recede into distribution. This increasing specialization was in turn made possible because of certain technological and resource characteristics of the power industry in south-central Brazil, namely, its increasing dependence on large-scale and often far-flung hydroelectric plants.

This book, then, is an exploration of how the technology of the Brazilian power sector influenced the handling of its problems. Note that my use of the word "technology" refers to the effects of a production technique already in use, rather than to the change brought about by technological innovation or adaptation. The power story in Brazil was defined and guided by both the spatial arrangement of the various suppliers and the structure of the specific task assigned to each. The technology of distribution, for example, has properties particularly suited to a company like the Light, which was uncertain about its future and uninterested in making heavy commitments. Similarly, certain aspects of hydro power facilitated coexistence between the public and private sector. One such aspect was long transmission lines: in the climate of distrust that prevailed between foreign and state utility, transmission distance helped to keep each sector from encroaching on, or stifling, the other. Furthermore, just as the distance between generating plant and distributing market made it possible for electric power to contain two potentially antagonistic supplying companies, so the distance between the generating plants themselves made possible the existence of more than one state generating company. The rivalry of these state companies had some aspects of private sector competition, and may therefore have had efficiency-stimulating effects on the development of state enterprise in electric power.

The technological nature of generation also helps to explain the impressive achievement of Brazilian state enterprise in electric power. Hydro plants have strong political appeal, but at the same time their construction and operation are relatively invulnerable to political meddling. Moreover, the challenging yet limited nature of the individual hydro project—in contrast to state construction programs or state-sponsored business— enabled the sector to attract competent managerial talent otherwise scornful of state-sponsored activity.

In other words, it seems to have been of considerable significance that the state entered the power business in hydro generation only, leaving distribution for the moment to the foreign company. Just as important as this functional division of tasks between the two sectors was their resulting functional interdependence. The vertical "deintegration" of the power industry imparted a certain institutional stability to that sector —a stability that enabled it to grow and to emerge from the period of inadequate rates and intense nationalism with the foreign company still in operation, and with a successful new power producer in the person of the state.

This *modus vivendi* was not a particularly happy one, nor does it possess long-term stability. A high price was paid by both sides for coexistence. The company could not get the rates it deemed adequate, and the country could not expel the disliked foreigner from its side. The policy-making process in electric power was thus shot through with the exasperations of both sides. But precisely because the period was so ridden with problems and conflicts, the progress and limited stability that it nevertheless yielded are remarkable. Although many observers predict that the power industry in the south-central region will soon reintegrate, with the state power sector buying out the Light, such an occurrence would not detract from the hypothesis that deintegration helped lead the power sector out of its impasse. Indeed, the competence and strength gained by the state power sector through its apprenticeship in hydro generation will increase the probability that the sector will be able to take on distribution without being weakened by it.

The first two chapters of this study are a prelude to the remaining five. In the first chapter, the major actors in the power sector are identified, and the power bottleneck and its interaction with the economic growth of the region are described. In the second chapter I look at the rate problem, which is the traditional culprit in the story of deficit-ridden public services in inflationary developing countries. It turns out that resolution of the problem came about only *after* the major achievements and adaptations of the postwar period had occurred. For this reason I try to show the merciless difficulties that a successful resolution of the rate problem entailed, and to indicate how its conspicuousness obscured other less attention-getting areas in which interesting forms of accommodation and progress were taking place.

The remaining five chapters represent the heart of the book. They focus on the technology of the industry, along with the particular form it took in conforming to the geography of south-central Brazil. At times—for example, in the discussion of the efficiency-inducing aspects of competition between the various state companies—technology is only one of several factors accounting for the story. In other cases—for example, the relative political invulnerability of a single hydro project —the role of technology has outright dominance. In either case, technology caught my eye as a way to explore events in the Brazilian power sector.

The reader is bound to ask whether the hydro solution is being suggested for all struggling state power enterprises in developing countries. The answer is no, not only because of the unique circumstances of Brazil's historical development, but because of the special character of its geography—the size of the country and its concentrated abundance of hydro potential. Should the work therefore be properly identified as a narrow case study, with no pretensions of relevance to more general questions of economic development? The answer again is in the negative, for this study is meant to illustrate the general thesis that technologies vary as to their political vulnerability, their ability to draw out and train competent talent, and their capacity to brook the coexistence of politically antagonistic institutions. The lesson of this particular case is not that hydro should be favored in developing countries, but that the technological configuration of a project, program, or economic activity is a valuable source of information in the study of opportunities for economic development.

1. The Setting

Power for metropolitan Rio and São Paulo has long been supplied by Rio Light and São Paulo Light—the only subsidiaries of the Toronto holding company, Brazilian Traction, Light and Power. In 1962 the two systems accounted for almost one-half the power generated in Brazil, while covering only 0.4 percent of the country's area and containing 15.2 percent of its population (see Table 1.1).[1] Power consumption per capita that year was 1,314 kwh in the São Paulo Light system, or three and a half times the per capita consumption in Brazil as a whole (365 kwh). In the Rio system per capita consumption was 783 kwh in 1962, or more than two times the national average.

The two utilities were the major retail suppliers of power for the states of São Paulo, Rio de Janeiro, and Guanabara (the old Federal District). In 1960 these three states accounted for 57.7 percent of Brazil's national income (less the agricultural sector) and 60.0 percent of income from the industrial

1. Unless otherwise noted, all statistics in this chapter are based on four sources: Brazilian Traction, Light and Power Company, Ltd., *Annual Reports;* Getúlio Vargas Foundation, which is the source for all national income figures in Brazil, as published in *Revista Brasileira de Economia* and *Conjuntura Econômica;* International Engineering Company, Inc., "São Paulo Light, Rio Light: Transmission and Distribution Expansion, 1965–1970–Economic and Technical Soundness Analysis," (processed, Rio de Janeiro, 1965)–cited hereafter as International Engineering; and CANAMBRA Engineering Consultants, Ltd., "Power Study of South-central Brazil" (processed, December 1963), 5 vols.– cited hereafter as CANAMBRA. (In December 1966, CANAMBRA completed its final seven-volume report; see bibliography.)

Table 1.1 Importance of the Light system in Brazil: area, population, power production and consumption.

Category	SP Light		Rio Light		SPL & RL	
	Amt.	% of Brazil	Amt.	% of Brazil	Amt.	% of Brazil
Area (square km)	21,000	0.25	9,800	0.15	30,800	0.4
Population (1000's) 1960	6,146	8.6	4,712	6.6	10,858	15.2
Energy sales (gwh) 1962	7,536	31.8	3,600	15.1	11,136	46.9
Consumption per capita (kwh) 1962	1,314	360.0	783	215.0	—	—

Source: International Engineering, p. II-13

sector.[2] Per capita income in 1960 was $216 for São Paulo, $354 for Guanabara, and $116 for the state of Rio de Janeiro—in comparison to the national average of $122.[3]

The region served by Brazilian Traction, Light and Power, known in Brazil as the Light, was the center of Brazil's postwar economic boom. Between 1947 and 1962 gross internal product for the country as a whole grew at an annual rate of 6.0 percent. For the state of São Paulo, gross internal product grew at 7.5 percent per annum, and for Rio de Janeiro and Guanabara it grew at 7.1 percent.[4] During this same period industrial product for Brazil as a whole grew at a rate of 9.6 percent. In São Paulo the rate was 11.8 percent; in Rio de Janeiro and Guanabara it was 8.1 percent.

The Shortage of Power

The power supply to metropolitan Rio and São Paulo was almost always on the brink of crisis during the postwar period. Up to 1946 the two systems had been able to keep pace with the growth of demand for electricity, and even to stimulate it because of the slack capacity in their plants. In 1938 available generating capacity in the São Paulo Light system was 53 percent greater than peak demand; in 1942 it was 33 percent greater than peak demand. In 1946 peak load for the first time reached the level of installed capacity.[5] Throughout the succeeding twenty years the systems were never able to satisfy fully the demands made upon them. In its Annual Report of 1947, the company announced that it was operating without

2. The national income estimates of the Getúlio Vargas Foundation do not exist on a state-by-state basis after 1960.

3. Domestic income at factor cost; purchasing power parity rate of 220 cruzeiros to the dollar in 1960. CANAMBRA, "Memorandum for Discussion of Economic Factors in the B-2 Forecast" (typescript, March 24, 1964, revised June 3, 1964), p. 6.

4. Rio de Janeiro and Guanabara figures are available only for the period 1950–1960 and are based on internal income series, as opposed to the real product indices used for the São Paulo and Brazil calculations.

5. Henrique Andrade, "A atual crise de energia em São Paulo," *Engenharia*, 9:1 (April 1953). The author is an employee of São Paulo Light.

adequate reserve capacity, that there was a grave risk of being unable to maintain service in case of equipment breakdown, and that rationing had already been introduced in São Paulo. This was to be the case in varying degrees for the next eighteen years.

After 1946 the two subsidiaries never ended a year without a backlog of unattended requests for power connections. In four years—1956, 1957, 1958, and 1965—the company reported that it was able to supply the connected load, as opposed to demand for new connections, with no restrictions. During these years, however, external circumstances had usually limited demand.[6]

By comparing the yearly observations on rainfall conditions with those on the condition of power supply, one discovers that inadequate rainfall was not the sole contributor to the power shortage (see Table 1.2).[7] Though shortage always worsened during low rainfall years (1952–1955, 1963–1964), restrictions were prevalent in average rainfall years as well, making clear that installed capacity was never enough. Figure 1.1, for example, shows the continuous existence from 1946 through 1954 of substandard voltage and frequency during the peak hours, which was one method of limiting load to fit within the bounds of installed capacity. Even for the years when significant additions to installed capacity entered service, restrictive measures were not always dispensed with.

An impressive sign of the precariousness of the system occurred during 1964, when the government-owned Furnas Plant

6. In 1957 power sales diminished considerably because of strikes and labor unrest in the São Paulo textile industry, one of the major industrial power consumers, during the season of its heaviest demand for power. In 1965 demand for power was considerably less because of an industrial recession.

7. Up to 1954 both Rio and São Paulo Light were, for all practical purposes, completely dependent on hydropower. With the commissioning of the 160-mw Piratininga Thermal Plant in 1954, São Paulo Light could count on 22 percent nonhydro capacity. That percentage rose to 30 in 1960, with the expansion of Piratininga to 410 mw. Rio Light remained completely dependent on hydro capacity except for a 25-mw floating plant (Piraquê), representing 3 percent of the system's present capacity. The plant was not always available to the Rio system.

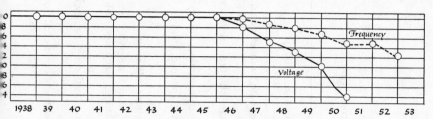

Figure 1.1. São Paulo Light: substandard voltage and frequency during peak hours owing to lack of generating capacity, 1946–1953. *Source:* São Paulo Light.

entered service with almost all of its 600 megawatts of installed capacity available to São Paulo Light, amounting to approximately 43 percent of the existing capacity of that system. Demand for power was considerably slack that year because of a general recession. However, 1964 also saw the second driest cycle of the century, so that even after this large injection of new capacity São Paulo Light still had to maintain strict rationing measures. Sales increased by only 3.3 percent, in comparison to the annual average increase of 7.6 percent for the 1947–1963 period. The company's purchased power, as a percent of total sales, jumped from 3.9 percent in 1962 to 46.6 percent in 1964, with the major share of the increase represented by purchases from the newly completed Furnas Plant. The small increase in sales and continued rationing—in comparison to the great injection of new power—show that Furnas came into operation just in time to make up for the unusually low level of the São Paulo Light's reservoirs. Despite the abnormally low streamflow, however, these figures show the brinkmanship by which Rio and São Paulo were supplied with power during the postwar period.

The power shortage that prevailed throughout the postwar period plagued the consumer in the Rio-São Paulo metropolitan area. "There are deficiencies in transmission and distribution, and in the servicing of new customers," said the Director of the Water Division (Divisão de Águas) of the National Department of Mineral Production (Departamento Nacional de Produção Mineral). "There is a waiting list of 6,000 requests

Table 1.2. São Paulo Light: annual changes in power sales, industrial production, and installed capacity, 1948-1965.

Year	Yearly percentage change			Rainfall and runoff conditions; ability of company to attend load
	SPL: kwh sales	SP state ind. prod.	Installed capacity (SPL)[a]	
1948	13.0	14.0	17.3[b]	Average rainfall; capacity inadequate to meet demand; rationing
1949	12.4	8.8	0	Rainfall somewhat below average; shortage in generating capacity continues
1950	4.7	8.1	14.7	Rainfall better than previous year; rationing (quotas)
1951	6.0	11.1	12.9	Rationing continues at somewhat reduced level
1952	5.7	0.1	0	Strict rationing
1953	3.3	12.6	0	Lowest runoffs in 30 years; stringent rationing
1954	9.1	10.6	28.0	Runoff less than previous year; major reservoir lowest in history (13%); stringent rationing; large injection of new capacity
1955	13.7	14.4	0	Runoff less than previous year; rationing somewhat reduced
1956	17.8	13.0	35.6	Abundant rainfall; no restrictions on connected load; backlog of unfilled requests

Year			
1957	4.9	6.6	0	Rainfall better than previous year; no restrictions on connected load, but sales down owing to strikes in textile industry
1958	14.0	27.1	0	Abundant rainfall; connected load reaches limits of installed capacity
1959	8.5	12.2	0	Rainfall more than previous year; restrictions of industrial peak demand
1960	13.0	16.0	31.8	Rainfall slightly above average
1961	9.4	—	4.7	Rainfall more plentiful than in recent years
1962	9.1	—	0	Rainfall above average; restriction on peak load during high load periods
1963	2.8	—	0	Low rainfall and flows; drought; rationing; main reservoirs almost empty
1964	-1.0	—	43.8 (Furnas)	Severe drought; rationing; restrictions discontinued at end of year owing to Furnas and normal rainfall
1965	-3.4	—	15.2 (Furnas)	Normal stream flow; first time in years that connected load could be supplied without restrictions; energy sales less than expected owing to temporary industrial recession

Source: Power statistics, International Engineering; income statistics, Getúlio Vargas Foundation; rainfall conditions and capacity of the system, Annual Reports of Brazilian Traction, Light and Power Company, Ltd.

a. As of the end of the year.
b. Capacity had increased by 20.0% in 1947.

for new connections, for example, in the city of Rio . . . We get complaints about the problem of new connections and extensions, complaints about the rates, complaints about decreases in the voltage, and complaints about variations in the frequency of power received." [8]

It would seem that this twenty-year shortage of power should have seriously retarded economic growth, especially in a region that had enjoyed a surplus of power for many years. In 1949 a Brazil-United States Technical Commission had already noted that in São Paulo further industrial expansion was seriously handicapped by the inadequacy of power facilities.[9] In 1954 the Joint Brazil-United States Economic Development Commission described graphically what it was like to be engaged in industrial production in a region with chronic power shortages: "At times of serious system overload the power company has no option but to disconnect certain circuits . . . without warning to the power users concerned . . . Tiremakers lose a day's production when such stoppage occurs, and another day is required to clean out the machinery. Stoppage of power to glass furnaces cuts off the air circulation used to cool the walls of furnaces, endangering the strength and life of these walls . . . [In polystyrene factories] the material flowing through the production equipment solidifies, causing a shutdown of no less than 10 days and up to 3 weeks, while polystyrene is manually chipped out of the vessels . . . [Another] difficulty arises from low voltage and low frequency during periods of overload. Motors burn out, much equipment operates improperly with very widespread losses . . . [Textile] looms operate improperly because shuttles slow down at such

8. A. Rogério Teixeira Mendes, in one of a series of interviews conducted in 1961 by ELETROBRÁS, the federal government power holding company, as part of a study for modification of the legislation concerning electric power. Centrais Elétricas Brasileiras, S.A., "Entrevistas a que se referem fls. 4, 5 e 6 do Relatório do Grupo de Trabalho da ELETROBRÁS," File document (typescript, Rio de Janeiro, 1961)—cited hereafter as ELETROBRÁS Interviews.

9. Joint Brazil-U.S. Technical Commission [Abbink Mission], "Report of the Joint Brazil-U.S. Technical Commission" (mimeo, Rio de Janeiro, Feb. 7, 1949), p. 143.

times, resulting in cloth whose quality is substandard." [10]
Of course, the years when these observations were made—
1953, 1954, and 1955—were the worst years in the power history
of the south-central region: power cutoffs reached five to seven
hours a day in Rio and São Paulo, and unforeseen cutoffs were
common. Such severe conditions did not prevail throughout
the postwar period, but substandard voltage and frequency
were permanent features of the shortage, as well as quotas and
other less severe forms of limiting the load.

After observing these various manifestations of a long-term
power bottleneck, one is a little surprised to read the figures
on economic growth during the same period—as well as those
on the growth of power consumption itself (see Table 1.3).
Between 1947 and 1960 real product in the state of São Paulo
increased at a rate of 7.5 percent, while industrial product
grew at an annual rate of 11.8 percent. During this same
period of deficit in power supply, consumption of electric
power in the São Paulo Light area grew at a rate of 9.5
percent, while sales to industry grew at a rate of 12.8 percent.
Industrial consumption accounted for about 55 percent of the
annual sales of São Paulo Light during this period.

The Rio Light area demonstrated similar, though less impressive, rates of growth. In the states of Rio de Janeiro and
Guanabara, income between 1950 and 1960 grew at an annual
rate of 7.1 percent, and industrial income at 8.1 percent. Power
sales kept up with economic growth at an annual rate of 8.0
percent, and sales to industry grew at 9.0 percent per year.

It is just as difficult to discover the power bottleneck in the
year-by-year increments of economic growth (see Table 1.2).
One would at least expect to find substantially diminished
increases in industrial production during the years of worst
crisis for the power system—1952, 1953, and 1954. But no relation emerges between the annual percentage increases in
power sales during that period and the increases in industrial

---

10. Joint Brazil-U.S. Economic Development Commission, *The Development of Brazil* (Washington, D.C.: Institute of Inter-American Affairs,
1954), p. 158.

Table 1.3 Rio and São Paulo systems: annual growth rates, 1947–1962[a].

Area of growth	São Paulo[b]	Rio[c]
Installed capacity	8.1	7.4
Power sales[d]	9.6	8.0
Power sales, industry (1954–1962)[e]	12.8	9.0
Real product (1947–1960)[f]	7.5	7.1[g]
Real product, industry (1950–1960)[h]	11.8	8.1[g]
Urban population (1950–1960)	5.5	4.4

Source of raw data: Income statistics, Getúlio Vargas Foundation; power statistics, International Engineering.

a. The year 1947 was selected to start because it was the first year for which income statistics were available on a state-by-state basis. It roughly coincides, moreover, with the divide that begins the period studied here—the change from chronic excess to shortage in power facilities. The power series is carried through 1962, even though the income series goes only to 1960, because there was only a slight difference between the rates of growth calculated on a thirteen-, fourteen-, and fifteen-year basis, starting in 1947. The power series is not carried beyond 1962 because of the abnormal conditions of industrial recession and severe drought in 1963–1965.

b. Power figures refer to the concession area of São Paulo Light; income statistics, to the whole state of São Paulo.

c. "Rio" refers to Rio de Janeiro and Guanabara states. Power figures refer to the concession area of Rio Light; income statistics, to the two states of Rio de Janeiro and Guanabara.

d. Power sales do not include the bulk sales of each utility to the other, because that would cause double counting.

e. This series starts in 1954 for São Paulo and 1953 for Rio. In those years the company changed its method of categorizing consumers. Sales to industry accounted for an average of 55 percent of the sales of São Paulo Light during this period. Industrial sales in the Rio system represented a much smaller percentage of the company's sales, averaging 30 percent.

f. Income statistics are not yet available on a state-by-state basis after 1960.

g. The series used here is "internal income" rather than "real product" and starts in 1950 rather than 1947. It includes everything but agriculture, which is insignificant in the Light zone.

h. Industry here is "secondary sector."

production. The year in which power sales were most affected by the drought, 1953, was the year of greatest percentage increase in industrial production in São Paulo for the period 1949–1955. Indeed, the years of extreme power crisis coincided with a considerable increase of new industry in São Paulo. Many of these industries located with their own generators, on the promise that as soon as the rains came, they would have public power. The growth impulse was apparently so strong that it could not be contained by the absence of one of the major basic services.

In a view of the largely discredited theories about infrastructure as a prerequisite to economic development, it is interesting to note that the south-central region's great surge of development occurred *not* when power was in ample supply but during the period following, precisely when facilities were inadequate. Industry was not deterred from locating in São Paulo, for example, during a period of five-hour daily blackouts. Although expansion of installed capacity did not keep up with economic growth, neither did it fall below a rate of growth considered reasonable for expansion of power facilities in industrializing countries. The figures on growth of installed capacity during this period (see Table 1.3) show a rate of growth of 8.1 percent per year in the São Paulo Light system, and 7.4 percent in the Rio system. These rates indicate more than a doubling of power capacity every ten years, which is the rough rule-of-thumb for projecting growth of power production in developing countries. The power shortage, then, was not due to complete stagnation in the power sector; rather, installed capacity was growing at an average rate made unacceptable by the unusual rate of growth of the economy.[11] This

11. The power company was usually blamed for the power crisis; it was accused of a deliberate policy of not expanding capacity. Economic growth was sometimes pointed to as the culprit as well, with just as much exasperation. "The cause of this crisis is the uncontrollable development of São Paulo," reported the president of the State Electric Power Council of São Paulo at its first meeting in 1952. São Paulo, Secretaria de Viação e Óbras Públicas, Departamento de Águas e Energia Elétrica, Conselho Estadual de Energia Elétrica, "Atas do Conselho Estadual de Energia Elétrica" (typescript, São Paulo, June 5, 1952), p. 2—cited hereafter as CEEE Minutes.

discrepancy helps explain the strange combination of chronic shortage with healthy growth of power sales and industrial output.

One more question is posed by the statistics. If reserve capacity ceased to exist in 1946, how was it possible for power sales to increase at a rate higher than the rate of increase in installed capacity? Such a discrepancy in growth rates is usually attributed to the progressive using up of reserve capacity or an increase in the load factor.[12] Reserve did not exist, however, in the case of the two Light systems. Even during the years immediately following the commissioning of new capacity, restrictions were not necessarily dispensed with (see Table 1.2), which means that new capacity was loaded up rapidly. Between 1947 and 1962 the load factor of the two systems increased by about 8.5 percent.[13] Although this increase can explain part of the discrepancy between rates of growth for installed capacity and power sales, the load factor in the Light systems was already quite high in 1947—63 percent in São Paulo and 58 percent in Rio. There was not much leeway, in other words, for expanding power sales by filling up the off-peak hours.

Second, that the power system was based on hydro imposed a constraint on the possibility of increasing power sales by evening out the load, especially during times of inadequate rainfall. During off-peak hours, the company often needed to recoup the levels of its reservoirs to the extent of sacrificing some of the revenue that could be earned from attending all of off-peak demand. Indeed, some state officials believed that São Paulo Light had allowed its major reservoirs to reach

12. The load factor is the ratio of average load to peak load. An increase in the load factor for a given installed capacity means that demand for power is more evenly spread across the hours of the day or the days of the week. It therefore means more kilowatt hours sold per unit of installed capacity.

13. International Engineering. Again 1963 and 1964 are excluded from the calculation, because the diminution occurring in the load factor during those years was caused by the reduced sale of power (decrease in average load) owing to the industrial recession, rather than by any increase in installed capacity—i.e., in ability to serve peak load.

dangerously low levels in 1953 and 1954, and that this was a result of the company's short-run interest in squeezing as much revenue out of its system as possible.[14] This hydro-based difficulty of increasing off-peak demand (and therefore selling more power for a given level of installed capacity) was reinforced in the Light systems by considerable reliance on a water supply that was electrically pumped from streams and reservoirs at lower altitudes (pumped storage). Inasmuch as these pumps were driven by the system's own power, the pumping could only be done during off-peak hours, because demand always touched the limits of installed capacity during the peak hours. Much of the company's off-peak capacity, therefore, was used up in its own off-peak demands for pumping.

Other factors may have contributed to the discrepancy between the rate of growth of installed capacity and that of power sales. Not one year passed without new customers being connected to the net, as is apparent from the company's Annual Reports. Even during the most severe power crisis of 1952–1955, as well as during the 1963–1964 drought and industrial recession when sales actually decreased, the connection of new customers did not cease. In fact, during this period the governor of São Paulo followed a policy of allowing the company to continue new connections, in order not to discourage the industrial influx into São Paulo. The new connections to the net were made at the sacrifice of the rest of the consumers, including the already existing industrial consumers, by making cuts and quotas even more severe.[15] In face of inadequate installed capacity, in other words, the increase in sales was achieved by a continual decrease in the quality of service rendered to each customer.[16]

14. Companhia Brasileira de Engenharia, "Plano de eletrificação do estado de São Paulo" (mimeo, São Paulo, 1956), I, 202.
15. Ex-Governor of São Paulo to the author.
16. This accommodation of new consumers was an often cited complaint in the São Paulo State Electric Power Council. During the 1952–1955 power crisis a CEEE member representing the São Paulo industrial interests suggested that measures be taken to limit new connections. "Despite all restrictions," he said, "there was an increase of 30,000 kw

What was important about this increasingly defective share of power received by each consumer was that the industrial sector—the greatest contributor to economic growth—was the consumer most able to adapt to defective supply, through the use of voltage regulators, for example, and more important, the supplementary use of his own generators. In 1956 the São Paulo Electrification Plan reported that supply to industry had been accomplished increasingly by the use of "own power," especially since 1950.[17] During the 1952–1955 crisis the São Paulo Federation of Industries (Federação de Indústrias do Estado de São Paulo) reported that by 1954 São Paulo industry had installed more than 100,000 kw in diesel generators. They represented about 20 percent of the installed capacity of the São Paulo Light system.[18] Ten years later during the 1963–1964 crisis most major industries in Rio de Janeiro and São

---

in connected load so far this year [1953]. This means an increase on the order of five or six thousand kilowatts a month. While the connected load was increasing, the generating plants continued with the same insufficient capacity—or even a reduction in capacity owing to the diminution of reservoir levels. We can only conclude from this that the newly connected load is receiving energy taken away from existing consumers —in other words, at the cost of an increase in the hours of rationing." CEEE Minutes, July 31, 1953, p. 10.

17. Cia. Brasileira de Engenharia, "Plano de eletrificação," p. 242.

18. CEEE Minutes, March 19, 1954, pp. 3–4. Figures on own-power installed capacity will always err on the high side as a measure of the inadequacy of the public power system, for two reasons. The load factor of the industrialist's own private generator is much lower than that of the public system, because of his uneven use of the equipment. Any given amount of own-power capacity, then, represents far fewer kilowatt hours generated than the same amount of capacity in a public plant, which has a higher load factor. Second, many electric-power-intensive industries build own-power facilities regardless of the state of the public power system. Their installations, therefore, do not count as a measure of incapacity in the public system. Such plants, however, being larger and of a more permanent nature, are more likely to get into the statistics on own power than are those of the more marginal producers of this type of power, who are simply supplementing the faulty supply of the public system. The latter case is more interesting as a measure of the degree of inadequacy in the public system. These two factors may overstate the importance of own power as a measure of public power shortage, but there may be a natural correction of this bias in view of the fact that own-power facilities are rarely accounted for completely in the statistics.

Paulo were equipped with standby power.[19] At the end of 1963 the CANAMBRA group estimated the installed capacity of own-power installations in the state of São Paulo at 125,648 kw, or about 9 percent of the capacity of the São Paulo Light system. The group estimated, moreover, that 20,000 kw of this capacity would exist regardless of the adequacy of public power supply, so that a more accurate estimate of private capacity installed because of the shortage of public power would be 105,648 kw, or about 8 percent of the capacity installed in the public system of São Paulo Light.[20]

The prevalence of own power helps to explain why the power bottleneck did not produce a greater echo in the statistics on economic growth and industrial expansion. It does not explain the relatively rapid growth of power consumption itself, given the chronic inadequacy of the public system. In addition to our former demonstration that the shortage was not a case of standstill in the growth of installed capacity, it can be added that supplementary own-power enabled the industrial and commercial consumer to continue buying an increasingly inadequate and unreliable supply of public power. This may have contributed to maintaining the growth of power sales over so long a period at a rate higher than that of installed capacity. In this connection, is is interesting to note one of the conclusions of a São Paulo commission appointed to study rationing measures at the beginning of the 1952–1955 crisis. The commission discussed the greater desirability of monthly quotas, compared to cutoffs of the distribution circuits, as a means of reducing power consumption. It reported that "numerous firms had acquired their own supplementary generating units, with capacity lower than their normal demand for power.

19. U.S. Department of State, American Embassy, Rio de Janeiro, Airgram (processed, Feb. 18, 1964), p. 2.
20. CANAMBRA, "Power Study of South-central Brazil," II, 2–10, 2–11. This figure is not at all high, given the inadequate capacity of the public system. It seems to relate, however, only to own-power producers who are not in any proportion consumers of public power. It would thus not include the aspect of own power that is most relevant here—the supplementing of defective public supply with private generators.

In such cases the private firm's generating unit could supply the quantity of power forbidden by the power quota. However, in the case of rationing via cutoffs of the distribution circuits, the privately installed generators would not have the capacity to supply the peak demand of the firm. During such cutoffs these private generators would therefore become an unutilizable investment." [21]

As a result, the commission recommended quotas rather than cutoffs as a way of reducing power consumption that would harmonize with the industrial sector's ownership of supplementary generating units. Although the 1952–1955 crisis became so severe that both quotas and cutoffs were necessary, quotas alone were in existence throughout much of the postwar period. Hence, with a marginal addition by each industrial establishment to the supply of power received from the public net, inadequate public supply could be used to the fullest, and industrial growth could be freed somewhat from the restrictions of public installed capacity.

One more factor may have contributed to the continued high rate of growth of power sales in relation to the level and rate of growth of installed capacity. During the 1952–1955 crisis the State Electric Power Council (Conselho Estadual de Energia Elétrica) concerned itself frequently with requests by the Light company to authorize the relaxation of rationing restrictions. Whenever there was a slight improvement in rainfall or water storage conditions, the company did not want to miss the opportunity of converting that momentary increase in power availability into revenue. The state authorities, however, were concerned about the risk of allowing such frequent and fine changes in rationing restrictions. It was very difficult to announce a slight relaxing of power rationing without having an overenthusiastic response by the consumer, which could plunge the system into even greater crisis. State authorities were more interested in allowing reservoirs to accumulate a minimum level of water storage than in converting into power any slight increase in their levels. They wanted to insure against future crisis, even if it meant giving up temporary

21. CEEE Minutes, Nov. 14, 1952, p. 4.

relief of the existing shortage.[22] Yet it was to the company's financial interest to squeeze the maximum possible number of kilowatt hours from existing capacity even if that made the system precarious. It was inclined to favor not only the premature relaxing of rationing measures but also the granting of new connections that could not be adequately serviced. The company's interest in pushing its system to the brink must have been important in maintaining the rate of power consumption at such a puzzlingly high level. This short-run outlook may have been conditioned in part by the Light's dissatisfaction over the rate it was earning and a general insecurity about its prospects for long-run survival as a foreign utility in an atmosphere of rising nationalism. Both considerations would focus its attention on the short-run methods of earning revenue, as well as those that required a minimum of investment.

In sum, metropolitan Rio and São Paulo were "on the brink" in matters of electric power during the whole postwar period. The region was able to live with its power crisis because of the size and intensity of its growth boom, the extremes of utilization to which its power facilities were pushed, and the sizable expansion in installed capacity. On the one hand, the power problem was serious enough to require a long-run solution; but on the other, the crisis was not so crippling that it allowed no time for a solution requiring years to bear results—namely, the construction of hydro plants by the state.

The Companies

Throughout most of the postwar period the Light continued as sole generator and distributor of electric power for the metropolitan areas of Rio and São Paulo. Up to 1956, not only existing generation and distribution but even the construction of new generating facilities for the two regions were the function solely of the Light (see Figure 1.3).[23] In that year the company began a construction program that would add 470 mw

22. CEEE Minutes, Aug. 6, 1954, p. 8; Aug. 20, 1954, pp. 2–3; April 23, 1954, p. 3.
23. The three plants started before 1956 by the CHERP and USELPA companies had little importance in the Light system.

to its existing capacity of 1,661.5 mw—representing an increase of 28 percent in the combined installed capacity of the two systems.

Eight years later, in 1964, the situation had changed considerably. Forty-five percent of São Paulo Light's sales were provided with energy from the state-owned plant, Furnas, which had entered into operation that year.[24] The Light's last construction program, started in 1956, had been terminated the previous year with the coming into operation of the 90-mw Ponte Coberta Plant of the Rio Light system.[25] In the intervening years the company had not initiated further expansion of its generating facilities, nor had it any plans to do so. By 1961 it announced that the generating resources it would have upon completion of the 1956 construction program would be capable of supplying the load *only* through 1963. Two years before its generating supplies would be inadequate to meet load growth, the Light had no plans or program of its own to breach that inadequacy. It was counting for future generating supply on the various power projects in construction by the government; it was giving up its position as sole generator for the Rio-São Paulo region.[26] Even after winning the rate legislation it had long struggled for, and after seeing the change in April 1964 to the most sympathetic government it had worked under in fifteen years, the Light in 1965 reiterated its new specialization in distribution. "In accordance with government policy," the company reported, "additions to Brazil's electrical generating facilities are entrusted to government organizations." [27] Even with the rate increases, moreover, it was not clear that the Light had settled down to stay.

24. The percentage figure exaggerates somewhat the importance of Furnas to the system at that time, because the year was exceptionally dry and the Light company's reservoirs were almost empty. But considering that half of Furnas' capacity was still to come into service (300 mw in 1965, another 300 mw some time after 1970), this drought-caused exaggeration of Furnas' importance gives an idea of the long-run contribution that the plant would make to the Light system.

25. The 250-mw expansion of the Piratininga Steam Plant was completed in 1960, and the 130-mw expansion of the Cubatão Plant in 1961.

26. *Annual Report, 1961*, p. 10.   27. *Annual Report, 1965*, p. 12.

The Light's retreat from generation expansion was complete. Of the seven hydro plants included in the 1963–1966 power construction program for the south-central region[28]—as well as the fourteen plants already under construction or expansion —all were being undertaken by government-sponsored power entities. Not one of the twenty-one plants was a project of the Light—nor, for that matter, of any other private company (see Table 1.4). Within a period of eight years the state had become the exclusive supplier of additions to generating capacity for the Rio-São Paulo area.

Quite a different picture emerges from looking at figures on the private-public share in power sales rather than in additions to installed capacity. In 1965, when the Light announced its new specialization in distribution, the two systems bought from outside sources only 24 percent of the power they distributed, most of that share being represented by Furnas. The installed capacity available to the Light's systems from outside sources did not reach any significant percentage of the company's capacity until the initiation of the Furnas Plant in late 1963, 1964, and 1965.[29] "State-sponsored power" for the Light will be in fact a future development—though in a quite nearby future. How, then, is it possible to discuss the achievements of the state power companies before they represent a majority contribution to the power supply in the Rio-São Paulo area?

First, there were two state companies—USELPA and CHERP of São Paulo—which got started early in the postwar period. (USELPA is Usinas Elétricas do Rio Paranapanema— the Paranapanema River Hydro Company—and CHERP is Companhia Hidrelétrica do Rio Pardo—the Pardo River Hydro Company.) Between them, they started and finished three

28. This program was based on the recommendations of the CANAMBRA report, adopted as official government policy in Federal Decree No. 53,958, June 9, 1964. The south-central region was defined by CANAMBRA as the four states of São Paulo, Minas Gerais, Rio de Janeiro, and Guanabara, plus small parts of the states of Goiás, Mato Grosso, and Paraná.

29. The 900 mw of the Furnas Plant represented 42 percent of the combined capacity of Rio and São Paulo Lights.

Table 1.4. South-central region: expansions in generating capacity, recommended and under construction (December 1963).

Plant	Capacity (mw)	Company
Under construction		
Hydro plant expansions		
Três Marias	130.0	CEMIG (Minas Gerais)
Limoeiro	14.4	CHERP (São Paulo)
Euclides da Cunha	47.2	CHERP
Hydro plant construction		
Furnas	912.0	Furnas (Federal)
Jupiá	1,400.0	CELUSA (São Paulo)
Barra Bonita	122.0	CHERP
Bariri	123.9	CHERP
Ibitinga	117.0	CHERP
Graminha	67.6	CHERP
Funil (Paraíba)	210.0	CHEVAP (Federal)
Chavantes	360.0	USELPA (São Paulo)
Fumaça	35.2	Cia. Brasileira de Alumínio
Thermal plant construction		
Santa Cruz	150.0	CHEVAP
Campos	30.0	EFEE (Rio de Janeiro)
CANAMBRA recommendations		
Hydro plant expansions		
Peixoto (Units 5-10)	300.0	CPFL[a] (Federal)
Três Marias	130.0	CEMIG
New projects		
Estreito (Units 1-6)	600.0	Furnas
Jaguara (Units 1-7)	483.0	CEMIG
Funil (Grande)	88.0	CEMIG
São Miguel	59.0	CEMIG
Piraju	107.0	USELPA
Rosal (Units 1-2)	48.0	EFEE
Total recommended	1,815.0	
Total recommended & under construction	5,534.3	

Source: CANAMBRA, I, 4.

a. CPFL is Cia. Paulista de Fôrça e Luz, one of the ten former American and Foreign Power subsidiaries in Brazil. On April 22, 1963, an agreement was made between the company and the Brazilian government, guaranteeing the purchase of AMFORP by Brazil. The sale was closed in March 1965. The properties are now run by ELETROBRÁS.

plants during the nineteen fifties, and started two expansions, as well as three more new plants (see Figure 1.2). Although the companies were not set up with the intention of solving São Paulo's metropolitan power problem, their projected interconnection with São Paulo Light was an important justification in helping them get their projects authorized and financed. In late 1962, the first high-tension interconnection between the Light and a state-sponsored power company was inaugurated —the connection of USELPA's Jurumirim Plant to São Paulo Light via a 230-kv, 100-mva transmission line; another interconnection, not as important, was made with CHERP. Although the two companies' combined production amounted to only 10 percent of São Paulo Light's production in 1962, their marginal importance nevertheless helped the Light to meet its load demands from 1962 on.[30] In the CANAMBRA plan, moreover, and in the construction programs already under way in 1963, the two companies represented 18 percent of the expansion in installed capacity in the south-central region between 1963 and 1966. Thus, USELPA and CHERP, though without much weight in the energy sales of the Light, are important in that they represent state power projects completed and in operation by the late nineteen fifties.

Included in this small category of state power companies with a history of selling power is the CEMIG company of Minas Gerais, of the same generation as USELPA and CHERP. (CEMIG means Centrais Elétricas de Minas Gerais—The Minas Gerais Power Company.) CEMIG does not bear directly on the study of power supply to metropolitan Rio and São Paulo, although it will in the future be part of the interconnected network covering the south-central region. But some reference to CEMIG is indispensable in a study of state power in the industrialized section of Brazil, for it is the only state company in this area to have taken on both generation and distribution, and it is considered one of the best-run enterprises in Latin America.

Just as the Brazilian Northeast has long supplied the coun-

30. *Annual Report, 1962*, p. 9.

NAME OF PLANT AND INSTALLED CAPACITY IN MW

COMPANY	1945	46	47	48	49	50	51	52	53	54	55	56	57	58	59	60	61	62	63	64	65	66	67	68	69	70
São Paulo Light			Cubatão 65 / 65									260	Expansion			65 / 65	Expansion 250									
												160	Piratininga													
Rio Light			Fontes 35 (Expansion)			Ilha 45 (Expansion)			70 / 270								46.7 / 46.7 Ponte Coberta									
						Nilo Peçanha																				
Furnas															Furnas				300/300/300				Estreito 600 (1971)			
CHERP												Euclides da Cunha	47.2	Expansion	47.2											
												Limeiro	14.4 Expansion	14.4												
														Graminha	67.6										
														Barra Bonita		122										
																	Bariri	123.9								
																		Ibitinga		117						
USELPA								Salto Grande						60												
													Jurumirim					180				Chavantes 360				
CELUSA																		Jupiá					1400	Ilha Solteira		2500 (1973)
CHEVAP																	Funil		Santa Cruz				150		210	

Figure 1.2. Power supply available to metropolitan Rio–São Paulo: additions to installed capacity, 1947–1970.

try with fine statesmen, so CEMIG was unrivaled as a supplier
of managerial talent to the state power sector. The five major
figures in the state power sector of Brazil were all members of
the founding team of CEMIG. Three of them later formed the
Furnas company, which would make the first significant contribution of state generating facilities to the Rio-São Paulo area.[31]
Hence, the longer operating history of CEMIG is an excellent
supplementary source of information on the quality of the state
programs now being undertaken to supply Rio-São Paulo load
growth, and on the kind of experience that underlies them.[32]

There is another, more important reason why it is possible
to discuss state power as a significant event during a period
when its percentage contribution to supply was almost negligi-
ble. The construction of a hydro plant is an important activity
in itself, in contrast to the business of selling power. Even
though Furnas, for example, had not finished its plant and
was not in the business of selling power until late in the period
under study, it was by no means a company without a history.
For five years it had been one of the largest construction-
contracting companies in Brazil; and as the conclusion of its
plant drew near, the company worked hard at finding a way
of prolonging the activity of construction—which could be

31. The five managers from CEMIG were Lucas Lopes, John Cotrim,
Flávio Lyra, Benedicto Dutra, and Mauro Thibau. Cotrim, Lyra, and
Dutra moved on to become, respectively, president, technical director,
and commercial director of Furnas. Dutra was appointed chief deputy
(Chefe do Gabinete) in 1964 to the Minister of Mines and Energy,
Mauro Thibau. Lucas Lopes, after leaving CEMIG, became Minister of
Finance during the presidency of Juscelino Kubitschek and was instru-
mental in developing and implementing the government's Target Pro-
gram (Programa de Metas), in which electric power received major
priority. Mário Bhering, also a member of CEMIG's founding team and
later its president, was appointed president of ELETROBRÁS by the
Costa e Silva government when it took office in April 1967.

32. CEMIG developed in unusual circumstances, characterized by
an abnormally high industrial load. Its facilities are in an area with a
large concentration of power-intensive metallurgical industries, many
having their own plants. Some of these industrial power plants have
at one time or another been integrated into the public system. The
growth of CEMIG is very much bound up with the development of
these power-intensive industries.

accomplished, of course, only by starting on another plant.[33]

Just as significant events often show up better in marginal rather than average relationships, so in the Brazilian power sector of the nineteen fifties and sixties it was only in the percentage figures for *additions* to installed capacity that one could see reflected the fury of activity in state power. When I discuss state power companies here, therefore, it is for the purpose of describing the activity surrounding these additions to the power supply of metropolitan Rio and São Paulo. A brief biography of each of the state companies involved in the region's power supply is now appropriate, as well as a description of the Light system itself.

Brazilian Traction, Light and Power

Rio and São Paulo Light are wholly owned subsidiaries of the Brazilian Traction, Light and Power Company of Toronto, having been incorporated in 1912.[34] The equity capital of the company is mainly common stock—roughly 36 percent being held in the United States, 25 percent in Canada, and the remaining third represented by bearer share warrants held primarily in Europe. The company has no operations outside Brazil, and it terminated its tramway concessions in 1963.

The Light went to Brazil at the turn of the century with the initial purpose of substituting power for animal traction in the urban transport systems of the cities of Rio and São Paulo. The São Paulo and Rio subsidiaries of the Canadian

33. When the company wanted to construct the Estreito Plant, downstream from Furnas, one important justification for the project was that in the course of constructing Furnas, "the Federal Government invested a great amount of money and effort to set up a technical staff and organization, which constitute today a most valuable asset to the country. . . . To leave idle a staff so highly qualified, which underwent lengthy preparation for this task, would be tantamount to abandoning a valuable store of technical knowledge, which if dispersed, could be recovered only with great difficulty." "A usina de Estreito," *O Estado de Minas,* Jan. 20, 1963. Although this article was a defense of the right of Furnas rather than CEMIG to develop the Estreito site, it is an excellent example of the importance of construction activity to the company's existence.

34. On Aug. 23, 1967, Rio and São Paulo Light were merged into one firm, Light–Serviços de Eletricidade S.A.

holding company took advantage of the hydro potential of the nearby rivers—the headwaters of the Tietê near São Paulo, and the Paraíba and its tributaries near Rio (see Figure 1.3). The most important power sources of both companies came to be these hydro developments on the Serra do Mar, a mountainous escarpment that rises close to Brazil's central coastline and then levels off to an interior plateau. This geography causes many of the region's rivers to flow westward toward the interior instead of eastward to the sea. The rivers flow eventually into the Atlantic Ocean, but outside Brazilian territory, via the southward-flowing Paraná River, and, finally, the Prata River.

The idea of the Light was to turn these rivers backward at their headwaters, letting them fall over the edge of the scarp to generate electric power. The diversion schemes were achieved by a complex system of dams, canals, pumping stations, and surface and underground generating plants—a system that was expanded each time an increase in capacity was desired. The São Paulo diversion, Cubatão, was the more spectacular of the two: in comparison to the 320-meter head of Rio Light's Lages development, Cubatão allowed the Tietê headwaters to plunge a distance of 720 meters, giving rise to a cheaper and larger development (900 mw) than that at Lages (550 mw). In addition, Cubatão was based on a complete turnabout of the headwaters of an inward-flowing river, whereas the Lages development was based initially on a stream that already tumbled over the scarp and was later expanded by diverting the Paraíba, which flows northeastward in a valley paralleling the scarp and the ocean coast.

The Light came to be considered a dynamic force in the development of Rio and São Paulo, not only because it created an abundance of power in the third and fourth decades of the country but because it had taken a new and rapidly developing technology, hydropower, and made of it a perfect fit for south-central Brazil's topography. In so doing, it had transformed an important obstacle to development of the south-central region, the coastal scarp, into a major asset, at least in terms of the supply of electric power. Besides turning back

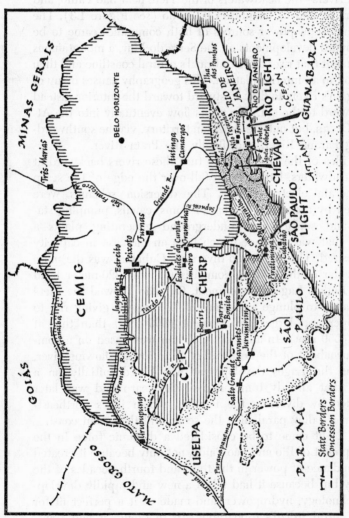

Figure 1.3. Concession zones, power plants, and state boundaries: São Paulo Light, Rio Light, CHEVAP, CHERP, USELPA, CELUSA, CEMIG, and CPFL (AMFORP). *Source:* Brasil, Ministério das Minas e Energia, "O suprimento de energia elétrica à região centro-sul do Brasil no período 1962/1970." *Relatório do Grupo de Trabalho,* printed in *Engenharia* (São Paulo, April and May 1962).

the waters, the Serra development represented the magnificent human conquest of a highly resistant natural environment— especially in São Paulo which, unlike Rio, lay at the top rather than at the foot of the scarp. The almost complete lack of a transport system between that city and the coast made even more difficult the design and execution of a project in the midst of a highly malarial environment. It was perhaps this dramatic conquest of the natural environment, more than the providing of electric power, that gave to the Light its reputation as a major contributor to the development of the south-central region.

São Paulo Light is the largest electric utility in Brazil. It serves the greater São Paulo area and several towns extending from Sorocaba in the west to the border of the state of Rio de Janeiro in the east. The system operates 410 mw of oil-fired thermal capacity (the Piratininga Steam Plant), and 960 mw of hydroelectric capacity. There are two 230-kv tielines to adjacent systems—one eastward to Rio Light, the other westward to USELPA. Late in 1963 the first circuit of 345-kv transmission between the São Paulo Light system and the Furnas Plant was placed in service. The Furnas Plant, 310 kilometers to the north of São Paulo, will supply a large share of the load growth of São Paulo.

Rio Light serves the state of Guanabara (the city of Rio de Janeiro) and a portion of the state of Rio de Janeiro, which includes the government-owned steel complex at Volta Redonda, the middle Paraíba Valley, and various small towns near the city of Rio de Janeiro. Its generating plants are principally hydro, located 70 to 130 kilometers from the city of Rio and totaling 761 mw of capacity. The only thermal generation is a 25-mw floating plant (Piraquê), used jointly with a company serving the state of Rio de Janeiro. Rio Light is a 50-cycle system, in contrast to the 60 cycles of São Paulo Light and other systems in the south-central region. The 230-kv transmission tie with São Paulo Light has a 50-mw frequency changer at Aparecida, approximately midway between the two cities. The same line can be used to transfer 150 mw between parts of the two systems when operated on the same frequency. The system is now undergoing conversion to 60 cycles.

USELPA

Among the companies of the state of São Paulo is USELPA, founded in August 1953, with 99 percent of its capital held by the state. Its immediate aim was construction of the Salto Grande Hydroelectric Plant on the Paranapanema River, which forms the border between the states of Paraná and São Paulo. The 60-mw plant was one of the forty-one projects recommended by the Joint Brazil-United States Economic Development Commission,[35] and it received a $10 million loan from the International Bank for Reconstruction and Development (IBRD). The plant was concluded in 1957, one year after the company began construction on its second plant, Jurumirim, which also received financial assistance from the IBRD with a loan of $13.4 million. This 180-mw plant, lying downstream from Salto Grande, was commissioned in 1963. Immediately before completion of Jurumirim, USELPA started construction of its third plant, Chavantes, situated midway between Jurumirim and Salto Grande. The project, assisted by a $22.5 million loan from the IBRD, will have a capacity of 360 mw and is scheduled for completion in 1969.

USELPA currently has a capital participation of both the states of São Paulo and Paraná, the Paranapanema River forming the divide between these two states. The company supplies most of its power wholesale to nine utilities covering the southwestern part of the state of São Paulo, plus a portion of northern Paraná. In addition, USELPA is responsible for electrification of the isolated Upper Araraquarense area and the south coastal areas; it supplies an important block of power to São Paulo Light. The main interconnection with São Paulo is a 230-kv line from the Jurumirim Plant. In 1962 USELPA generated 535,200 megawatt hours and served a

35. Joint Brazil-United States Economic Development Commission (Comissão Mista Brasil-Estados Unidos para Desenvolvimento Econômico), *Projetos: Energia* (Rio de Janeiro, 1954), X–XIII.

population of 2,221,700, representing a rather low per capita generation (241 kwh).

CHERP

The creation of a state power company to build two plants on the Pardo River was authorized by the state of São Paulo in May 1965. The CHERP company was to continue work started on two hydroelectric plants by the Pardo River Section (Óbras do Rio Pardo) of the São Paulo Water and Power Department (Departamento de Águas e Energia Elétrica). The Limoeiro Plant was completed in 1958, with 14.4 mw of installed capacity, and Euclides da Cunha was completed in 1960, with 47.7 mw of installed capacity. Immediately before completion of each of the plants, work was begun to double their capacity, which was completed in 1966. The company had in the meantime undertaken construction of a 67.6-mw plant on the Pardo River—Graminha was started in 1959 and completed in 1967. In 1956 the Water and Power Department delegated to CHERP the responsibility for executing two projects on the Tietê River, which flows westward through the state of São Paulo. The 122-mw Barra Bonita Plant was begun in 1957 and completed in 1965, and a plant of equal size, Bariri, was started in 1960 and completed in 1966. CHERP started another plant on the Tietê in 1961, the 117-mw Ibitinga Plant, scheduled for completion in 1968.

CHERP supplies wholesale power to about fifteen small utilities in northeastern São Paulo, extending into the state of Minas Gerais, and its generating capacity is entirely hydroelectric. The company has a limited interconnection with São Paulo Light, not as important as that between USELPA and the Light. In 1962 CHERP generated 391,200 megawatt hours and served a population of 1,119,400, giving a per capita generation of 341 kwh.

CELUSA

The CELUSA company (Centrais Elétricas de Urubupungá —The Urubupungá Hydro Company) was created in January 1961 to develop the hydro potential of the Paraná River at the

falls of Urubupungá, where the river forms the western divide
of São Paulo with the interior state of Mato Grosso. Tributary
to the Paraná are the Paranapanema (being developed by
USELPA), the Pardo and Tietê (CHERP), and the Grande
(Furnas). The CELUSA complex will consist of two plants
with a combined capacity of about 4 million kw–Jupiá, with
1.4 million kw, and Ilha Solteira, with 2.5 million kw. Construction on the Jupiá Plant was started in 1962 and is planned for
commissioning in 1968. The same size as Furnas, Jupiá shares
with that plant the distinction of being the largest hydroelectric plant in Latin America; work on Ilha Solteira has
already begun.

The principal shareholder of CELUSA is the state of São
Paulo, with 98 percent of the company's stock; the remaining
two percent is held by the states of Goiás, Santa Catarina,
Mato Grosso, Minas Gerais, and Paraná. CELUSA received
a $13.2 million loan for Jupiá from the Inter-American Devel-
opment Bank in 1964, and in 1967 received another loan of
$34 million from the bank for the construction of Ilha Solteira.
Jupiá will transmit power to metropolitan São Paulo via a
doubled-circuited 400-kv transmission line, 572 kilometers long.
Another line, 340 kilometers in length and 138 kv, will extend
from Jupiá to Mimoso, a city in Mato Grosso. The company
plans initially to sell the bulk of its power to São Paulo Light
and expects later to expand service to the less developed areas
of the interior. In September 1966 the various São Paulo state
power companies were merged into CESP–Centrais Elétricas
de São Paulo (the São Paulo Power Company).

CEMIG

CEMIG was organized in 1952 by the state government of
Minas Gerais, in order to carry out a state-wide electrification
program. It has the largest area of influence of the major
generating and distributing systems in the south-central region;
within the area are a number of independent utilities and
producers. CEMIG has seven principal generating plants, all
of which are hydroelectric. The company's installed capacity

in 1963 was 465 mw, supplemented by about 225 mw in small
plants of one megawatt or more, which are owned by interconnected utilities or industries generating their own power.
In 1963 generation in CEMIG's area of influence was 2,915,400
mwh, population served was 8,785,000, and per capita generation was 332 kwh. The company's initial interest was the major
industrial loads, especially the metallurgical ones, of the south-
central region of Minas Gerais, and for several years industrial
consumption accounted for 80 percent of its sales.

FURNAS

In the mid-nineteen fifties CEMIG discovered the Furnas
site on the Grande River, a short distance before the river
becomes the Minas-São Paulo state border. The proposed
project, a 1.2 million kilowatt plant, was eventually considered
too large for the CEMIG market; therefore a federally sponsored company, Central Elétrica de Furnas, S.A., was created
in 1957 with the express purpose of developing the hydro
potential at the Furnas gorge. CEMIG's champion of the
project, John Cotrim, became its president, and two other
CEMIG directors moved into its top positions.

Furnas was to be the key project in an integral development
of the Grande River. Several large hydro plants were envisaged
for the river at transmission distances from São Paulo (316
km.), Belo Horizonte (265 km.), and Rio de Janeiro (429
km.), which would make possible the integration of the south-
central region into one interconnected power system. The
river's central location, bisecting the south-central region, was
its major attraction. In 1958 the World Bank granted a $73
million loan to Furnas to finance the foreign exchange costs of
the project. The company prided itself on being the only
authentic "mixed" state enterprise in Brazil, in that two private
shareholders accounted for 60 percent of the preferred stock,
most of that share being held by São Paulo Light. After several
subsequent increases in share capital, however, the percentage
held by São Paulo Light dwindled to the usual one or two
percent typical of private participation in the state companies.

The Furnas Plant was completed in late 1963, and by 1965 six of its projected eight units were in operation, amounting to 900 mw of the eventual 1,200 mw of installed capacity. At the same time, the company started construction of the down-stream Estreito Plant (800 mw), for which it received a $57 million loan from the World Bank. Furnas also took the lead in regional planning for power development in the south-central region. Together with the major utilities of the region, the planning department of Furnas conducted the first study to determine the supply of power for the entire region. The study became the basis for a later plan for power development, prepared by the Ministry of Mines and Energy.

CHEVAP

The CHEVAP company (Companhia Hidrelétrica do Vale do Paraíba—The Paraíba Valley Hydro Company) was created in September 1960, with the purpose of building a 210-mw hydro plant on the middle reaches of the Paraíba River in the state of Rio de Janeiro. In 1956 the federal government insti-tuted a special commission to study the site, and the company grew out of this commission. The Funil Plant was to help relieve the power supply problem in the metropolitan Rio area, as well as to provide a new power source for the less built-up regions of the state of Rio, some of which were con-sidered likely areas for future industrial expansion. Construc-tion of the plant was started in 1960, and the completion date was pushed back several times, from 1965 to 1969.

In the middle of 1961 CHEVAP was entrusted with the task of building a 150-mw thermal plant, Santa Cruz, on the out-skirts of the metropolitan Rio area. Because of the emergency state of the Rio system, and because no new source of power would be coming into operation in the near future, the Min-istry of Mines and Energy decided in 1961 that a thermal plant was the only possible solution to the impending crisis in power supply. Responsibility for the plant's construction was given to CHEVAP, and construction commenced in 1962 with a $15.5 million loan from the United States Agency for International Development (AID). Santa Cruz, like Funil, was also victim of various delays, and commissioning was possible only in late 1967. Because of various political and administrative problems, CHEVAP was taken over by the federal government in August 1965, through the majority stockholding control of ELETROBRÁS; in 1967 management and administration of the company were handed over to Furnas, which was by then a subsidiary of ELETROBRÁS. (ELETROBRÁS–Centrais Elétricas Brasileiras–is a federal government holding company, incorporated on June 11, 1962, to coordinate power policy and take charge of the federal government's stockholding participation in the various federal and state power companies.)

The Steering Committee

In 1956 the newly formed government of Juscelino Kubitschek created a Development Council (Conselho de Desenvolvimento) to draw up a target program (Programa de Metas) for growth in various sectors of the economy. Power was one of the main targets, and for the first time the south-central region was looked at as a whole in matters of power. As a result of the council's considerations, the Furnas project was considered an excellent candidate, since it was well located for supplying the whole region. Late in 1959, four years before the plant was to come into operation, the Furnas company took the initiative in bringing together the principal utilities of the south-central region in order to conduct a study of power supply for the region. The studies were to serve as the basis for coordinating the operation of the region's power systems (which the Furnas Plant would make necessary) and for planning expansions in capacity. The participating utilities, under the leadership of Furnas, were CEMIG, the Light, AMFORP, USELPA, and CHERP (CHEVAP and CELUSA were not in existence at the time). The Furnas-sponsored studies became the basis of a recommended power development program drawn up by a Working Group (Grupo de Trabalho) in the Ministry of Mines and Energy. The group's

recommendations were accepted as a guide for policy by the
ministry and were approved by executive decree.[36]

In the meantime, CEMIG had been seeking financing from
the United Nations Special Fund for a survey of the hydraulic
potential of the state of Minas Gerais. The World Bank, which
would be executing agent for the Special Fund financing,
suggested to the Brazilian government that the CEMIG survey be extended to all the river systems of the south-central
region. The bank thought that such a study should be used to
build a regional power plan for the south-central region, covering a period of at least fifteen years. The suggestion was
adopted by the Brazilian government, the Special Fund
granted $2.5 million for the study, and the Steering Committee
on Power Studies for the South-Central Region was created
to carry it out. The Comitê Coordenador de Estudos Energéticos da Região Centro-Sul was composed of representatives
from the World Bank, the Ministry of Mines and Energy, the
four state governments, and ELETROBRÁS. Because of its
cumbersome name, the committee was always referred to as
The Steering Committee (O Comitê Coordenador), or simply
The Committee (O Comitê).

In June 1962 the World Bank, in collaboration with the
Brazilian authorities, selected a consortium of three American
engineering firms to carry out the studies—Gibbs & Hill of New
York, and Montreal Engineering and G. E. Crippen Associates
of Canada. The consortium was called CANAMBRA, to describe the nationality of the companies and the area to be
studied—Canada, America, Brazil. Although the group's reports were issued under the name of CANAMBRA, they were
in truth the result of close collaboration with The Committee.
By December 1963, CANAMBRA presented the first stage of
its two-part task—a five-volume report on the power situation
in south-central Brazil and a recommended program of construction through 1966, which would meet the forecasted
growth of the market through 1970. The second stage of

36. "Relatório do Comitê de Estudos Energéticos da Região Centro-
sul," Federal Decree No. 51,058, July 28, 1961.

CANAMBRA's work was a final report, prepared by December 1966, which gave further study to the power market and recommended a long-range program of construction to meet the forecasted market requirements.[37] Both reports were presented to the Ministry of Mines and Energy and approved immediately as official government policy.

The Committee is included here among the power companies of south-central Brazil for two reasons. Brazilian participation in and promotion of its activities was to a great extent the activity of the Furnas company. To Furnas was delegated the representation of ELETROBRÁS in The Committee, or as local power officials said, Furnas "took over" from the newly created and comparativly weak ELETROBRÁS. Because Furnas had built such an interconnectable plant, it was highly interested in, and wanted to have a strong influence on, the course of future power projects and interconnections in the south-central region.[38] In other words, the regional planning accomplished by The Committee was to a certain extent one of the "projects" of the Furnas company.

The Committee served an important function as a meeting ground for the power enterprises of south-central Brazil. It was not easy for these utilities to work together—state company with state company, as well as state company with foreign. Because of the work of The Committee, however, it was necessary that they meet periodically to decide on certain matters,

37. CANAMBRA Engineering Consultants, Ltd., "Power Study of South-central Brazil" (processed, December 1963), 5 vols., and "Final Report on the Power Study of South-central Brazil" (processed, December 1966), 7 vols.

38. One sometimes heard subdued complaints from CANAMBRA technicians that they were being pressured to hurry their work by the managers of Furnas and that they therefore could not be as precise as they would like. This Brazilian "speed-up" of the working pace of American technicians was "because Furnas wants to have a Plan in hand so it can start lobbying for its power program." The more time that elapsed before the plan came into existence, this strategy implied, the more chance there would be for those favoring solutions that deviated from the plan. Local power officials and managers sometimes grumbled that "it was Furnas who gave the orders in the Committee" (quem manda no Comitê é Furnas).

especially those having to do with the placement of transmission lines and substations, for these decisions were the most important for future interconnection. To achieve agreement on such matters was a most difficult problem, because it meant that each company had to give up some of its "sovereignty" for the future collective operation of the system. During these meetings many conflicts between the companies, both present and potential, came out into the open. At the same time, many were brought to some kind of resolution. The project carried out by The Committee was thus a bringing together of several independent and often antagonistic companies—based on the necessity of cooperating for regional planning and for coordinated operation of their power systems.

There was considerable variance in the quality of the south-central region's state power companies. Furnas and CEMIG outranked the others. CHEVAP was a conspicuous failure. USELPA never achieved the reputation of a Furnas or a CEMIG, and CHERP stood somewhat behind USELPA. CELUSA, not having completed its first plant, is difficult to rank, but the company does not seem to have yet gained the political insulation that made Furnas a success. The state's achievement in the power sector, in sum, is not monolithic, nor does it lack a number of less efficient companies and some uneconomical contributions to power supply.

2. *The Rate Problem: Obstruction and Accommodation*

In 1948 the Brazilian government requested the collaboration of United States technicians to make an analysis of factors in Brazil that tended to promote or retard economic development. The result was the establishment of the Joint Brazil-United States Technical Commission, the so-called Abbink Mission. The mission arrived in Brazil in late 1948, and one of the first problems it noticed was the incipient bottleneck in power supply. It pointed to the rate situation as a major cause, but implied that the growing imbalance between power supplies and industrial growth could not help but eventually resolve that impasse. "The need for a rate increase," the mission reported, "does not always become fully evident until large-scale expansion is contemplated, when the question arises of how to pay interest and amortization on the needed funds." [1]

The implication was that the hitherto satisfactory state of power supplies had deprived the rate situation of the urgency needed to mobilize action and overcome resistance to rate reform. Only when large-scale expansion became urgent would the inadequacy of rates be considered intolerable. The mission, in short, did not seem worried about the rate situation, though recognizing its difficulties. Expressing faith in a kind of unbalanced growth, it appeared to be saying that the up-and-coming crisis in power would help the rate problem take

1. Joint Brazil-U.S. Technical Commission [Abbink Mission]. "Report of the Joint Brazil-U.S. Technical Commission" (mimeo, Rio de Janeiro, Feb. 7, 1949), p. 147.

care of itself. Throughout the following fifteen years, however, the rate situation did not change. The Light objected continuously. "The public utility companies," it argued "are subject to rates set by the authorities, who insist on keeping them frozen, or grant only inadequate increases, while all other prices in the economy are rising. The utilities, therefore, are the principal victims of the inflationary process; they have no way of getting around it, or softening its effects. In order to prevent their services from deteriorating—let alone to expand at a pace that keeps up with the growth of demand—they must therefore put forth a tremendous financial effort. And this effort involves a permanent struggle against the lack of comprehension and concern, and even the ill will of others." [2]

Suddenly on November 4, 1964, the Brazilian government put an end to the rate problem. With three executive decrees it provided for automatic protection of rates against inflation and for an immediate provisional rate increase pending a detailed updating of the power companies' capital accounts.[3] In one fell swoop the government had authorized what the Light had been fighting for during a period of almost fifteen years.

Given the political difficulties of making public concessions to a foreign company, this sudden and complete resolution of the rate problem is remarkable. The explanation is almost disappointingly simple. The government of November 1964 had been installed by a military coup in April of that year. Because of its military backing, it was willing and able to enforce unpopular measures. More important, the new power policy-makers had always been on the side of rate increases and had not been unsympathetic to the Light. [4] Through the

2. São Paulo Light S.A.—Serviços de Eletricidade, *Relatório Anual de 1960.*
3. Federal Decrees Nos. 54,936, 54,937, and 54,938.
4. These new policy-makers were Mauro Thibau, Minister of Mines and Energy; Benedicto Dutra, Deputy to the Minister of Mines and Energy (Chefe do Gabinete); Octávio Marcondez Ferraz, President of ELETROBRÁS. The most important measures promised by the new Minister of Mines and Energy were those to "promote the adaptation of the utilities' financial situation to existing economic realities . . . and

years they had consistently criticized nationalizing solutions of the power problem, being convinced that state enterprise was, as a rule, incompetent. Sympathy for rate increases within the government, then, was to a certain extent a simple function of the arrival of new policy-makers who were already in favor of such change.

Because of this brief and arbitrary resolution of the rate problem, the executive decrees of 1964 do not seem very interesting as a case study in stalemate-breaking. They are interesting, however, for the questions they raise about the preceding period. A respectable expansion in power had been undertaken in the fifteen years between the Abbink Report and the final breaking of the rate stalemate in 1964. Large-scale expansion, in short, had been achieved *without* the rate increase that had seemed necessary to finance an expansion in supply and which the Abbink Mission assumed would fall into place as the need became evident. Although the expansion in the later years of this period was carried out by the newly formed companies in the state sector—and was therefore not necessarily dependent on a previous improvement in the rate situation—how is it possible to account for the respectable rate of expansion of the Light itself, as well as the fact that the company hung on as long as it did even after it had stopped investing in new generating capacity?

Without intimate access to the books and experience of the Light, it is impossible to answer these questions with any accuracy. The company's published records show that the profit rate diminished considerably between 1947 and 1965, as well as the share of capital expenditures as a percentage of

permit private power companies once again to finance out of their own earnings the improvement and expansion of their facilities." "Diretrizes básicas no setor de energia elétrica" [June 6, 1964], *Revista Brasileira de Energia Elétrica* (May-October 1964), II, 7. In a similar tone, the new President of ELETROBRÁS announced that his organization would follow a realistic policy, "based on the decision to serve the consumer well. The consumer will be made to pay the real cost of electricity, instead of transferring the burden to the general taxpayer. In other words: he who buys pays." "Política realista para a ELETROBRÁS," *Revista Brasileira de Energia Elétrica* (May-October 1964), II, 2.

total revenue (see Table 2.1). It is possible, however, to show that exclusive emphasis on basic rate reform—though perfectly justifiable as an end to be pursued—may somewhat obscure the degree of accommodation that was worked out between the government and the utility during this period. This accommodation explains how the private company could expand, or at least stay put, given the impasse in the rate situation. Perhaps more important, it shows that there was more of a possibility for "coexistence" between the state and the foreign company than was indicated by the lack of progress on the question of basic rate reform.

The basic rate increase was the most politically difficult way of financing the large-scale expansion needed in the power sector. Other ways of channeling resources to the private utility were employed—namely, the "additionals" or surcharges on the rates, and the foreign exchange privileges. These measures were not as efficient or substantial as the rate increases sought by the company, but they may have been the only real political alternative, short of nationalization, given the intense public hostility to the foreign company. After orderly nationalization of the American-owned power utility in Mexico, for example, a spokesman for the company admitted that "increased rates, no matter how small the increment, always brought adverse public reaction in Mexico. They could even lead to a political crisis which could cause foreign capital to look for a more stable environment." [5] In other words, the most efficient way of channeling income to the foreign company might possibly have led to a *decrease* in supply. Thus, the real alternative in Brazil was not necessarily between adequate rate increases and the makeshift arrangements that actually occurred; it may rather have been between these actual arrangements and a nationalization in the Mexican form.

The additionals and foreign exchange privileges are an essential part of the history of the "deintegration" of the

5. Quoted by Miguel Wionczek, "Electric Power: The Uneasy Partnership," in Raymond Vernon, ed., *Public Policy and Private Enterprise in Mexico* (Cambridge: Harvard University Press, 1964), p. 84.

Table 2.1. Brazilian Traction, Light & Power Co.:
net revenue and capital expenditure, 1947–1965[a].

Year	Net rev. (% of total rev.)[b]	Capital expend. (% of total rev.)
1947	27.9	51.5
1948	26.5	31.7
1949	25.5	33.3
1950	24.4	41.3
1951	23.3	44.5
1952	24.4	51.0
1953	17.7	50.8
1954	14.2	37.1
1955	13.0	27.4
1956	23.5	21.6
1957	15.1	26.4
1958	8.3	27.1
1959	6.6	43.5
1960	10.4	16.6
1961	9.6	17.3
1962	0.9	15.6
1963	-0.8	11.8[c]
1964	-0.3	9.7
1965	8.9	12.1

Source: Dollar figures in Brazilian Traction, Light & Power Co., *Annual Reports.*

a. These figures are for Brazilian Traction rather than the two electric power subsidiaries, São Paulo Light and Rio Light. They therefore include the company's Brazilian operations in telephones, water, gas, and streetcars, which represented a minority of the company's receipts and fixed assets and were subjected to the same downward trend owing to the lack of adjustment of utility rates to inflation.

b. Total revenue: gross earnings from operations, plus interest on temporary investments and miscellaneous income. Net revenue: total revenue minus operating expenses (which include taxes, depreciation, and amortization).

c. Capital expenditure is positive, even though net revenue is negative, because of financing from depreciation allowances and borrowing.

power sector. By keeping the foreign company at least in distribution, such makeshift accommodations facilitated a solution to the power shortage that did not require a previous time-consuming attack on the rate problem. That state enterprise could concentrate on generation, as will be seen later on, endowed its first ventures in power with a considerable probability of success.

One further word is needed about the evolution of the rate problem for the Light, and the role of the additionals and foreign exchange privileges in supplementing the company's earnings. According to the 1934 Water Code,[6] the first comprehensive legislation on power in Brazil, the return allowed on a power company's investment was set at 10 percent. This return was to be calculated on a capital base evaluated at original cost, and the basic rate was to be set so as to yield that return. The concept of original or historic cost, rather than the 10 percent return, had been the target of criticism of the rate structure, for the real value of the original cost of the company's investment was continuously eroded by inflation, which averaged an annual rate of 18.4 percent between 1946 and 1961.[7] Without some provision for periodic correction of the value of the company's assets, historic cost became an inadequate basis for calculation of a fair return.

The necessity for providing periodic correction of historic cost was the essence of the Brazilian rate problem—even though this statement oversimplifies the question of rate legislation and its effect on the foreign utility's ability to expand. Whether the company was earning adequate returns despite legislative and administrative problems was, and still is, a much debated question. What is important here is that there was no procedure for increasing the basic rate; this vacuum, in turn, was both cause and effect of the lack of well-functioning rate-regulating machinery in the government.

With the enactment of the Water Code in 1934, rate-making

6. Código de Águas, Federal Decree No. 24,634, July 10, 1934.
7. *Conjuntura Econômica*, September 1964. The index used is the cost of living in the state of Guanabara. After 1961 the rate of inflation accelerated considerably.

authority passed to the federal government. The Water Division (Divisão de Águas) of the Ministry of Agriculture—transferred to the Ministry of Mines and Energy when the latter was created in 1961—was charged with the task of passing on the rate increases requested by the utilities. The Water Code introduced in Brazil the concept of federal regulation of power utilities as public services; it was also intended to introduce orderly, uniform rate-making machinery—in the spirit of the Federal Power Act of 1920 in the United States, and the subsequent legislation of 1930 that reorganized the Federal Power Commission as an independent organ.

For various reasons the Brazilian power legislation did not facilitate the orderly dealing with rates that had been desired. The legislation was not designed for the inflationary atmosphere that was soon to play havoc with the historic-cost basis for calculating the rate. Furthermore, the legislation covered more completely the power utilities that would obtain concessions *after* its enactment than those, like the Light, that had existing concessions. Although the latter were intended to come under subsequent implementing legislation, such legislation was decreed after a considerable lapse of time, and then only partially. Utilities like the Light were in a kind of limbo throughout much of the period, in terms both of rate-making procedure and of obtaining new concessions. Only in 1957, with Decree No. 41.019, was comprehensive implementing legislation for the Water Code decreed, setting down in law the procedure by which rates should be fixed and the specific reasons for which surcharges could be added. The principle of revaluing the inflation-eroded capital base of the power utilities, and of authorizing consequent increases in the basic rate, was not established by law until the decrees of 1964. Moreover, to the extent that the Light had been anxious to avoid government scrutiny of its books, it had not avidly sought the protection of the law, which perpetuated somewhat the unsettled state of rate-making. Finally, the federal government was not adequately staffed to carry out effectively the rate review function it had assumed. The result of these circumstances was that rate-making occurred to a considerable extent outside the legal framework, most increases being the outcome of specific campaigns by the company in the Ministry of Agriculture.

From the enactment of the Water Code in 1934 until the rate decrees of 1964, Rio and São Paulo Light achieved only one increase in the *basic* rate—in June 1955 for Rio Light, and March 1956 for São Paulo Light. The increase occurred with the "nationalization" of the two companies, which meant the conversion of their accounts from dollars to cruzeiros and a consequent updating of their investment value. That is, the exchange rate that the company was allowed to use for purposes of the conversion resulted in more than doubling the value of its fixed assets.[8] Corresponding rate increases were authorized, calculated on the new capital base. Although the conversion provided a basic rate increase for the Light, it did not represent any progress on the basic rate problem. The company could only be "nationalized" once; it could not use the 1955–1956 rate increase as precedent for further action in the field of rate reform.

Two mechanisms kept the Light going, in lieu of a fundamental adaptation of the rate structure to inflation. One was the additionals or rate surcharges allowed for increases in certain costs, such as labor, fuel, foreign exchange for debt service, and purchased power. The other was preferential exchange rates granted for remittances of profits and debt service and for the importation of equipment. Rate increases based on the additionals had accounted for significant increases in cruzeiro rates and were crucial to the company's operation.[9] It is estimated, for example, that São Paulo Light's average return per kilowatt hour increased between eleven and twelve times in the face of a twelve-and-a-half-fold increase in the cost of

8. The exact increase in value for Rio Light was 2.12. The increase for São Paulo Light may be assumed to have been similar. Banco Nacional de Desenvolvimento Econômico (BNDE) Project Files, Doc. DP-8/61, Jan. 25, 1961, p. 22—cited hereafter as BNDE Files.

9. United States Department of State, Agency for International Development [AID], "Brazil—Rio Light S/A and São Paulo Light S/A," Capital Assistance Paper: Proposal and Recommendations for the Review of the Development Loan Committee, Document #AID-DLC/P338 (June 9, 1965), p. 54.

living during the same period (see Table 2.2). If this increase is compared with the change in the percentage share of the additionals in the company's return, it can be seen that the additionals get full credit for the increase (see Table 2.3). In 1956, immediately after São Paulo Light's basic rate increase, the additionals represented about 5 percent of the company's total receipts, and the basic rate represented 95 percent. By 1964 the percentages were exactly reversed: the additionals accounted for 95 percent, the basic rate, for 5 percent.

The second important area in which the company was able to defend itself against its losses in the basic rate was the foreign exchange market. Between 1939 and 1954 the cost of living increased almost six times.[10] During the same period, however, the rate at which the company could convert cruzeiros into dollars for debt service and profit remittance remained the same. In 1953 a free rate of exchange was established alongside the already existing official rate. But a provision of the legislation allowed the Light to be classified as an "essential industry"; it therefore could import equipment, remit interest on foreign debt, and transfer profits—all at preferential exchange rates that represented about one half the cost of exchange to the nonpreferred sectors (see Table 2.4).[11] Even after 1961, when the preferential rates were abolished, the company did not really lose from having to remit considerable sums of money through the exchange market, because increases in the cost of foreign exchange used to service registered debt were reflected in electricity rate adjustments.[12] By 1964 the foreign exchange additional represented 23.5 percent of the total receipts of São Paulo Light.[13]

10. The exact increase was 5.76, based on data from the Getúlio Vargas Foundation.

11. In its justification for a loan to Rio and São Paulo Light in 1965, the AID Brazil Mission pointed out that the special exchange rate had represented a significant advantage for the company during the 1950's, when the power rate picture, in contrast, was so bleak. "Rio Light and São Paulo Light," Appendix to the Financial Section, p. 19.

12. This foreign exchange additional was codified in Federal Decree No. 41,019, Feb. 27, 1957.

13. São Paulo Light S.A.—Serviços de Eletricidade, *Relatório Anual de 1964.* Total receipts = basic rate plus additionals.

Table 2.2. São Paulo Light: indices of average return
per kwh and the cost of living, 1958–1964[a]
(1958=100, current cruzeiros).

Year[b]	Gross return per kwh[c]	Net return per kwh[d]	Cost of living[e]
1958	100.0	100.0	100.0
1959	134.7	139.1	137.5
1960	162.9	159.9	185.2
1963	656.2	645.7	678.1
1964	1434.4	1189.0	1267.9

Source: São Paulo Light, *Annual Reports,* for total receipts and tax figures: International Engineering for kwh sold; Getúlio Vargas Foundation for cost of living index.

a. The ideal year in which to start this comparison would be 1956. It could be assumed that because the basic rate was increased in that year, the company's rates were close to adequate. The closest year for which comparable company figures were available, however, was 1958. The comparison ends in 1964 so as not to include the basic rate increases that became effective in the April billings of 1965. The income figures of the annual reports of the parent company are more complete but also include return on the streetcar, telephone, gas, and water services—some of which were in perpetual deficit.

b. Information not available on a comparable basis for 1960 and 1961.

c. Total receipts divided by total kwh sold.

d. Total receipts minus taxes charged to consumer and passed on to government, divided by total kwh sold.

e. For the city of São Paulo. The increase in this index for these years was slightly higher than increases in the general wholesale index (1264.7 in 1964) and in the industrial products index (1230.2 in 1964). I therefore use the cost of living index to provide the most conservative comparison to the Light's increase in kwh receipts and to give an idea of the increase in the average rate paid by the consumer as compared to the increase in the cost of living.

Table 2.3. São Paulo Light: change in percentage share of additionals and basic rate in total receipts, 1956–1964.[a]

Year	Basic rate (%)	Additionals (%)
1956	94.60	5.4
1957	85.86	14.14
1958	82.78	17.22
1959	60.78	39.27
1960	51.69	48.31
1961	33.10	66.90
1962	23.03	76.97
1963	12.56	87.44
1964	5.79	94.21

Source: São Paulo Light S.A. — Serviços de Eletricidade, *Relatório Anual de 1964.*
a. Total receipts exclusive of tax surcharges collected by the company and passed on to the government.

I emphasize the above figures in order to dispel the erroneous image of complete stalemate between the host government and the foreign utility—an image portrayed by the basic rate picture. Important concessions were being made to the company throughout the period of rate stalemate. Although they may not have been great enough to turn the Light into a rapidly expanding company,[14] they at least indicate the absence of a determined attempt on the part of the state to suffocate the company—an accusation often made by critics of

14. Many observers believed that the rate problem was not the basic cause of the company's stagnation. Some thought that only a considerable and improbable lessening of popular hostility and government obstructionism could turn the Light back to a rapidly growing enterprise. Others thought that the company's pre-Water Code (1934) profits had been so spectacular that no improvement in its financial position within the context of public utility regulation could ever duplicate the conditions under which it had operated before the Water Code. Both points of view may find some support in the company's reaction to the new rate decrees of 1964. When the Light finally did get the rate change it had fought for, it did not change its decision to restrict its activities to distribution—a decision that had grown in the first place out of its adaptation to the inadequacies in the basic rate.

Table 2.4. Preferential foreign exchange rates for equipment imports and foreign debt service in essential industries, as compared to nonpreferential rates (under Brazilian exchange auction system, 1953–1961).

Year (as of 12/31)	Preferential rate[a] (Cr$ per US$)	Pref/free rate[b] (%)	Pref/general rate[c] (%)
1953	25.82	48.5	—
1954 (3/1/55)	33.82	43.4	—
1955 (1/1/56)	43.82	64.9	—
1956	43.82	66.9	—
1957	51.32	56.1	54.2
1958 (1/31/59)	100.00	68.3	38.9
1959	100.00	49.3	46.1
1960	100.00	51.2	43.7
1961 (3/14/61)	200.00	62.8	62.8
1961 (7/1/61)	318.00	(preferential rates abolished)	

Source: International Monetary Fund, *Annual Report on Exchange Restrictions,* 1953–1962.

a. For (1) remittance of principal and transfers of interest (not exceeding 8% p.a.) on registered debt for investments in petroleum or printing industries, or in sectors considered essential to economic development or national defense; (2) equipment imports for petroleum and printing industries, or in sectors considered essential to economic development or national defense.

b. Almost all invisible transactions, and all capital transactions not effected at the preferential rate.

c. For raw materials, equipment, and other production goods, and for general consumption goods whose supply was not sufficient in domestic market. The General Category rate was established in 1957; it unified four previously existing categories covering these items.

state action in this field. What the government was taking away with one hand, it was to some extent returning with the other.

The case of foreign power in Mexico reveals a similar combination of accommodation and obstruction. "The state's responses to the difficulties of the power industry," wrote Wionczek, "were complicated and equivocal . . . Administrators made it perfectly clear that, on political grounds, they rejected a radical revision of the rate structure and the constant upward adjustment of electricity prices to conform to the general inflationary trend. At the same time, however, attempts were made to compensate the private sector of the industry for inadequate rates . . . The foreign companies were given unrestricted access to state-generated power under very favorable pricing conditions; at the time of periodical collective contract negotiations, the government persuaded the electric trade unions to restrain their demands; through Nacional Financiera, the Mexican government's development bank, the firms received sizable medium-term domestic credits carrying an interest much below the current market rate; and finally, the government acted on behalf of, or jointly with, the private companies in obtaining foreign loans, and extended its unconditional guarantee to all the major loans granted them by international agencies." [15]

Obstruction: The Basic Rate

Any reform of the basic rate would have required the displacement or complete modification of a concept fundamental to rate-making in Brazil—that is, return must be calculated according to the original cost of the investment. It was not that the original cost concept was necessarily cherished by Brazilian power officials; rather, any attempt to change the basic rate would have required a profound and difficult consensus on rate-making concepts, and thus on the sensitive question of the foreign power company.

15. Wionczek, "Electric Power," p. 78.

In evaluating the resistance to updating the original-cost principle, one must realize that enactment of historic cost into law in 1934 was not a case of malice aforethought, as some critics of the Water Code later said. The Water Code was often considered a piece of super-nationalistic legislation, product of a period of similar enactments designed to keep the nation's hands on its natural resources, but fashioned in such a way, according to these critics, as to suffocate development. From this point of view, the original-cost provision of the Water Code was just one more way of guaranteeing the eventual undoing of the electric power companies, which, in terms of kilowatt hours produced, were principally foreign.

Far from being xenophobic, however, codification of the original-cost principle might even have been termed an "aping" of the foreigner. Original-cost was in vogue in the United States during the nineteen thirties, when the major concern surrounding rate-making was deflation rather than inflation.[16] The Brazilian rate "squeeze" of the nineteen fifties and sixties thus represented a growing outdatedness of the regulatory legislation, brought on by inflation rather than by a long-standing attempt to snuff out the life of the foreign utility. This legislative lag was no doubt latched on to by those who wanted to persecute the power companies, for no form of persecution could have been easier than *not* to exert oneself to support a very difficult reform. The persistence of the rate lag, however, was in no way a sign that the "suffocation" school had won out.

The concept of making certain prices automatically inflation-proof was in itself just starting to gain ground in the late

16. "The protagonists of original cost in the United States have emphasized the fact that prices have fallen as well as risen in the past . . . It is significant that the champions of original cost won from the United States Supreme Court the right to employ their method . . . only after the deflation of the '30's . . . Brazil . . . adopted an original cost rate base, reflecting the drift of thinking on this issue in the deflationary '30's." David Cavers and James Nelson, *Electric Power Regulation in Latin America* (Baltimore: Johns Hopkins Press, 1959), pp. 115–116.

nineteen fifties. Only then was inflation beginning to be considered a somewhat permanent phenomenon of growth in Brazil, against which certain prices should and could be insulated. The delayed action following the realization of the relative permanence of inflation was not without reason. To legislate protection against inflation would have meant that the government was admitting defeat in the struggle against the phenomenon, which could have been politically disastrous. A prominent Brazilian economist pointed out the effect of this political constraint on the rate problem: "When speaking candidly, the government will agree that the concept of original cost as a basis for remuneration of the public utilities is an incoherent position in an atmosphere of chronic inflation. But the desire to hide the symptoms of the inflationary process is even stronger." [17]

It was not only public utilities that were the victim of political resistance to inflationary adaptation. The National Development Bank (Banco Nacional de Desenvolvimento Econômico), for example, was well aware of the fact that its loans were in effect subsidies, because inflation turned the rate of interest negative. This negative-interest lending was to a certain extent deliberate policy—or rather, deliberate avoidance of monetary correction clauses—out of the conviction that Brazil's industrial development ought to be subsidized. But even when the bank finally attempted to introduce monetary correction into its loan contracts, it took many years to succeed because "we couldn't get away with it politically." [18] In order to break this impasse, the bank began to favor participation in its borrower's equity, rather than lending, as a way of assisting companies seeking financing. It made repeated efforts to convince São Paulo industrialists of the validity of this plan, arguing that the bank's lending capital could thereby escape inflationary erosion. The industrialists responded that if

17. Mário Henrique Simonsen, "Tensões em países subdesenvolvidos: O papel da economia nos setores público e privado e as tensões surgidas da administração de uma economia mista," *Desenvolvimento e Conjuntura* (Oct. 1962), p. 99.
18. BNDE official to the author.

the bank wanted to prevent borrowers from reaping inflationary gains on its loans, it should attempt to control the inflationary process, instead of becoming its partner by buying into
the private companies seeking financing.

If it was so difficult for the country's own development bank
to institute the principle of monetary correction in its loan
contracts, one can imagine the resistance to applying such a
principle to the electric power rates of a foreign company. As
one congressman said, in opposing an inflation-adjusted power
rate, "Now Brazil still has not accepted the automatic sliding
scale for wages, which ought to be one of the natural consequences of the galloping inflation that we are experiencing;
we still have not allowed automatic increases in the earnings
of government workers. If we do not recognize this principle
for the price of labor, then why should we start with the price
of electricity, where the major benefactor will be the [foreign]
power companies?" [19]

Basic rate reform, then, required legislative consensus on a
question that would make the foreign company one of the first
to benefit from the new idea of making certain prices inflation-
proof. It was therefore probably the most resistance-strewn
path for channeling increased earnings to the company. Indeed, given the obstacles to regular increases in the basic rate,
the less "immediate" alternative of state construction of hydro
plants was often considered a *shortcut* solution to the power
problem, despite the massive capital requirements and the
long gestation of these projects. In mid-1955, for example,

19. Brasil, Congresso, *Diário do Congresso Nacional,* Sec. I (Aug. 25,
1959), p. 5569. The deputy was Barbosa Lima Sobrinho, Socialist party
(PSB), from the state of Pernambuco. Wionczek, "Electric Power,"
p. 83, made similar comments in discussing a 1957 Mexican government report on the power problem, which proposed a steep upward
revision of power rates and almost automatic annual increases in line
with future cost increases: "If the state did not consider it politically
feasible to put such government-owned enterprises as the railways and
the petroleum industry on a sound financial footing by increasing the
prices charged for their services, how could it be expected to launch a
much more difficult operation involving sizable increases in the profits
of foreign-owned companies and real or imaginary hardship for millions
of electricity consumers."

when the São Paulo State Electric Power Council was discussing a proposed program of state-constructed generating plants, the representative of São Paulo industry said, "Being as I am a believer in the possibilities and the efficiency of private initiative . . . I could object to the exclusive solution of this problem by the government. At this point, however, we must recognize a simple matter of fact: existing legislation neither stimulates nor permits a massive flow of private capital to the public utilities, notably those producing and distributing electric power. And because the modification of this legislation is a matter of great complexity—extremely disputed and requiring long-drawn-out consideration—I am of the opinion that it is simply not possible to wait around for this modification and not do anything in the meantime about building new generating plants." [20]

The political difficulty of reforming the rate structure centered also on the public admission that such reform was required. That is, to press for legislation correcting the capital base on which the company's return was calculated would have been to argue that the foreign utilities were not earning their just due, which was anathema to public opinion. It was this necessity to commit oneself publicly on the question of the foreign power company that lumped the varying shades of reasonable and unreasonable opinion among politicians and policy-makers into one resistant mass. Of all the ways of allowing a utility to earn money, raising the basic rate drew the highest political attention and penalties. Letting the rate lag, therefore, was far from being a sign of persecution. It could simply represent an unwillingness to bear the political penalties of reforming the rate, regardless of the politician's sentiments on the matter. The stalemated rate situation, in sum, was very much a result of the certainty of public resistance on the question of the basic rate.

There was a surprising reasonableness concerning the Light

20. CEEE Minutes, July 25, 1955, Annex No. 2. The speaker was Aldo Mário Azevedo of the São Paulo Federation of Industries (Federação de Indústrias do Estado de São Paulo).

from a wide spectrum of policy-makers and power bureau-
crats—or at least, a lack of hostility. They would privately
admit that the basic rate structure was inadequate and at the
same time query, "But do you think that the Light *really* isn't
earning?" [21] It was as if all believed that a kind of equilibrium
in the power sector had been deviously established, and that
it was perfectly possible to make marginal accommodations to
maintain that equilibrium—accommodations such as additionals increases, preferential exchange arrangements, BNDE
financing, and other less visible arrangements. According to
this view, the continued existence of the company was the
simple proof that, having encountered the closing of one major
channel of earnings, it had busily opened up and developed
others. These government officials would invariably preface
their opinions on the Light with a wise, sad smile and the
comment, "The Light is a company that's *very* complicated"—
as if to say that the company had acquired an impenetrable
aura in order to camouflage its extra-legal way of earning
money.[22]

21. In 1957 São Paulo Light requested financing from the BNDE for
two additions to its generating capacity. After making its own study of
the company's earnings figures, the bank reported that between 1948
and 1953 the Light had earned profits greater than the 10 percent legal
limit. Any financial cooperation, the Project Division of the bank suggested, "ought to be formulated with considerable care, owing to the
company's demonstrated capacity to invest. It is capable of financing
by itself a part of the expansion for which it is requesting our assistance."
Parecer DP-109/58, Sept. 13, 1958, Appendix II (July 28, 1958), BNDE
Files, p. 20.

22. This conviction of the Light's propensity to complicate was exemplified in a BNDE analysis of a loan request from the company. In 1953
the Light had asked the bank for a Cr$500 million loan to complete an
expansion of the Cubatão Hydro Plant. While the request was being
studied, the company communicated to the bank that it would also like
to use the requested funds for any general expansion programs that it
might be undertaking. "The Light always presents its problems in the
most complex manner possible," a bank memo stated. "In the present
case, for example, the principal project of the company is the Cubatão
Plant—a project that is quite easy to analyze. It is conducive, therefore,
to a rapid and informed pronouncement by the bank. The company,
however, complicates the whole question by deciding to use the Cubatão
loan for other projects as well . . . It preferred to leave the whole matter
[of presenting an analysis of these other projects] more or less up in the

The company itself had for years participated in this "devious" equilibrium. Up to the early 1950's the Light still hoped that it might succeed in having the Water Code declared unconstitutional. It envisioned a return to the pre-Code days of the "gold-clause" when rate adjustments automatically followed variations in the world price of gold.[23] Until that occurred, the company preferred dealing with the government on the basis of its influence rather than through established regulatory channels—a logical tactic, since it was one of the most capable and powerful institutions in Brazil. If the Light were to press for regularization of rate legislation, or to press too firmly for rate increases, it would have no grounds for refusing the government's attempts to look at its books. Such an examination of the books would of course be necessary for the purpose of determining an adequate rate. The company preferred to be the victim of, but an outsider to, the legislation, rather than to bring down government control upon its head in order to earn more through the rate structure.

In the mid-1950's, however, the Light began to promote legislative reform of the rate structure. Two changes drove the company to the law. One was the government of Getúlio Vargas, which moved into office in 1950. The Light had expected to deal with the new Vargas administration as it had with the old—on the basis of influence. But the new government began to sponsor legislation that disturbed the devious equilibrium. The most unsettling case was Law No. 1,807 of January 1953, which ended the system of a fixed special rate for a considerable proportion of the company's foreign exchange dealings. Although excepting the Light from the general rate, the law left the periodic determination of the special rate, and the Light's privilege to it, up to the authorities. This was an insecure arrangement for a company that

---

air—surely in order to serve its own purposes—purposes that, as far as we are concerned, do not coincide with those of the bank." "Processo No. 172-A/53—Assunto: Pedido de financiamento feito pela Brazilian Traction, Light and Power Company, Ltd.," May 8, 1954, BNDE Files, p. 11.

23. Lawyer of Rio Light to the author.

had to count principally on the foreign exchange market to compensate for its losses in the power rate.

This new certainty about the foreign exchange market transformed the power rate situation into a bigger problem and a more serious barrier to expansion in generation. Even though the Light continued to receive preferential treatment under the new legislation, the removal of long-term certainty about its favored position contributed to the company's unwillingness to undertake correspondingly long-term expansions, which were precisely the type of financial commitment needed in hydro generation.

The second factor that drove the company to seek protection within the law was the postwar surge of economic growth in the Light's concession areas. As long as the market had expanded calmly, the company did not need as much of a long-term promise of return through an adequate rate structure in order to function adequately. It was the jolt of the economic upsurge, plus Vargas' undermining of the "influence" way of doing things, that forced the Light to seek just treatment under the law. Only then did the company begin to fight for a living rate, as well as give in a little on the idea of government scrutiny of its books.

But by that time the Light's way of doing things was a difficult pattern to change or erase from the minds of power officials, who still believed that the company was making more than sufficient earnings through the makeshift accommodations that had been worked out. This point of view was succinctly expressed by one of the BNDE's most respected nationalist economists: "It seems to me that the existing legislation does not at all hinder the expansion of power facilities. The principal allegation is that historic cost prevents the establishment of a realistic rate in the power sector. But in reality, this does not at all occur—for a very simple reason. Historic cost in this country is only applied to the small utilities, which are the only ones truly regulated by the government. The large power companies have never applied historic cost since 1938. They have simply increased rates above the levels existing at that time. The increase always covers all the increases in expenses. Strictly speaking, we can say that historic cost is not now taken into account in the large utilities in the determination of the rate—and it never was. An examination of the books to determine the balance of their assets has never been made. How can we say, then, that the rate is being based on the original value of the utility's investment?" [24]

In terms of the possibilities of rate structure reform, a kind of vicious cycle had developed: the more the basic rate deteriorated, the more adept the company became at capturing income outside the rate. The more certain it seemed to government officials, therefore, that any modernization of the rate structure would be a stupidly magnanimous concession. Nobody, after all, expected to see a more law-abiding equilibrium develop, where the advance in legitimate earnings would be accompanied by a relinquishing of "illegitimate" earnings. So it was that the question of updating the capital base of the power companies in order to facilitate realistic rates turned otherwise flexible power officials into the camp of the obstructionist foreign-company haters—or turned the interest of concerned policy-makers into disinterest. Attitudes on the basic rate question were thus the least typical of relations between the power company and the government. Focusing on them simply reveals two opposing camps on the power ques-

24. José Ribeiro Lira, ELETROBRÁS Interviews, Nov. 22, 1961, p. 14. A more passionate expression of this approach was made by the governor of Guanabara, Carlos Lacerda. In August 1965 the Ministry of Mines and Energy sent a communication to the governor, characterizing his objections to the recent rate increases as "rate demagoguery." In his reply to the minister, the governor wrote, "What Your Excellency referred to as 'rate demagoguery' is not only the failure to grant fair rates to the concessionaire. It is, at the same time, the failure of the concessionaire to give an accounting of the exact cost of the kilowatt hour. The Light has never given information about this, and the Federal Government has never been able to find out. Even Your Excellency, at this moment, would be unable to say what a kilowatt hour costs the Light, as you admitted in my office. This 'demagoguery,' in short, cuts both ways. It is not honest to favor one side, in the name of combating the other." "Do Governador da Guanabara ao Ministro de Minas e Energia," Ofício GGG No. 672, Aug. 18, 1965, reprinted in *Jornal do Brasil,* August 19, 1965.

tion, rather than the many fine shadings of opinion that existed and out of which arose the working arrangements described below.

Accommodation: The Additionals

If electric power was to be so highly politicized, it may have been just as well that this politicization at least occurred around such a specific subject as the basic rate. For policy-makers this meant that there were other areas where one could negotiate in relative peace.[25] The additionals were one of these areas more amenable to change. The mechanism is not at all novel, being in wide use in both the United States and developing countries, as well as in public services other than electric power. In fact, Brazil, in comparison to other Latin American countries, is considered to have made substantial progress in providing for these periodic electricity rate in-creases based on increases in operating expenses.[26] What is interesting about the history of the additionals in Brazil, how-ever, is its neat demonstration of a type of problem that was by its very structure, more open to solution. The story of the additionals also makes clearer the contrasting difficulties resid-ing in the basic rate question as a class of problem. Finally, the additional cases set the background for understanding the less publicized areas of interaction between foreign company and government.

The story of the additionals starts in 1945, even before the basic rate had become a problem. Utility workers in Rio and São Paulo were demanding a cost-of-living increase in their wages, which the companies resisted. They could not, they said, absorb such an increase in their operating expenses if

25. A similar explanation is often given for President Vargas' national-ization of the petroleum-refining industry; that is, PETROBRÁS, the state monopoly, was established in order to calm virulent nationalist dissatisfaction over the possibility of foreign exploitation of Brazilian petroleum. If nationalist pressure was given in to on the sensitive matter of petroleum, according to this view, resisting such demands in regard to other sectors would be politically easier.

26. Cavers and Nelson, *Electric Power Regulation*, p. 125.

they were not reimbursed with compensating increases in the rate. Decree-Law No. 7,524 of May 5, 1945, granted both the salary increases and the rate increases. Subsequently, rate surcharges for increases in wages became standard practice, as well as the sequence in which they came about: union insistence on a wage increase, the company claim for a corresponding rate increase, and the almost simultaneous granting of the two. Public explanations always focused on the necessity for the wage increase and the social maladies that would be consequent upon not granting it. There were never attempts to justify the company's claim that it could not absorb the increase or to describe the maladies that could be brought on by insufficient rates.

The next foothold gained by the additionals occurred during the planning of the Piratininga Thermal Plant for São Paulo, the only significant thermal contribution to the Rio-São Paulo system. In 1950 the Light went to the Water Division—the federal rate-regulating authority—and indicated that it was ready to build the plant, but it would not undertake such a venture without the guarantee of a "fuel clause," ensuring automatic rate increases in compensation for any future increases in the cost of fuel. It could not risk subjecting the remuneration of such a major component of its kilowatt-hour cost to future inflationary caprice.[27] The Water Division, faced with an impending crisis in the São Paulo power supply, promised to grant the fuel clause in exchange for immediate construction of the thermal plant. Soon after construction had begun, the surcharge for fuel was formalized. The fuel clause was thus the only way for São Paulo to get the added capacity, and the plant was the only way to avoid the imminent power crisis. Additionals for increases in the cost of fuel were henceforth accepted as justification for rate increases.

The next additional to appear was compensation for increases in the cost of foreign exchange used for making pay-

27. In 1962, when the Piratininga Plant represented 30 percent of São Paulo Light's installed capacity, fuel costs accounted for 60 percent of the average operating expenses of the system per kwh sold.

ment of interest and principal on registered foreign debt.[28]
This additional was a concession granted by the government
in exchange for international financing of the region's power
supply. To deny it would have been to miss the opportunity
to capitalize on the newly discovered appeal of Brazil's power
sector to international financial circles.

The last additional, compensation for increases in the cost of
purchased power, must have been the easiest to achieve, for
it bound the interests of the government to those of the Light
in a very direct way. The third parties from which the Light
started to buy power on an important scale were the state-
sponsored companies—first the plants of the São Paulo state
company, USELPA; later, on a much more significant scale,
the federal power company, Furnas.[29] It was therefore in the
direct interest of the government's new undertakings in power
to allow the Light to increase its rates when the bulk suppliers—
the state-sponsored generating companies—increased theirs.

An interesting aspect of this additional was that, as the
Light became more and more dependent on purchased power
because of the successive entry into operation of Furnas generating units, its rate would draw closer and closer in substance
to what the basic-rate modernization aimed for in form. After
this last purchased power additional had fallen into place, the
only major lagging component in the rate structure was the
capital base on which the Light's rate of return was calculated.
Under the system of historic cost, the older the company, the
longer its capital base had been exposed to inflationary erosion.
But the younger the company, the less erosion its capital base
had suffered, and its rate would thus be less inadequate than
that of the older company. The initial entry of the state gener-

28. Federal Decree No. 41,019, February 26, 1957. The provision
for this additional was a codification of already existing parctice.
29. The first occasion for granting such an additional was the interconnection of São Paulo Light in 1956 with the Cia. Paulista de Força
e Luz, a subsidiary of AMFORP, which supplied the interior of the
state of São Paulo. The following year the principle of a purchased power
additional was codified into Federal Decree No. 41,019. It was obvious
by then that the major future source of purchased power for São Paulo
Light would be the generating plants of the state and federal governments.

ating company into the Light's retail rates would then result in a rate increase to the consumer caused by an increase in the cost of the Light's purchased power. This increase represented at least a partial updating of the capital base component of the total rate, disregarding for the moment the effects of the uneven way this modernization was distributed between the Light and the supplying state company.

The purchased power additional not only brought in through the back door a gradual modernization of the total rate, but it opened up for Brazil's new state undertakings access to international financing institutions, without requiring a previous solution of the basic rate problem. Through the purchased power additional, the state generating companies obtained guaranteed protection against consumer resistance to future rate increases. The increase would be paid by the distributor (the Light) and passed on as an additional to the consumer.

At the same time that pro rate-reform policy-makers were battling in vain for acceptance of the concept of rates charged on an updated capital base, this modernization of the rate was taking place to some extent in practice. The change as such was unresisted, because it was being called by a different name: additionals surcharge for increases in the cost of purchased power. It should be noted that the difficulty of calling certain public utility charges by their proper names is not unique in Brazil. It is standard practice in the United States, for example, not to include the cost of metering and billing the individual residential consumer in his monthly bill. The most logical procedure would be to charge $1.00 per month per residential customer for the cost of metering and billing, but customers complain that the company is trying to charge something for nothing. "The proposal of a metering and billing charge," wrote a specialist on public utility rates, "meets with such opposition on the part of the customers who contend (erroneously, but bitterly) that it is an attempt to charge them 'something for nothing,' that the company modifies its plan by introducing a $1.50 minimum bill . . . From the standpoint of cost analysis this method is decidedly inferior to an unqualified customer charge. But this inferiority is held to be outweighed by its greater palatability from the standpoint of public taste." [30]

The purchased power additional shared in common with the other additionals an important feature: though a step in the direction of providing the company with a fair return, the surcharge specifically avoided saying so. Policy-makers did not have to betray their basic stand on the company's "lack of merit" nor their belief in the devious equilibrium.[31] Reform of the basic rate, in contrast, would have had to be argued on grounds of the inadequacy of the company's current return—something that most public officials would have hesitated to proclaim in public.

The additionals cases, then, always diverted attention from the more basic question of the company—either by threatening to withhold a reward (such as the thermal plant in the fuel-clause case, or international financing in the foreign-exchange case), or by linking the increase to the cause of groups who were much less antipathetic than was the foreign company (such as labor in the wages-increase case, and government power undertakings in the purchased-power case). The company appeared almost miraculously de-politicized in these arrangements, a neutral intermediary through which certain "goods" were received and paid for—a thermal plant, international financing, a living wage to workers and labor peace, and adequate earnings for government power undertakings. This clear definition and almost immediate delivery of the concessions made by both company and government were what rendered the additionals approach so workable and helped to

30. James C. Bonbright, *Principles of Public Utility Rates* (New York: Columbia University Press, 1961), p. 312.

31. This argument was used by Charles Lindblom in support of the "incremental" approach to political decision-making on matters of economic policy. He wrote: "Incrementalism sidesteps problems posed by disagreement on values because decision-makers deal directly with policies . . . no virtue attaches . . . to prior discussion of and agreement on objectives or values." "Decision-Making in Taxation and Expenditure," *Public Finances: Needs, Sources, and Utilization,* A Conference of the Universities-National Bureau Committee for Economic Research (Princeton: Princeton University Press, 1961), p. 309.

bestow bargaining equality upon two parties who were inherently unequal.

The additionals had an added advantage in that the authorities could always keep their eyes on them, precisely because they were tacked onto the basic rate with high visibility, instead of being swallowed up in it. Whereas the additionals surcharge was to meet a new cost that had just been incurred, the basic rate increase was intended to update a cost undertaken long ago—a cost that many observers believed had long since been recuperated. "The Light is just a heap of scrap iron," was the common response to pleas for updating the company's capital base. Finally, the additionals guaranteed an immediate benefit. The basic rate increase, in contrast, promised only an "atmosphere" that was supposed to call forth the desired benefit: long-run expansion of power facilities.

These distinctions were important for power policy-makers whose resistance to rate reform was based principally on their disbelief about what the company was really earning. Being able to see where the money was coming from, and where it was going—more important, seeing that it did go out immediately after being received—did not jar with their more intuitive belief in the devious equilibrium. Hence, they often showed a willingness to allow increased power rates and at the same time a resistance to increases in the *basic* rate. The National Confederation of Commerce (Confederação Nacional de Comércio), for example, came out in favor of rate increases in 1963. Rather than purchase or take over the power companies, maintained the confederation's director, the government should allow an increase in rates. Along with this increase, however, he recommended that steps be taken "to make sure that the proceeds from the rate increase be committed to a special investment fund. The utilities should not be allowed to include these proceeds in computing their profits for remittance abroad." [32]

The additionals were not originally a mechanism by which

32. "Emprêsas de energia elétrica precisam de melhores tarifas," *O Jornal,* July 4, 1963.

the company could add the cost increase onto the rate automatically. Each rate change based on a cost increase had to be first passed upon by the Water Division, which could approve, reject, or stall the request. By granting additionals in individual cases, therefore, the government was not necessarily stepping aside to let the company maneuver in one more murky area of earnings. On the contrary, it was doling out measured permissions to charge higher rates, so that its power of approval to a certain extent increased, rather than lessened, the visibility of the company's operations. Only with Decree No. 41,019 in 1957 were the additionals codified into law and their application made automatic. The company thereby gained the right to raise the rate immediately upon undergoing the cost increase, although the Water Division retained the right to revoke the increase if subsequent study showed it to be unjustified.

When the additionals were codified and given automaticity, they had already been accepted in practice for thirteen years. Their enactment into law was thus the end, not the beginning, of this process of modification in rate legislation. The most difficult stage of the solution—public recognition and justification of the practice—had been left to the last. Nobody could then effectively oppose a decree whose only novel contribution was to start calling something by its real name—that is, to proclaim the right of the utility to receive compensation for increases in operating expenses, rather than to justify the increase in each case in terms of the specific event requiring it. That it was politically possible to impart automaticity to the additionals at a time when it was still impossible to achieve basic rate reform was another testimony to the benefits of a piecemeal approach to the problem.

Accordingly, it is no accident that the only basic rate increase that the Light received during the twenty-year period leading up to the 1964 rate decrees was an individual instance that circumvented the legislative process. The occasion for the increase was a unique event—the above-mentioned conversion of the company's accounts from dollars to cruzeiros. The increase required no public concession or argumentation, and no precedents were established. That the company achieved in this transaction a more than doubling of the value of its fixed assets represents a significant accommodation by the government. During the same period the President had sponsored a bill in the Congress proposing basic rate reform; it would have allowed the power utilities to apply monetary correction indices periodically to their capital bases for the purpose of making corresponding rate increases.[33] The proposal was a full-fledged basic rate reform, which even proposed an increase from ten to twelve percent in the legal return allowed on invested capital. The bill, however, encountered a wave of nationalistic opposition in the Congress and, despite its original backing by the Executive, was not enacted into law. In short, the basic rate problem did not provide a feasible sequence for attack, comparable to the piecemeal approach possible with the additionals. Except for the freak case of the conversion of the company's accounts from dollars to cruzeiros, basic rate reform required both a public proclamation beforehand of what was going to be done (enactment of laws allowing re-evaluation of the capital base) and permission to increase rates on the basis of that re-evaluation.

Accommodation: Foreign Exchange

That the Light's struggle for earnings was deflected from the field of power rates to the foreign exchange market was no accident. The company's exchange rate privileges were, among other things, manifestations of the Brazilian government's practice of exercising developmental priorities through a system of multiple exchange rates. In direct contrast to the power rate, the exchange rate was blessed by inflation with the ability to facilitate politically difficult economic decisions. Selective control of the rate of depreciation of the country's foreign currency was an important instrument of Brazil's development in the nineteen fifties. Through this control, resources were

33. Projeto 1,898 of 1956. See Ch. 6 for history of this bill.

transferred from the established exporting interests to the developing industrial sector of the economy. Because of the political power of the exporting interests, such transfers of wealth could never have been pursued as explicit development strategy.[34]

Continuing inflation not only provided the opportunity to make repeated decisions about development priorities, determined by the extent to which the exchange rates for various categories were allowed to accompany the rate of inflation. In addition, the transfer of resources from the exporters to the industrialists was accomplished by the relatively painless act of not letting the relevant rate for both accompany the inflation, whether the rate was for machinery imports or coffee exports. In electric power, not letting the price of electricity accompany inflation took resources away from the power company. In the foreign exchange market the same politically easy stand of not letting the rate move channeled resources back to the company. The Light, by improving its position through the exchange market, was simply transferring some of its earning activities from a market where lagging prices were disadvantageous to one where they were advantageous.

The most obvious explanation of the differing fortunes of the Light as between exchange rates and power rates was the relative invisibility of exchange-rate decisions. In the first place, foreign exchange regulations were expressed in general terms that defined favorable rates of exchange for types of transactions, rather than for the parties making the transactions. For example, the special rates provided in Federal Law No. 1,807 for equipment imports, foreign debt service, and profit remittance were granted to enterprises of special interest to the development of Brazil—petroleum, printing, transport, communications, and electric power. Second, the granting of licenses to buy exchange at preferential rates was not a public procedure, as was the granting of power rate increases. And last, the incidence of the cost of the exchange subsidy

34. This analysis was developed in Celso Furtado, *Desenvolvimento e subdesenvolvimento* (Rio de Janeiro: Fundo de Cultura, 1961), Ch. VI.

was not clear, as it was in the case of power rate increases. That the consumer was also indirectly paying for the bargain rates at which the company purchased exchange, inasmuch as he had to pay so much more for less privileged import categories, was not nearly as apparent as an increase in the monthly light and power bill. At the same time, channeling revenue to the company through the exchange market rather than through the power rate implied a subsidy to the large consumers of electric power, who constituted the industrial and manufacturing sector. They would not necessarily be against the power company's privileged position in the foreign exchange market as long as that meant the continuation of their privileged position in the power market.

This exchange rate lag is interesting in that it illustrates how inflation undoes certain growth processes in some areas, such as the power rate and the growth of power supplies, and opens the opportunity to reorder them in others. Inflation made power rate increases difficult and at the same time provided an avenue of escape through the foreign exchange market. Power rates were left lagging because no one risked raising opposition by letting them rise; but in the exchange market, rates for the power company were not raised—or were preferential—in order to achieve the same transfer of resources, which no one dared attempt in any other way. Thus, the foreign exchange market provided a less politically sensitive way of returning to the company roughly what the artificially low power rates took away.[35]

Power officials and development planners often admitted that the foreign exchange market was a crucial component in the devious equilibrium between the power companies and

35. Wionczek, "Electric Power," p. 79, also pointed out the beneficial aspects of channeling income to a foreign power company in this fashion: "The government's indirect financial assistance to the private companies [including foreign exchange privileges] was tantamount to subsidization by the rest of the economy of one of the activities vital to the country's development. Such a policy had tremendous advantages: unsophisticated public opinion was not aware of its cost; and the latent hostility of the Mexican society toward the foreign owners of the utilities was held in check."

the government. A BNDE director who was not unsympathetic to the Light addressed himself to the argument that the company had exploited the fixed rate it had enjoyed for foreign exchange remittance between 1939 and 1954. In the first place, he said, the fixed exchange rate was general economic policy in the country during that period. The Light took advantage of it, yes, but along with everybody else. Second, he said, the Water Code and inflation had made the company's remuneration so small that, without this subsidized remittance, it would have been completely without resources for new investment.

A more critical bank evaluation of the Light pointed out that the obsolescence of Brazilian rate legislation resulted in discrimination against the domestic utilities and worked to the benefit of the foreign companies. Whereas both domestic and foreign companies were afflicted with frozen rates, it maintained, only the foreign had the opportunity to recoup the consequent losses because of their voluminous exchange dealings. "In the case of São Paulo Light, the corrosive effects of inflation were much less than those suffered by kindred utilities with completely local capital." [36]

This discussion of accommodation with the power sector may leave a misleadingly optimistic impression, as often happens with attempts to add some grays to a black picture. The crude equilibrium that carried the power sector through the postwar period was doubtless not a healthy one. It was based on an excessive, unhealthy dose of frustration and mutual distrust. Power officials felt vastly inferior to the Light in technical, financial, and legal power, and were often convinced that in their dealings with the company they were being "taken." Because they considered themselves unable to discover, understand, or control what the company was doing, their regulatory function was bound to deteriorate somewhat into generalized pin-pricking. That approach was one way of righting accounts with the Light, instead of bringing about any

36. "São Paulo Light S.A.: Pedido de financiamento de Cr$1.3 bilhões," BNDE Files, p. 13.

genuine modification in the procedures of regulatory control.

One of the prominent Brazilian proponents of rate increases aptly expressed the impatience that existed over the devious equilibrium that reigned between the government and the Light. "Either we decide once and for all to give to private enterprise the conditions for survival and expansion," he said, "or else the country has to face up to the take-over of these services by the government. We can not continue doing things this way . . . talking about private enterprise and at the same time depriving it of the possibilities of survival . . . Do we want the power utility to be taken over by the government? Then let's put the cards on the table and start negotiating agreements with the companies. The present situation just can not be continued. When a private power company asks for financing from a bank, there is a public outcry! When it seeks financing abroad, again a public outcry! The company is damned if it does, and damned if it doesn't." [37]

The additionals and foreign exchange accommodations may have fortified the elements of irrationality in the government's relations with the Light, which were already difficult because of vivid public hostility. The handy scapegoat provided by the additionals increases, such as labor demands, international financing, an emergency thermal plant, and adequate earnings for the state-sponsored generating companies, could simply strengthen the habit of taking necessary but unpopular steps only when it was possible to put the blame on someone else. The additionals strategy catered to the consumer's unwillingness to see the connection beween paying higher rates and receiving adequate power; it did not help to break down resistance to utility rate increases as a necessary prerequisite for adequate power supply. The consumer was told, in effect, not to get excited about his latest rate increase because it

37. The final sentence reads literally, "One is taken prisoner for having the dog, and one is taken prisoner for not having the dog" (Prêso por ter cão, prêso por não ter cão). John Cotrim, in a speech delivered to the National Economic Council (Conselho Nacional de Economia), quoted in "Problema da eletricidade no Brasil—crise à vista," *Correio da Manhã*, May 29, 1960.

really did not go to the company but passed right through it. The implication was, of course, that any rate increase that stayed with the company was worth getting angry about.

To a certain extent the difference between additionals and basic rate increases must have passed over the heads of most consumers. All the consumer knew was that his monthly bill was increasing. In this sense the company got the worst of both worlds: it received the consumer's wrath for charging a rate increase, or perhaps even a tax surcharge passed on to the government, which it considered an unsatisfactory substitute for the basic rate increase to which it felt entitled. At the same time, the additionals surcharge only heightened public opposition to the more vital increase the company wanted. It is no wonder that the Light never considered the additionals as rate increases. When it got its 1955–1956 basic rate increase, for example, it reported the event as "the first increase in electric rates since 1933." [38] In short, the additionals strategy adapted itself to the atmosphere of mutual hostility rather than providing opportunities of eliminating it. [39]

The additionals and foreign exchange accommodations tended to make the company specialize in those costs for which it was guaranteed remuneration, such as foreign financing, fuel, purchased power, and labor. It would not necessarily seek the most efficient combination of factors, but rather the combination that would qualify for the maximum possible additionals coverage. The case of the fuel additional seems to be the only one in which the additional-induced substitution of factors may not have redounded to the benefit of the system. The Piratininga Thermal Plant represented 30 percent of the capacity of São Paulo Light after 1961. When used to meet

38. Brazilian Traction, Light and Power Co., *Annual Report, 1955*, p. 11.

39. Wionczek, "Electric Power," p. 79, refers to the shortcomings of this informal accommodation between government and foreign company in the Mexican case: "Policies of this type were doomed in the long run because the private companies regarded whatever they received in the way of special consideration as too little, whereas the state considered its concessions as more than ample. Very soon the patterns of mutual disappointment emerged."

base rather than peak load, the plant generated power at a cost considerably higher than that of hydro generation in the same system. The justification of this more expensive alternative at the time the plant was built emphasized the shorter period required to put the plant into service, given the emergency power situation; the plant would also ease the system's complete dependence on hydro resources. It was recognized that Piratininga would have to be used as base capacity during dry years, when there was not enough water to feed the existing hydro capacity. More important, it would also have to serve base load if the company did not at the same time undertake the necessary expansion in its hydro capacity. Yet if base load were to be regularly attended by the Piratininga Plant, the result would be a higher average generating cost and consequent rate increases, as well as an annual expenditure of $7.3 million in foreign exchange for fuel imports.

There is some evidence that because of the fuel clause, the Light operated Piratininga more than was necessary during years of normal or above-average rainfall, when it nevertheless had the alternative of substituting cheaper hydro generation.[40] The more expensive thermal and its consumption of foreign exchange was substituted for hydro so that the company could cover a greater percentage of its kilowatt-hour costs. That the Light built Piratininga in the first place with the promise of a fuel clause, however, means that the distortions of this additional were not wholly unfortunate. The resulting disincentive with respect to hydro operation was also an incentive for thermal construction, at a time when the basic rate was not encouraging *any* construction of new generating facilities. The fuel additional thus helps explain the fact that the company invested in the expansion of thermal capacity despite its complaints about the rate situation.

The purchased power and labor additionals account to some extent for the eventual specialization of the Light in distribu-

40. This tendency to substitute the higher-cost thermal for the lower-cost but less revenue-yielding hydro was verified by American technicians studying the two systems.

tion. Since distribution is much more labor-intensive in operation than generation, the company received compensation
through the rate for a greater share of its distribution costs than
of its generation costs. The additional for purchased power also
promised a more secure earning position to the distributing, as
opposed to the distributing-generating, company. Not that
these accommodations made distribution so lucrative that the
Light happily withdrew from generation; as far as that company was concerned, the rate was not high enough to induce
it to expand even its distribution capacity in pace with the
growth of demand. But the additionals did provide an opportunity for temporizing, by allowing the Light an adequate
return in the branch of the industry in which it had a tendency
to concentrate anyway. With the foreign company accommodated in distribution, there was time for the state to build its
plants, and for the rate reformers to carry out their struggle
for change—two tasks which, as will be shown below, were
not entirely unrelated.

A different interpretation of these events could run as follows:
the additionals and foreign exchange accommodations, rather
than providing time for a long-range resolution of the power
problem, actually caused the basic shortage in the first place.
It could be said that the result of relying on additionals and
foreign exchange accommodations as imperfect substitutes for
basic rate increases was the eventual withdrawal of the Light
from expansion in generation, and the government was thus
forced to go into generation as a producer of last resort. This
interpretation, however, does not stand up. The decisions of
the state to construct hydro plants and the accommodations
in the form of additionals and foreign exchange privileges
occurred during the same period. If anything, state activity in
power preceded the period when these accommodations took
on major importance. It is thus more accurate to say that the
rate problem—or rather, its persistent insolubility—was more
an effect of the government's knowledge that it would build
power plants, than a cause of the new undertakings by the
state. That the government and the consumer knew that state-

sponsored generating construction was under way diminished the sense of urgency over the rate problem and the pressure for reform. A speech by the president of Furnas in 1960 seems to indicate that this was the case: "The Furnas and Três Marias projects," he said, "have resulted in a false sense of security and euphoria. The success of these large government projects is causing the public to be overly optimistic about the electric power problem. The real situation is quite a different story: there is danger of a grave power crisis within a few years, principally in the south-central region. This is due to the absence of a rational approach to the financial problem of the power industry in Brazil." [41] State construction may have initially prejudiced the already severely handicapped cause of rate reform, but as will be suggested later, state-sponsored power in the end contributed to the victory of that cause.

In conclusion, the additionals and foreign exchange accommodations explain three facets of the power situation in the Light region: they partially account for the expansion that took place despite the deteriorating rate situation; they reveal a picture of government-company relations not quite as black as that suggested by the basic rate problem; and they set the stage for the eventual specialization of the Light in distribution and of the state in generation. They also help to explain why the foreign utility stayed, and how it was able to coexist with the state companies—a coexistence that, although uneasy, provided considerable benefits for the state companies' first ventures in the power sector.

41. From a speech by John Cotrim, May 12, 1960, to the National Economic Council, "Problema da eletricidade no Brasil—crise à vista," *Correio da Manhã,* May 29, 1960.

3. The Latitudes of Distribution

In late 1964 the Light applied to the United States Agency for International Development for a loan to carry out a major expansion of its distribution facilities. The projected investment followed the rate breakthrough achieved with the executive decrees of 1964. The Light's loan application was based on a detailed study of the system conducted by an engineering consultant firm, International Engineering.[1] The proposed expansion was intended as much to update the existing distribution system as to provide for future demand, for the company's facilities had deteriorated considerably through the years of rate stalemate, especially since 1959. After that year, for example, no major projects were completed in the primary overhead distribution net of Rio Light. In the underground net of the same system, overloading was so severe by 1957 that explosions occurred in the underground transformers, forcing the company to undertake a limited expansion.

During 1963 and 1964 the Rio system was spared some of the pressures of load growth, owing to the drought that brought rationing from April 1963 to October 1964. For twelve consecutive months, starting with the rationing in April, power consumption was less than for the corresponding months of

1. International Engineering Company, Inc., "São Paulo Light, Rio Light: Transmission and Distribution Expansion, 1965–1970—Economic and Technical Soundness Analysis" (processed, Rio de Janeiro, 1965)—cited hereafter as International Engineering. The information here and in the next four paragraphs is taken from this study, pp. R2.5.2.4–R2.5.3.3., S2.5.2.4–S2.5.3.

the previous year. Yet even with this artificially diminished load, operating conditions at Rio Light's substations deteriorated in 1964, as compared to previous years.

In 1964 overload and undervoltage conditions typified operation of the receiver and distribution substations of Rio Light. Only 25 percent of peak load was delivered at voltages not less than 95 percent of normal. Approximately 50 percent of peak load was served at voltages below 93 percent of normal, and there were extreme cases involving approximately 8 percent of the load in which voltage was between 80 percent and 90 percent of normal. As for transformer capacity at receiver and distribution substations, approximately 27 percent of total installed capacity was subject to various amounts of overload, with some units carrying up to 45 percent above rated load for extended periods of time. On subtransmission circuits approximately 65 percent of the total number of overhead circuits were loaded at 95 percent or more of design capacity. About 30 percent of the circuits were operated at loads 20 to 60 percent above rated values. Underground cables were similarly overloaded, with extreme cases ranging up to 40 percent of cable capacity. In the overhead distribution system, overload conditions of up to 25 percent existed at about 25 percent of the units, causing an estimated total overload of 50,000 kva. This overloading of the overhead line circuits had existed since 1956, worsening progressively after 1959. In the underground distribution system of Rio Light, conditions were particularly severe in the solid network systems feeding the residential and commercial areas of greatest load growth. Approximately 30 percent of the transformers operated with overloads of up to 25 percent. There was almost no reserve capacity available in any of the vaults, and overload conditions resulting from feeder failure were extremely severe. There were in all 50,000 kva of overloading in the overhead system of Rio Light, which affected over 40 percent of the circuits, while in the underground net the overall absence of reserve capacity, coupled with overloaded conditions in 30 percent of the vaults, constituted a danger to human life and equipment.

In the São Paulo system there were 1,800 breakdowns of equipment, called outages, in the years 1963 and 1964, owing to system overload during the hours of high demand. These outages totaled 965 hours, which could represent a loss of 3 to 5 percent of industrial production per year. In 1956 reserve capacity in the substations of São Paulo Light's distribution system was about 27 percent. By 1964 it was less than 5 percent. At peak load in that year approximately 30 percent of the substations were loaded to full capacity. A further 22 percent of the substations carried overloads of 20 percent of rated capacity, and 12 percent showed overloads of from 40 to 50 percent of rated capacity. Although reserve capacity in 1964 was 25 percent of total capacity in the distribution circuits of the system, overload conditions existed in many distribution circuits. About 65 percent of the total number of circuits were overloaded to various extents at the time of circuit peak, and on 22 percent of these circuits overloads of about 20 percent were present; on 15 percent of the circuits, overloads of more than 40 percent existed. The shortage of transformer capacity was estimated at over 100 mva. Approximately 30 percent of the overhead and underground circuits were overloaded.

There was, then, no doubt about the need for substantial catching up in the Light's distribution systems. What was remarkable in this complex tale of overload was not so much the revelation of extreme deterioration in the power network, but rather that distribution—in contrast to generation—was so "overloadable." Since overload conditions started in 1956, this could only mean that for nine years the Light made a considerable substitution of overloading for investment in new distribution facilities. It was partially by means of this substitution that the company met the growth in power consumption that occurred during those years. The option to overload, instead of invest, helps to explain the Light's staying power through such a long period of financial and political adversity.

Distribution is particularly replete with such options, which helps to explain the precarious persistence of the Light for so many years. In generation, one can not overload until better times come; it is technologically impossible to wait and see. Yet frequent "second thoughts" about investing are quite natural for a foreign company supplying a public service in a developing country, with the company always uncertain about how long present profits or problems may continue. The technology of distribution is more adaptable than that of generation to such hesitations, and to their corresponding short-run enthusiasms. It offers a less extreme solution for pessimism than getting out of the business. Perhaps more important, the technology is equally capable of responding to small increases in investment optimism. In distribution it is just as easy to change one's mind and expand, as it is not to expand.

In addition to "overloadability," there are three other "latitudes" [2] in distribution, all of which imparted an important flexibility to the functioning of the Light in its particular circumstances. They are the relative brevity of the construction period, the substitutability of operation for construction activities, and the possibility of substituting consumer for company capital in extending the distribution net. These four latitudes are conspicuously absent in hydro generation.

Overloadability of Equipment

International Engineering's findings on overloading were an excellent demonstration of how a distribution system can be subjected to considerable abuse. The capacity constraints of generating facilities are much more arbitrary, so that a generating plant can not be overloaded to the same extent as can distribution facilities. In a hydro plant, furthermore,

2. I am borrowing this term from Albert O. Hirschman, *Development Projects Observed* (Washington: Brookings Institution, 1967), Ch. II. "I propose to designate by the term 'latitude' this characteristic of a project (or task) that permits the project planner and operator to mold it, or to let it slip, in one direction or another, regardless of outside occurrences . . . While lack of latitude retains the great advantage of determinateness, of preventing mere slippage, of accelerating decision making, and in general of providing project directors and managers with firm discipline and guideposts for action, the presence of latitude has in some situations been shown to foster training in rational decision

waterflow adds another constraint to the capacity of the equipment during times of insufficient streamflow. In distribution, however, one can squeeze more production from existing facilities without increasing investment, even though the extra production occurs in increasingly hazardous and uneconomic conditions. This latitude of overloadability thus equips the company for weathering periods of hostile political climate.

There is no doubt that the overloading described in the Light study is not a desirable way for a power system to grow. The resulting poor quality of power supply causes particularly severe losses in the industrial sector and increases public hostility toward the power company. But for the Light it may have been the least costly way out, given the political constraints of the Brazilian power situation. Moreover, the success of the state's first venture into power had much to do with the fact that it went into generation only, as will be explained later. Thus, even if complete nationalization of both branches of the power company had occurred smoothly and with just compensation, the state as generator-distributor might still have been a poor power manager. If this judgment is correct, the overloaded distribution system with its foreign managership was a less costly path of economic growth than state takeover of the whole industry.

Overloadability in distribution can help to stabilize power developments only if the foreign company is uncertain about its future. The American and Foreign Power Company (AMFORP), in contrast to the Light, knew for almost three years that it was to be purchased by the Brazilian government. An informal agreement to this effect had been made by Presidents Goulart and Kennedy in April 1962. The idea behind

---

making or the adaptation of imported models of economic behavior to local conditions and requirements" (pp. 86, 127). This kind of latitude can lead to greater mastery and adaptation of technology. The latitudes of distribution, however, allow the *retreat* from an already acquired pattern of standards by a technologically advanced enterprise. In general, such latitudes are similar to those described by Hirschman in that the nature of the task imparts flexibility to certain operations in which such flexibility may be of benefit.

the negotiations was that the Brazilian government would
re-establish good faith in international lending circles with
the orderly purchase of the AMFORP properties, in order to
compensate for the disorderly expropriations of AMFORP and
IT&T properties in 1959 by the governor of the state of Rio
Grande do Sul.[3]

The execution of the Kennedy-Goulart agreement was delayed for several reasons, and not until early 1965 was the sale
closed.[4] The AMFORP people therefore knew with certainty
for almost three years that they would be leaving Brazil in
the near future. They undermaintained and neglected the
replacement of equipment, retaining as much of their revenues
as possible. When the rate situation and general political
climate improved radically with the decrees of November 1964,
the company—according to my theory about overloadability—
should have changed its mind and decided to stay. When one
of its Brazilian directors was asked why the radical change in
the investment atmosphere did not lure AMFORP to stay on,
he replied that this was out of the question. Knowing for so
long that it would be bought out, he said, the company had
let its system run down completely.[5] Even with the new rate

3. "The purchase of AMFORP originated with the untimely expropriation of the Rio Grande do Sul Power Company [Companhia de
Energia Elétrica Rio Grandense, the AMFORP subsidiary in that state].
The company, of course, claimed the indemnification to which it had
full rights according to Brazilian Law . . . At the same time, the government of Brazil was attempting to obtain foreign financing in the United
States; the American government happened to be unable to meet these
desires . . . Brazil then took the initiative in proposing a solution to the
Americans: Brazil would acquire, with just compensation, all the utilities
already taken over or in the process of being taken over." Explanation giv-
en by the president of ELETROBRÁS, Mauro Thibau, in a public meeting called to justify government purchase of the AMFORP subsidiaries,
Revista Brasileira de Energia Elétrica (May-October 1964), II, 26–29.
    4. Federal Law No. 4,428, October 14, 1964, authorized ELETRO-
BRÁS to buy the AMFORP properties. The contract for sale was signed
on November 12, 1964, and the sale was closed in March 1965.
    5. "The subsidiaries are in precarious conditions technically, owing to
the impasse [in negotiations for the purchase] that existed for more than
three years. There has not been any expansion during this period, in
spite of the imminent collapse in power supply . . . This situation . . . is
caused solely by the nonreplacement of equipment." Another public

increases, it thus would have "cost a fortune" to put the facilities back into order.[6] AMFORP was overloading in preparation to leave rather than in order to wait and see. The Light, in contrast, although nine years overloaded, snapped quickly at the bait of the new rate increases.[7] Overloading, in sum, could be a *modus vivendi* only when the company was not certain about its departure.

This might be taken as one argument *against* orderly purchase of foreign utility companies, or at least against extended negotiations. The foreign utility, by learning that it is to be acquired respectably, is handed the opportunity to earn one last burst of profit in a manner quite prejudicial to the consumer and the purchasing government. Until its departure date, the company tends to retain as profit all funds that would normally be expended on maintenance and replacement. When the foreign utility leaves, it thus hands over the cost of this neglect to the new owner—the government. Perhaps the only way for a government to avoid this exploitation by the departing foreign utility, without resorting to sudden expropriation, would be sudden purchase.

There is an important redeeming factor in the capacity of a distribution system to be run down. The International Engineering study of the Light distribution systems was filled with fairly precise measures of the degree of overloading; one knew exactly how much expansion was needed to bring the system back to normal. Rio Light reported in 1962, for example, that 50 percent of the capacity of the step-down substations to be

explanation by the president of ELETROBRÁS and the Minister of Mines and Energy of the AMFORP purchase, "Concessionárias voltarão ao domínio da emprêsa privada," *Jornal do Brasil*, Sept. 16, 1964.

6. Official of AMFORP to the author.

7. This is not to suggest that the Light did not expect eventual expropriation or purchase by the Brazilian government. In 1962 the company reported that "it is anticipated that negotiations for the sale of the electric power subsidiaries will commence in the near future," and that the directors were authorized to carry out such negotiations by a resolution passed at the Annual Stockholder's Meeting in June of that year. *Annual Report, 1962*, p. 7. The companies actual sale or expropriation was never a certainty, however, as it was in the case of AMFORP.

built by it in the next three years was for the purpose of correcting the overloading of these stations.[8] In generation, however, estimates of expansion needs for inadequate facilities must be based on less precise measures. There is no equivalent, first of all, to taking overload readings from distribution equipment. Moreover, the lengthy construction period for generating facilities makes it unthinkable to undertake an expansion that will correct an existing gap in supply without taking into account the forecasted growth of demand. In other words, generation expansion has to rely much more heavily on estimates of future growth, because of the time required for execution of the expansion program. One can not even depend on unfilled power applications for estimates of the rock-bottom demand for generating capacity, because by the time the power plant has been completed, such applicants may have given up their projected ventures or initiated them elsewhere.

The precise measure of overload in a distribution system accommodates the risk-averting nature that the foreign distributing utility acquires after long exposure to the political and financial climate of a developing country. For when the climate takes a temporary turn for the better, the company is more likely to undertake expansion if it can be certain—and rapidly cognizant—of the exact amount of expansion required. In short, the technology that allows one to wait until the last minute before investing also facilitates an efficient and rapid last-minute response.

Brevity of Construction Period

Distribution's brief construction period is the complement of its overloadability. Because of this brevity, the penalty for overload is much less than in generation: the deficiency can be corrected more quickly. The correction can also be made conservatively, in accordance with a subdued optimism, be-

8. Alexandre Henriques Leal, "Expansão do sistema de distribuição," in Clube de Engenharia, "Semana de debates sôbre o problema de energia elétrica no estado da Guanabara; relatórios parciais" (processed, Rio de Janeiro, 1962), p. 5.

cause rapid rectification of an inadequate expansion can, if necessary, be made in the next period. Because of the brief construction period, furthermore, the utility is more likely than in generation to reap the returns on its investment before the next change in political climate. The Light's reaction to the 1964 rate decrees and to the new friendliness of the Castelo Branco government is a fine example of how distribution can benefit from rapid changes in the political-financial climate. In a period of months the company had initiated a $122 million expansion program in its distribution and transmission facilities, $40 million of which would be financed by AID. On the surface, it seemed rather naïve that after years of exposure to Brazilian nationalism the company should have made such a total commitment, based on an abrupt turnabout in political events. How could it believe that its new acceptance would continue longer than the current regime, or that its rate victories would hold under a future less sympathetic government?

A closer look at the Light's turnabout shows that it was not at all ingenuously optimistic. The company was undertaking an expansion that would require about two years to bring the distribution system back into satisfactory order. (Imagine correcting a nine-year neglect of generation with a two-year construction program!) The company stated, moreover, that its investment program did not mean it was turning once more into a development-promoting, market-seeking power company, reminiscent of the important role it played in the nineteen thirties. It knew very well that the political situation could change "tomorrow"; it did not intend to be caught out on a limb.

It was important for the power sector that the foreign utility was responsible only for distribution. An expansion program for generating facilities—or even the construction of one generating plant—would indeed have been an ingenuously optimistic commitment, even if based on a turnabout as favorable for the company as that brought by the April 1964 change in government. A $122 million hydro generating plant would have been a much more permanent commitment than the two-year

distribution expansion program of the same cost undertaken by
the Light in 1965. Hence, the 1964 change in climate in the
electric power sector elicited no increase in the supply of
generating facilities from the foreign company, simply because
of the long-range commitment required for even the most
conservative response.[9] In contrast, distribution's relatively
brief construction period made possible the Light's "small"
reaction to improvements in the political climate—a reaction
that could be commensurate with the suspected tenuousness
of the improvement, and still result in additions to capacity.

It is important to see that distribution's brief construction
period, along with its overloadability, makes it a particularly
apt activity for a company such as the Light, which by the
late fifties was not avidly interested in keeping ahead of the
growth of power demand. This is clearly illustrated by the
different consequences that errors in demand forecasting have
for the expansion of distribution, as opposed to generation,
facilities. In distribution, underestimation of demand and the
consequent inadequate expansion in capacity are not as grave
as in generation. Indeed, underestimation is so much less a
problem in distribution that in their distribution expansion
programs, utilities tend toward more conservative estimates of
demand growth. "This . . . prevents over-expenditures [in
distribution] resulting from over-installation and is justified
in view of the fact that if actual demand should develop faster
than forecasted, it is feasible to increase the distribution plant
on short notice. The installation of additional feeders, substations and appurtenant equipment can be accomplished in a
relatively short term (say up to one year), while the construction of large generating facilities requires about 5 years.
Accordingly, deviations of the actual growth from that forecasted can be easily detected [in distribution] and corrective
measures taken." [10] In distribution, therefore, an underestima-

9. I am referring here to the comparative length of time for investments to mature as between distribution and generation, and not to
comparative capital requirements or their divisibility.

10. International Engineering Company, Inc., "Cia. Auxiliar de Emprêsas Elétricas Brasileiras: Report on the Expansion of Eleven Power

tion of demand is an easily correctible mistake. Overestimation is the error to be avoided, for considerable investment will then be made in facilities that are postponable; one can even plan to be last-minute in distribution. In generation, it is not only unsafe to rely on last-minute solutions, but it often happens that in conditions of uncertainty the utility leans toward the more buoyant side of a demand forecast, in order to insure against being caught short on generating capacity.

This distinction explains the fears expressed by AID about possible optimism of the demand forecasts in its analysis of the Light's loan application for expansion of its distribution systems. "The essential issue . . . is to determine whether [the forecasts] are too high rather than too low," the analysis states, despite the long recital of overload conditions given by the International Engineering study. But AID's seemingly excessive timidity in the face of severe shortage is perfectly logical in view of the brevity of the construction period for distribution facilities. "An underestimate in forecasting," the above study continues, "can be swiftly corrected by a rapid expansion of the distribution system, and there are no significant economies of scale of establishing larger units in the first instance. This is in marked contrast to the issue of estimating power demand for a generation project where once begun, there is little margin for correction and there are significant economies of scale." [11]

Distribution, it has been shown, will be able to withstand a cautious, conservatively expanding company more than will generation. If the power sector must put up with a lagging company, then it is more desirable that the company be in distribution than in generation or generation-distribution. Since the technology of distribution makes lag a lesser error there than in generation, the foreign utility can more easily

Distribution Systems in Brazil" (processed, Rio de Janeiro, 1965), p. III–5.

11. AID, "Brazil–Rio Light S/A and São Paulo Light S/A," Capital Assistance Paper: Proposal and Recommendations for the Review of the Development Loan Committee, Document #AID-DLC/P338 (June 9, 1965), p. 21.

adapt its distribution programs to the rhythm of its hesitations. Thus, while distribution's overloadability induced the utility to last out periods of pessimism, its brief construction period made it worthwhile for the company to recoup its position during periods of optimism, even if they were expected to be short-lived.

The knowledge that inadequate distribution expansion could always be corrected in a hurry must have been an important element in the coexistence between host government and foreign utility. Although the continually inadequate service increased consumer hostility, the awareness by government officials of the ever-present possibility of quick redemption of the system may have considerably alleviated any compulsion to "do something drastic" about distribution. The government could accept an incipient deterioration of distribution facilities with less alarm than in the case of generation. It might even have been more willing to facilitate things for the distribution utility during friendly times, knowing that an expansion would give quick results. A rate increase, after all, can demonstrate spectacular results in distribution well within a four- or five-year term of elected office.

The technical "give" or latitude of distribution imparted a certain stability to the position of both utility and host country. Such stability was important because relations between the government and the foreign company were much less tolerant of governmental intrusion in distribution than in generation. Distribution of electricity for a single urban market can contain more than one supplier only with great difficulty, because of the locational compactness of the distributing facilities and the consuming units. Hence, it would have been difficult for the Brazilian government to supplement the distribution facilities of one market without displacing the existing utility. In generation, however, monopoly in the supply of a single market is not at all a necessity, especially in the case of a hydro system, where generating sources can be many and far flung. A new supplier, in other words, can be easily accommodated alongside the old one. Consequently, any government-built additions to the distribution facilities for Rio and São Paulo

would have implied more drastic institutional changes than
such additions to generation, where expulsion of the foreign
company was not a prerequisite for building more power
facilities. Government distribution, in short, would have been
a much less "friendly" solution than government generation.

Substitutability of Operation and Construction

It has so far been shown that distribution, in comparison to
generation, possesses considerable tolerance for lagging and
last-minute catching up. How feasible are such rapid switches
from expansion to stagnation and back again for a normally
functioning distribution company? Despite the resilience of
the technology to such shifts, it the cost excessive?

In generation, the answer would be obvious. To retreat from
a construction program, continuing only with normal operation
and maintenance, requires a drastic change in the number and
type of personnel. The administrative and labor requirements
for operating and maintaining a generating system are relatively
limited, and even more so for a hydro-based generating system.
This difference in labor needs as between construction and
operation-maintenance exerts itself not only at the lower skills
levels, where a vast number of unskilled laborers are hired to
do excavation and heavy construction work and have no counterpart function in operation, but it is just as important at
the more skilled levels and in administration. In fact, one
argument often used by Brazilian state power firms to justify
the undertaking of new hydro plants had to do with these
vastly different personnel and organizational needs of construction as opposed to operation-maintenance. If the company
did not start work on a second plant after finishing the first,
it was argued, it would have to disband a team of workers and
an organization put together at great cost.

In distribution, however, there is a certain substitutability
between construction and operation-maintenance activities.
Expansion programs and the retreat from them do not disrupt
the administrative structure of the company, nor do they require massive recruitment and organizational efforts. Although

operation and maintenance are not halted in order to switch
to construction, there will be some direct substitution of maintenance activities for construction to the extent that the system
is overloaded—assuming that overloading, as a substitute for
construction, requires a corresponding increase in maintenance.
Hence, the similarity between construction and operation-
maintenance causes quantitative, but not qualitative, changes
when a distributing utility switches back and forth from one
activity to the other. Because distribution operation-maintenance is labor-intensive, the quantitative changes in the
company's labor force consequent upon the startings and
stoppings of expansion programs are not significant enough
in percentage terms to require corresponding administrative
changes.

It has been shown so far that a generation and distribution
expansion program of equal cost require significantly different
minimum levels of commitment from the foreign utility; that
an expansion of the distribution net can be completed and
amortized in a shorter period of time; that instant sales are
certain, because the brief construction period makes demand
more foreseeable, and because the overuse of the system gives
exact figures for how much capacity is needed to catch up;
and that no radical changes will have to be made in the company's organization. One further aspect of distribution construction equips this branch of the industry for handling quick
changes in investment outlook. Construction in distribution
not only takes less time than in generation, but the expansion
program itself is divisible. "In a physical sense, the distribution
'project' is not one integral unit, which must be entirely completed before it is of value. Rather, project delays in these
distribution systems will tend to lead to a lesser quality of
service, overloading, and a backlog of requests for new connections." [12] The construction program in distribution, in other

12. AID, "Rio Light and São Paulo Light," p. 69A. This quotation
is part of a reassurance by the Rio Mission to Washington that the Light's
distribution expansion program was not an overly optimistic investment,
given the ever-present possibility of change for the worse in the political
climate.

words, can be used at various stages of its execution, whereas the investment in an uncompleted hydroplant is thoroughly unutilizable. The distribution expansion can be stopped short with almost no loss, for the half-completed project comprises facilities that can transmit power and generate new revenues. Such an expansion is a "project" only in terms of planning, in contrast to an expansion in generation, which is a task with a beginning and an end in every sense. The risk-averting foreign company could thus stop a distribution expansion in the middle if the political climate were to change, without losing much of its already invested capital.

The importance of distribution's flexibility in explaining why the power sector in Brazil was able to continue for so many years in seemingly precarious conditions may also throw light on the differences between the Rio and São Paulo systems. Of the two companies, Rio Light was always the "sick sister" financially.[13] Its equipment was more overloaded, crises were more frequent, relations between the company and the public authorities were more difficult, the cost of power was greater, the company was less efficient, and profits were considerably less.

There were several reasons for these differences between the two subsidiaries: São Paulo's more compact layout as a city and its closeness to the generating facilities; the greater magnitude of the São Paulo load (double the size of Rio's), allowing the company to benefit from scale economies; the fact that São Paulo's major generating plant, Cubatão, was an exceedingly economic development; the overbearing importance of industrial consumption in São Paulo, in contrast to residential and commercial consumption in Rio; the fact that Rio was a federal capital, with special problems and a frequent tendency to favor the consumer over the company; the problem in Rio of three jurisdictions dealing with power (the federal government and the states of Rio de Janeiro and Guanabara), with the related problem of the small territorial size of these political units; the complications surrounding expansion and

13. AID, "Rio Light and São Paulo Light," p. 41.

interconnection of the Rio system with its neighbors arising from its 50-cycle frequency, in contrast to the generally prevailing 60 cycles of the rest of the south-central region; and finally, the fact that Rio Light burdened itself with the deficits of its tramway company.

The problems of the Rio system may also have had to do with special circumstances that limited considerably the latitude characteristic of investment in distribution facilities. Because Rio de Janeiro was a federal capital, Rio Light had been required for purposes of appearance to install underground more of its distribution net than was economically desirable. Underground installations, although justifiable for centers of dense consumption like the heart of a city, are much more expensive than overhead facilities and are more complicated to expand. The excessive installation of underground facilities in Rio, therefore, made distribution expansion a less flexible investment than in São Paulo. Like a generation system, Rio's distribution net may thus have been less able to benefit from periods of limited investment optimism. Though the underground facilities may have been just as overloadable as the São Paulo net, they were less recuperable in periods of optimism, because of the heavier commitment required for their expansion. It was probably no coincidence that the only case of severe explosions and accidents in distribution due to extreme overloading occurred in the underground plant of the Rio Light system.

Substitution of Consumer for Company Capital

It has been shown that distribution facilities, in contrast to generation, could be considerably abused. This latitude was directly contingent upon the distributing company's ability to "overload" financially the consumer. A distribution system can be overloaded because, among other things, the consumer will adapt to the inadequate quality of the service; he buys the defective kilowatt hour at a cost that includes his adaptation to it. This cost may appear as the shortened life of power-using equipment and appliances, the purchase of voltage regulators and supplementary diesel generators, the financial losses to industrial and commercial users, or the inconvenience losses to residential users. Whatever the form in which it occurs, the consumer's adaptation cost represents his "contribution" to enabling the power company to sell a defective product—a contribution that makes it possible for the company to continue operating while expanding as little as possible.

This is not to imply that the substitution of consumer for company capital in "expanding" the distribution net is willfully pursued by the distributing utility. Rather, the adaptability of the consumer to defective service is a necessary component of the resilience imparted to the system by the overloadability of its equipment. In the case of the Light, this substitution became a shock-absorber for the deficient public power system, and allowed the distribution company to pass through periods of inadequacy.

There was an even more important area in which distribution allowed the Light company to exact a contribution from the consumer: that of forced consumer financing of the connection to the net. Upon receiving application for a large connection, the Light would inform the potential consumer that it had the power but not the financing to make the necessary installations. The applicant then had the choice of paying for the connection or of not having access to the public power system. A factory in the industrial zone of Guanabara, for example, requested in 1963 an increase in its load from 500 to 600 kva, allowing for a future increase to 1,000 kva. Rio Light informed the company that it would be necessary to expand the capacity of the secondary distribution net to accommodate this increased load—namely, to build a new receiving station. The industrial establishment would have to pay for this station if it wanted to increase its consumption.[14]

14. "Um fantasma ameaça o futuro da Guanabara: I—a rêde distribuidora estrangulada não deixa que crescam as indústrias," *O Globo*, April 24, 1963. Another factory situated on the President Dutra Highway between Rio and São Paulo asked in 1962 for an increase of 75 kva in its original connection of 75 kva, which the firm had already

This practice was not unique with the Light, nor peculiar to Brazil. Neither was it always a makeshift, emergency solution for financing distribution expansion. CEMIG employed this method of financing, with great success, in extending its distribution system to whole towns in Minas Gerais. Those who wanted to be connected to the CEMIG net had to subscribe to the company's capital, the amount of the subscription being determined by the expected consumption of the applicant consumer. The CEMIG approach to consumer financing was not as resented as that of the Light, precisely because it was a clearly defined policy of the company with procedures justified by law. The Light's approach, being more casual and undefined in law and public policy statements, was considered extortionate by many of the "forced" consumers.

The story of consumer financing is complex and of great interest in itself as another important interim solution for the expansion problem in power. There were several forms of such financing, varying as to whether or not the power company would repay, at what rate of interest, and after how long. All this depended on the relationship of expected revenues from the new connection to the investment required to install it. There was confusion and controversy concerning the status of the consumer's contribution—whether it could be included in the company's capital base for the purposes of rate-making, whether it could be converted into stockholding participation, and how such stockholding might be used as a way to "Brazilianize" the Light. There were considerable changes in the procedures for consumer-financing throughout the period, as the government tried to regularize the practice in law. Both the practice and the attempts to institutionalize it aroused intense antagonisms.

It is unnecessary here to analyze the intricacies of consumer financing. What is important is that such financing was an

---

financed one year before. Rio Light informed the firm that it would have to finance the expansion as well. Carlos Eduardo da Silva Corrêa, "A industrialização da Guanabara em face dos problemas de energia elétrica," in Clube de Engenharia, "Semana de debates," p. 25.

integral feature of the *modus vivendi* in the Rio-São Paulo power system, as the Light itself admitted. "Due to the lack of financial resources caused by inadequate tariffs," the company stated in its 1962 Annual Report, "many utilities have had to resort to consumer financing in recent years, and this has become an indispensable source of capital funds." [15] Consumer financing thus enabled the company to stay despite the problematical rate situation, and it allowed the economy to escape in part the strangling effects of the shortage of power. As a way of channeling capital to the power sector this was an alternative that existed only in distribution. There was no way in generation to condition an individual consumer's requested increase in load on his contribution of financing for the construction of a new generating plant.

Consumer financing in the Light system started in the early nineteen fifties. At the end of 1964 the amount outstanding was equivalent to approximately $22.7 million, comprising non-repayable contributions and repayable financing outstanding (see Table 3.1). Though the procedures surrounding consumer financing evolved haphazardly, the practice itself was part of a deliberate strategy of the company, called "maximum saturation of the primary distribution net." The primary net corresponds roughly to major distribution installations that can not in any way be related to the load of any particular consumer. The secondary net, in contrast, includes facilities that can be expanded through the forced contribution of the consumer requesting a new connection.

If a utility is interested in keeping capital investment at a minimum, it will not necessarily have reason to discourage expansion of the secondary net, as long as it does not have to supply the financing. Indeed, it might even be desirable to encourage consumer-financed expansion of the secondary net, for the company will then receive additional revenues from the new customers, without having to invest in the increased load. This would lead, of course, to an eventual overloading of the primary net, at which point it becomes necessary to make

15. *Annual Report, 1962*, p. 7.

Table 3.1. Rio and São Paulo Light: consumer-contributed financing as of December 31, 1964 ($1,000).

Type of financing	SP Light	Rio Light	Total
Contributions and donations[a]	$14,700	$5,200	$19,900
Shares to ELETROBRÁS[b]	540	170	710
Refundable consumer financing[c]	1,060	1,040	2,100
Total	$16,300	$6,410	$22,710

Source: Information from AID, "Rio Light and São Paulo Light," Appendix to Financial Section, p. 24.

a. When capital cost of project exceeds 36 or 42 estimated monthly billings (depending on the type of installation). Company has no liability to repay the contribution, but related plant is not considered part of the rate base.

b. Federal Law No. 4,156, November 28, 1962, provided that consumer contributions in cases where project costs were less than 30 months of expected billings should be "repaid" by the company in the form of an issue of voting stock to ELETROBRÁS, ELETROBRÁS, in turn, was required to issue its own nonvoting stock to the consumer. The consumer had his stock; ELETROBRÁS had its vote. The companies are still examining the various legal and practical implications of this arrangement, and the new government has changed the legislation so as to remove the control that ELETROBRÁS would thus gain in the councils of the Light. The figure quoted represents the potential liability of the Light in this category.

c. Projects where costs are between 30 and 36 or 42 months of expected billings. The company can elect to make the refund in the form of equity shares or loans (5 or 8 years). Figure quoted is the amount outstanding of such financing.

a minimal investment toward correction of the imbalance. Between 1959 and 1965, for example, no major projects were completed in the primary overhead distribution net of Rio Light.[16] The general aim of the company was to invest the least in the primary net, while encouraging consumer-financed expansion of the secondary net—to saturate, in short, the existing primary distribution facilities.

At the same time, consumer financing came to be an important carrier of electrification in general. Faced with the necessity of paying for its power connection, an industrial firm would often find it financially attractive to promote electrification of the whole vicinity surrounding its factory. The firm would become, in effect, the agent of the utility. It would gather together the inhabitants of the area, propose the introduction of electricity, and offer to finance the installations. The inhabitants would agree to reimburse the firm within a certain period for their share of the cost of the installations. The Light, in turn, would eventually reimburse the firm out of the revenue collected from it and from the other users of the new installations—but only during a limited period, usually five years. If by the end of that period the full amount invested by the firm had not been collected in revenues by the utility, the firm would take the corresponding loss.[17]

This type of arrangement was often made before the potential consumers were in place and cognizant of their obligation. Real estate operations would undertake such ventures themselves, financing the extension of the secondary net to a developing zone as part of their promotional and speculative activities. They were betting that their area would develop and that they could more than compensate their original invest-

16. International Engineering, pp. R2.5.2.4–R2.5.3.3.
17. This practice was described to me by an official of the Light. A specific instance was described by the president of a major heavy-equipment-producing firm in Brazil. The firm paid São Paulo Light for a new substation in the town where its factory was located, because existing power installations were "impossible." The firm arranged to improve the power supply to the whole town and divided the cost of the installations among the smaller factories and other consumers.

ment in the distribution expansion by means of the fixed charges they would exact from the new residents and consumers.

Consumer financing thus had an effect far beyond the makeshift response it was intended to be. The practice originated in the financial bottleneck of the power industry and the consequent crippling of expansion of power facilities. But this last-resort method of financing ended up disseminating electric power even more widely than might have occurred under the sponsorship of a normally expanding company. For no matter how optimistic a power utility might be, it would never have been carried away by the speculative frenzies that characterized the construction boom of the 1950's in Brazil. In power, on the one hand, a company undertook expansion if prospects were good; if not, it continued to earn revenues from investments made in the past. In construction, on the other hand, expansion and speculation on the future appearance of demand were the essence of the business and the spirit of the times. Although industrial expansion of the power net was certainly not impelled by the same degree of speculative enthusiasm, forced industrial-consumer contributions nevertheless meant that a much more lively sector than power was put to the task of financing the expansion of distribution facilities.[18]

Consumer financing, in sum, partially set free the expansion of the secondary distribution net from the encumbrances existing in the power industry. This was done by hitching up the secondary distribution system to the two most expansive sectors of the day—industry and construction. Those sectors made the

18. As shown in Table 3.1, consumer financing was more important in the São Paulo system than in Rio. Two factors explain this. By its very nature, consumer financing is more broadly applicable for expansion of the industrial load, in contrast to the residential and commercial loads. Of the two cities, São Paulo is the greater industrial center, the share of industrial power in total consumption being double that of Rio. São Paulo also has more room for territorial expansion, whereas in Rio, the sea and mountains close off much of the future possibilities for expansion, especially in the residential area of the city. In order for real-estate-financed extensions of the net to pay off, it was necessary to have lots of space in which to expand.

Light's "saturation policy" so successful that the resulting breakdowns and even explosions in the primary system forced the utility to expand that net, just to keep it functioning. Consumer financing thus turned an expansion of primary facilities into a kind of "repair," which was necessary in order to continue earning revenue from existing plant. Without consumer financing, the applicant consumer would have remained outside the net instead of hastening the breakdown of primary facilities. He also would have remained outside the revenue-collecting reach of the utility.

Up to this point it has been shown how consumer financing helped the rapidly growing economy adapt to the inadequate expansion in power. Also of interest is the effect of consumer financing on the power company's normal hesitations about expansion. The distributing utility, in effect, automatically received financing for a large part of the expansion of the secondary distribution net. Its own investment in the expansion of secondary facilities did not have to be made until the facilities had been installed and had already yielded the return necessary to make the investment. Although this may sound like an ordinary financing operation, there was a difference, and it was crucial. If the installation did not pay the return necessary to amortize the debt, the company was not obligated to repay the loan it had taken from the consumer. This investment, in short, was *not* dependent on expected returns. It could even be undertaken in an atmosphere of uncertainty about the future, and of threatened expropriation.

Pessimism about the future or the threat of expropriation could actually stimulate consumer-financed expansion of the secondary net. If the company were to be expropriated or bought out, it would not be around when the time came to repay the consumer-creditors for the profit-yielding expansions of secondary facilities. Pessimistic about its future, the company could look upon consumer-financed expansion as an excellent short-run strategy for cramming as many consumers into the net as possible. It could in this way earn a maximum amount of revenue before handing over the business to the host country. One could even say that the greater the pessimism about the future, the more the utility might encourage this type of expansion. For it would be less concerned about the eventual overloading of the primary net because of the certainty that it would not be around when that event occurred. In short, the consumer-financed expansion of the distribution system could not be deterred by the threat of expropriation.

In distribution, consumer financing allowed the foreign utility to "squeeze" the power consumer. In generation, there was no method by which the company could so directly force the consumer into paying for an addition to capacity. Like overloading, forced consumer contributions were perhaps not the most desirable policy for expanding distribution supply. They were, however, an alternative that accommodated the foreign utility's lack of interest in expansion. They also minimized to some extent the harmful effects of that lack of interest on the region's economic growth.

I have been arguing that distribution was particularly suited to the foreign utility under the prevailing circumstances, because of important substitutions allowed by its technology. This flexibility made it possible for the foreign company to temporize, and for the host country to be more temperate than it might have been if the activity involved were power generation.

There is one more aspect of distribution which made that branch of the business more responsive than generation to expansion impulses on the part of the foreign utility. That distribution was left to the foreign company, while the state embarked upon generation, was an interim arrangement well adapted to political sensitivities over power development and foreign companies. Generation expansion involves the granting of new concessions and new lands to the foreign company. According to nationalist sentiments, this means that the foreign utility is reaching out and acquiring more claims on the nation's natural wealth. Distribution growth, in contrast, is a kind of creeping expansion on the periphery of an already granted concession area—or even less offensive, it is an improvement of the net within the already existing concession. The focusing of anti foreign-utility sentiment on the acquisition of new hydro resources was an element in the Mexican case as well. Wionczek pointed out that a major objective of the Mexican government power planners, the *técnicos*, was "to prevent the extension of [foreign] company control over the water resources not yet incorporated in the large private generating systems . . . The *técnicos* feared that once the companies got hold of the remaining choice water resources, it would never be possible to dislodge them. If access to this potential wealth could be denied, according to their view, either the state or domestic private capital might one day be in a position to exploit these resources for the country's benefit."[19]

The difference in the geographical nature of distribution and generation expansion bears on that common government attitude of damning the foreign company for its poor service while at the same time imposing barriers to its expansion. In generation, the long-drawn-out struggle to obtain a concession to a hydro site could easily outlast the investment optimism of the company, let alone dampen it considerably. Many observers believed that the Light's inadequate expansion in generation had as much to do with the political difficulties of getting new concessions as with the inadequacy of rates. The Light, in fact, was at one and the same time damned for its faulty supply of power, prohibited the acquisition of new concessions, and accused of circumventing the law when it increased the capacity of its existing installations.[20]

19. Miguel Wionczek, "Electric Power: The Uneasy Partnership," in Raymond Vernon, ed., *Public Policy and Private Enterprise in Mexico* (Cambridge: Harvard University Press, 1964), p. 51.

20. The 1934 Water Code prohibited the granting of further concessions and water rights to foreign companies. In 1940 a new decree (Decree Law No. 2,059, March 5) permitted the granting of further concessions to existing foreign companies, provided that new waters were used only for expansions of existing installations. "This limitation made it necessary within economic limits [for the Light] to plan diversion of water from other drainage areas to [already existing] plants . . . This

In distribution it was much less painful for the government and the public to allow the company to provide adequate service. There was no reason to believe that the country was giving the company its natural resources free of charge. Instead of obtaining a concession to refine and sell a free-running resource, the foreign distributor had to buy all the inputs for which it would subsequently receive remuneration from the Brazilian consumer. Distribution expansion by the foreign utility could thus be more easily reconciled both with government submission to the company's continued presence and with its determination not to let the company strengthen its hold on the nation's resources. The two aims of "containing" the company and getting improved service from it were less conflicting in distribution than in generation, for the foreign utility would encounter less resistance in distribution during its expansionary moments. By withdrawing from generation expansion, the foreign company was letting go of the activity that aroused the greatest political resistance to growth in power supply.[21] The state, in turn, stayed away from distribution expansion, the activity that would have aroused the greatest opposition from the foreign utility. The division of labor between state and foreign utility may therefore have lessened considerably the poltical stresses that hampered the efficient functioning of the power sector.

---

led to schemes for concentrating the development of power at a few plants." Adolph J. Ackerman, *[Asa W.] Billings and Water Power in Brazil* (Madison, Wisconsin: pub. by the author and The American Society of Civil Engineers, 1953), pp. 71–72. Ackerman is an engineer who worked with the Light for several years.

21. As distinct from public resistance to the company's mere *presence*. This resistance was greater in distribution, where reminders of the foreign utility's presence were more frequent than in generation. But I am interested here in explaining the occurrence of *expansion* in face of strong public hostility.

4. Geographical Separation: State and Foreign Enterprise

Opponents of state-sponsored power in Brazil usually suggested that if the state insisted on going into the power business, it ought to restrict its activities to areas in which private enterprise could have no interest. Immediately before ELETROBRÁS was incorporated on June 11, 1962, having been authorized by law a year before, a governmental working group conducted a series of interviews among the leading electric power interests of the country. The group asked questions about ELETROBRÁS' future role as the holding company for the federal government's majority interest in the existing state-sponsored power enterprises.[1] The more nationalistic and state-oriented interests favored an active role for ELETROBRÁS, in both construction activities and financing procedures—a role that would increase the company's control over existing private and state-sponsored companies. The privately owned utilities, however, wanted to ensure that ELETROBRÁS would not muscle in on their individual domains.

Whereas privately owned utilities had previously opposed the creation of ELETROBRÁS, their only tack after its establishment was to try to interest the new company in areas removed from their own. The São Paulo Association of Hydro-

1. Centrais Elétricas Brasileiras, S.A., "Entrevistas a que se referem fls. 4,5 e 6 do 'Relatório do Grupo de Trabalho da ELETROBRÁS,'" File document (typewritten, Rio de Janeiro, 1961)—cited hereafter as ELETROBRÁS Interviews. ELETROBRÁS was authorized by Federal Law No. 3,890-A, April 25, 1961.

electric Industries (Sindicato da Indústria de Energia Elétrica
do Estado de São Paulo), in which São Paulo Light was the
dominant member, suggested that ELETROBRÁS become
involved in developmental power work in far-flung areas of
the country.[2] The president of Furnas, John Cotrim, recommended that ELETROBRÁS concentrate on building a first-
class power network in Brasília, the new federal capital.[3]
These suggestions coincided with an established line of
thought about the circumstances under which state-sponsored
economic activity was justifiable. To suggest that the state
work only in developmental power, in other words, was not
necessarily a thinly disguised defense of self-interest by the
private utilities. It is precisely the self-interest aspects of these
suggestions, however, which are of concern here, for they help
to explain one element of success in the state's coexistence
with private power.

To argue that the government concentrate on developmental
power projects, or on building a good system for Brasília,
amounted to sending it off into the wilderness in relation to
the location of established electric power interests in the south
and south-central regions. Brasília was situated on the central
interior plateau of the country, and developmental power
usually meant the backward regions of Brazil—the Northeast
or the interior. By advocating developmental power projects,
the established utilities were banking on interposing great
physical distances between the state's activities and their own
spheres of interest.[4] Far off in the backlands, ELETROBRÁS

2. Interview with President of the association, ELETROBRÁS Interviews.
3. ELETROBRÁS Interviews.
4. Electric power companies often feel uncomfortable with *any* other
utility close by, whether private or public. In 1955, for example, the
AMFORP subsidiary in the interior of São Paulo considered selling its
concession to the Praia site on the Grande River to the Light. The Praia
site was downstream from AMFORP's Peixoto Plant, in construction at
that time, which would be the company's largest hydroelectric development. AMFORP decided that the sale would not be desirable, because
"to have Light operating in the middle of our river would very seriously
reduce maximum effectiveness for our own use." "Discussions with Lite
Representatives on Peixoto Power," memorandum, Feb. 10, 1955, in

would be less likely to get into the affairs of these companies. Protecting the private sector from state impingement by locating state power in geographically distant places was particularly important in an industry where spatial monopoly was an essential component of monopoly of the market, at least in distribution.

The view that the only defense of the private utilities, faced with the existence of state power, was to urge the state to undertake projects outside the interest and geographical range of their concessions, had been held by the private utilities of Mexico during the emergence of that country's state power sector. "The private companies," wrote Wionczek, "could hardly be expected to work up any enthusiasm over the outlines of future CFE [Comisión Federal de Eletricidad—the Mexican state power commission] policies . . . What seemed to bother them most of all was CFE's trespassing on what they considered their own geographical preserve . . . According to the companies' interpretation, the Commission had been created to supply power only in areas that had not been developed by private interests. As a long-time official of one of the large companies . . . complained in 1961, after nationalization: 'Rural electrification was to be one of the responsibilities of the Comisión Federal de Electricidad . . . When the Commission should have been electrifying new areas for the social motive, it started to invade the concessions already being exploited by the power companies.' " [5]

It was not only a matter of putting as much distance as possible between the state and the existing private utilities. The latter actually hoped that the state would be caught up in another type of activity, with which it might gradually come to identify its responsibilities. For if the state became involved in "rural electrification" in Mexico or "a first-class power net-

---

American and Foreign Power Company, Inc., Files of AMFORP: Companhia Paulista de Fôrça e Luz (subsidiary in São Paulo), p. 3—cited hereafter as AMFORP Files.

5. Miguel Wionczek, "Electric Power: The Uneasy Partnership," in Raymond Vernon, ed., *Public Policy and Private Enterprise in Mexico* (Cambridge: Harvard University Press, 1964), p. 71.

work in Brasília," then its interest in the realms of the established companies might gradually lessen. The more active the state in its own projects, the less aggressive it might be toward the existing utilities.

In the case of Brazil, however, the major area of government action in the power sector was not developmental. With the exception of the Paulo Affonso Hydro Plant in the Northeast, the government's power projects usually were highly commercial ventures, closely related to the market of the existing utilities. CEIMG's plants sold to the AMFORP subsidiary in Belo Horizonte and to existing electricity-intensive industries; Furnas initially sold almost all its power to São Paulo Light, and CELUSA plans to do the same; USELPA and, to a lesser extent, CHERP also sold considerable blocks of energy to São Paulo; and CHEVAP planned to have Rio Light distributing a considerable share of its production. Indeed, when AMFORP began to draw up an expansion program in the mid-nineteen fifties, representatives of the Brazilian government advised the company that President Kubitschek "is interested at this time in providing additional power *only* for the central zone, embracing São Paulo, Minas Gerais, and the city of Rio, and they asked that the company submit an expansion program for that zone only." When AMFORP objected that it had to attend to *all* of its eleven Brazilian systems, the government representatives "insisted that a program for the central zone only be presented to them." [6] Far-off power development, in sum, was not the focus of the Brazilian government's investment program.

In light of the fact that distance between public and private power is an important condition for the coexistence of these two sectors, the circumstances of the Brazilian case would seem to represent an anomaly. Upon further examination, however, it appears that the technology of a hydro system provides an analogue to the distance between developmental and commercial ventures. In south-central Brazil hydro tech-

6. "Abstract from minutes of meeting held in Rio on May 14, 1956," AMFORP Files, pp. 1–2. Italics mine.

nology facilitated the separation of private and state utilities by allowing each to pursue a different task, while interposing the distance of transmission lines between them. This kind of separation of potentially antagonistic interests is more intricate than that achieved by having the state occupy itself with far-off projects. Not only does it keep the interests apart, as does the developmental power project; but at the same time the technology forces some degree of cooperation between the public and private sector, in that they both supply a common market.

The technology of hydropower offered two opportunities for separating the various components of the industry in Brazil and handing them over to different parties, with sufficient space in between so that they did not get in one another's way. First, there was the distance between distribution and generation facilities, discussed in this chapter, and second, the space between various hydro plants, or between clusters of them, discussed in the following chapter. With generation facilities far removed from distribution networks, the system could withstand several strong-willed companies likely to be at odds with each other at closer distances. It was not simply a matter of allowing state enterprises lots of space. Just as important was that, with the independence allowed them by space, these companies found it less difficult to accept their supplier relationship with the foreign distribution company. Because an atmosphere of distrust and recrimination pervaded the dealings of the state with the foreign company, any institutional development that lessened this hostility or its harmful effects was of major importance.

There were two reasons that coexistence between the Light and the state power companies was difficult. First, state companies were destined to be dissatisfied with their function as wholesale supplier to the foreign company. This situation subjected them to the accusation that instead of relieving the country of the grip of foreign capital, they were "selling out" by reviving and rescuing the foreign utility with new injections of bulk power. Such an objection was often made to the Furnas

Plant. "Why is the Furnas project being undertaken in the first place?" asked a deputy in the Congress. "To construct a hydroelectric plant with the intention of selling all its power, in bulk, to the two large companies, Light and AMFORP." "The same thing happened in the state of Bahia with the hydro project at Paulo Affonso," another deputy remarked. "We built a plant that would have been really extraordinary for the development of the Northeast—if it hadn't been for the handing-over of its potential to the companies affiliated with AMFORP. [The Furnas Plant] will be one more of these crimes against the Nation that have been going on in this Republic." [7]

Out of this discontent over the state company's relationship of supplier to the foreign company arose the second reason for the difficulty of coexistence between the Light and state enterprise. One would expect the state companies to threaten the Light's sovereignty in its concession area—the same kind of threat that the Mexican private utilities were complaining about. The Light, in turn, would protect its interest by using its superior technical and financial power to undermine the fledgling state companies. In view of these probabilities, it is remarkable that a working relationship was achieved between the public and private sector. That achievement is further remarkable in that it took place in a setting of mutual harassment. In order to understand the importance of the physical separation that kept conflict at a minimum, it is necessary to see how this atmosphere manifested itself on a day-to-day basis.

The Climate of Distrust

Rio Light had a reservoir, Santa Branca, on the headwaters of the Paraíba River in the state of São Paulo (see Figure 4.1). The purpose of the Santa Branca reservoir was to regulate

7. Brasil, Congresso, *Diário do Congresso Nacional*, Sec. I (July 7, 1959), p. 3,952. The first deputy was Oscar Corrêa, National Democratic Union party (UDN), from the state of Minas Gerais. The second deputy was Clemens Sampaio.

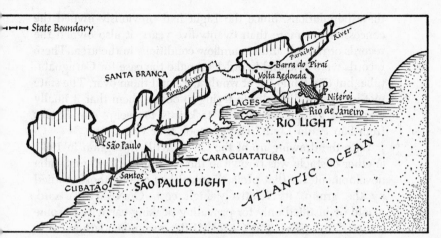

Figure 4.1. The Paraíba Valley: Caraguatatuba site, Santa Branca Reservoir, and Light concession zones. *Source:* International Engineering.

streamflow for the Light's downstream water-diversion scheme at Piraí. The state of São Paulo had been interested for several years in building a power plant at Caraguatatuba, upstream from the Santa Branca reservoir. Caraguatatuba would divert a part of the Paraíba headwaters over the coastal scarp, in a development similar to those undertaken by the Light at Cubatão and Lages. Effective resistance to the project arose among the downstream populations, who feared that their water supply would be decreased, and from the Light itself. São Paulo Light's dislike for state development of Caraguatatuba was based to some degree on a general aversion to state generation so close to its distribution concession—in this case, *inside* that concession. Rio Light also had reason to be uncomfortable about Caraguatatuba, for the project would divert the waters of a river that the company relied on for almost all of its hydro supply.

In order to overcome the resistance of downstream populations, the state of São Paulo had to prove that even with its proposed diversion at Caraguatatuba, there would still be enough streamflow left in the Paraíba to meet the needs of

these populations. Since the Light had previously owned the
concession for more than twenty-five years, it also owned the
records of rainfall and streamflow conditions in the area. These
records were essential in order to make the case for Caraguatatuba, but São Paulo Light would not hand them over. The state
met with such difficulty in trying to obtain them that it finally
employed a man whose sole task was to secure the figures
from São Paulo Light. The job took four years.

With the drawing up of the CANAMBRA program in 1963,
another obstacle was thrown in the path of the Caraguatatuba
development, for that project ranked low among those studied
by the group. Its relatively high cost, CANAMBRA said,
would be justified only for providing peaking capacity at some
future date.[8] Since the CANAMBRA recommendations were
to be adopted by the Brazilian government as official policy,
and any project included in the program was to have special
access to international lending agencies, such a low rating
meant difficult going for Caraguatatuba.[9]

When the state of São Paulo had finally secured streamflow
and rainfall records from São Paulo Light, it made a new study
of the Caraguatatuba project based on this more complete
information. The state then asked CANAMBRA to reconsider
Caraguatatuba, given the new information obtained from São
Paulo Light. In preparation for CANAMBRA's revisiting of
Caraguatatuba, one of the engineers of São Paulo's Water
and Power Department took great pains to install water
measuring devices on the private property of acquaintances,
downstream from the Light's Santa Branca reservoir. He was
certain that the Light would run down the reservoir the day

8. "The Caraguatatuba project . . . [has] an Index Cost of about $310
per kilowatt. Only Aiuruoca and Igarapava [two other plants considered
for construction] are more expensive," CANAMBRA Engineering Consultants, Ltd., "Power Study of South-central Brazil" (processed,
December 1963), I, p. V–26.
9. "International and Brazilian credit establishments are viewing this
study with great interest since it is expected that its conclusions and
recommendations will represent a valuable contribution to the evaluation of loan applications for future power projects located in the South
Central Region." CANAMBRA, I, p. iii.

CANAMBRA representatives came to look at the site, in order to give the impression that the river really did not have enough water to be diverted and at the same time serve the populations and hydro developments downstream.[10]

This mutual distrust between private and state utilities is illustrated again by the conflicting preferences of Furnas and the Light over location of the substation at which Furnas would deliver bulk power to Rio Light. Furnas wanted the station located near the southern end of the city of Rio, in Jacarepaguá, whereas Rio Light wanted it closer to the northern section. Further growth of the city's power market was likely to occur in the more industrial and less mountainous northern section. To locate a substation for a major supply of power at the southern edge of the concession, therefore, would make future expansion by the Light more complicated and expensive than if the station were placed closer to the northern zone. The Light resented the Furnas preference, believing that Furnas was purposely making things difficult in order to lessen the Light's control over future expansion.

A final example of distrust relates to the CELUSA Company, which wanted to locate the major step-down substation for its tie-in with São Paulo Light just outside that company's distribution zone (see Figure 4.2). It wanted, for either itself or other state companies, the future option to run distribution lines from this substation to the power-neglected areas peripheral to the Light's concession. Were the station to lie just inside the distribution zone, as the Light wanted, CELUSA would have much less flexibility in promoting distribution expansion around it. The Light naturally preferred to have the station within its borders, because of the greater control this would give it over such a major source of its future supply. Moreover, it preferred any alternative that lessened, rather than increased, the possibility of future activity by the state at the edge of its distribution zone.

The location and planning of such a connection between a huge plant and its major consumer should have been a matter

10. A São Paulo Water and Power Department engineer to the author.

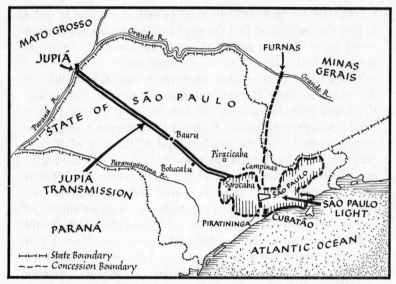

Figure 4.2.   The Jupiá Plant (CELUSA): transmission to São Paulo Light. *Source:* Brasil, Ministério das Minas e Energia, "O suprimento de energia elétrica à região centro-sul do Brasil no período 1962/1970." *Relatório do Grupo de Trabalho,* printed in *Engenharia* (São Paulo, April and May 1962).

of close cooperation between the two companies involved. CELUSA was worried, however, that the Light would use its influence to have the station located inside its distribution concession, and that out of sheer technical and financial superiority its preference would prevail. CELUSA was careful, therefore, not to consult with the Light about the substation. What the Light did not know, they believed, it could not subvert.

These last two examples point up how important is physical proximity in provoking distrust. They also seem to contradict the argument that hydro technology facilitated the geographical separation of state and private power companies. It turns out, however, that these cases of conflict occurred at a point where the two companies touched each other—that is, where the generator handed power over to the distributor. This point is the one exception to the generally prevailing condition of hydro technology, which keeps the two functions geographically separate.

The Propensity to Pre-empt

There is another common theme in these examples. They show how geographical contiguity makes coexistence in electric power very difficult. The reason for each conflict or harassment was not a problem that had occurred but one that was expected to occur. São Paulo Light did not want state development of Caraguatatuba because, with the site so uncomfortably close to the Light zone to which it would sell wholesale power, the plant's state managers *might* be tempted in the future to do their own distributing, that is, to challenge the Light for part of its distribution market. Rio Light was not in favor of Caraguatatuba because the state of São Paulo *might* not respect the Light's water-diversion needs for the Lages development. Rio Light disliked Furnas' placement of the substation near the southern edge of the city of Rio because it would complicate any future expansion the Light *might* undertake much more than if the substation was located closer to the northern zone. CELUSA wanted to deliver power to São Paulo Light at a substation outside the Light's concession area just in case it *might* go into distribution in the future. São Paulo Light wanted the CELUSA substation located inside its distribution zone in preparation for the time when it *might* be interested in developing that market itself.

There is a combination of certainty and uncertainty in these cases that makes physical proximity of different companies difficult, especially in circumstances where other factors are already contributing to conflict. What is uncertain is the growth and direction of future power demand, heightened in these cases by the new state companies' uncertainty about how interested it may be in supplying that future market itself. In face of such uncertainties, any power company wants to keep its options for future expansion as open as possible. Yet decisions about the geographical location of plants, stations, lines, and concession zones determine in the present the form to be taken by further expansions. The ideal position of the company would be to maintain a maximum degree of open-endedness about the future expansion of its system. But since the technology requires current decisions that are irrevocable in the future, the next best policy is to favor the alternatives that impose the least constraint on this open-endedness.

Because of the determinateness of locational decisions in electric power, utilities may be expected to make "pre-emptive" moves. Not only do they favor alternatives that leave their future as open as possible, but in addition they make decisions and take steps that might easily be postponed, in order to get to something before somebody else does.[11] If it were possible to indicate the pre-emptive power installations on a map of generating and distribution facilities, they would probably be clustered along the concession boundaries between various power companies. The cluster might be thicker according to the number of conflicting interests that coincide geographically at any particular point of the map.

The Poços de Caldas substation of CEMIG is the perfect example of a pre-emptive power installation (see Figure 4.3). For many years it was assumed that Poços de Caldas, a hot-springs resort town near the south-central border of Minas Gerais, would be the site of future aluminum manufacture,

---

11. A similar pattern has been pointed out in municipal water development in the United States, owing to the fact that appropriative doctrine gives water rights to those who make the first claim. "The appropriative doctrine (first in time, first in right) creates the incentive pattern for allocating waters by a principle of comparative disadvantage. Comparative advantage would have a city use first those waters most convenient to it relative to their convenience for others. The appropriative doctrine motivates cities to grab first for waters most in jeopardy, which of course are those more convenient to rival cities . . . Appropriative law, by granting future use as a reward for present use, motivates cities to establish their right of use thus as soon as the future rent is foreseen, long before there is present rent." Mason Gaffney in "Economic Analysis of Water Resource Problems," *American Economic Review* (Papers and Proceedings of the 79th Annual Meeting of the American Economic Association), LVII (May 1967), 192, 194.

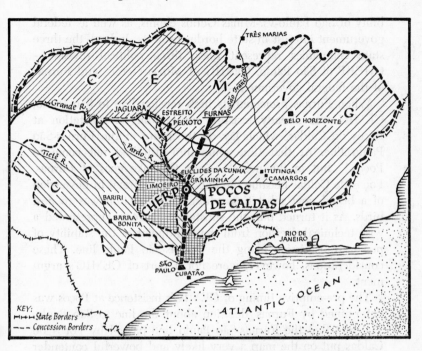

Figure 4.3 The Minas–São Paulo border: Poços de Caldas and the Furnas–São Paulo transmission line—concession zones of CEMIG, CHERP, and CPFL (AMFORP)—hydro plants at Furnas, Peixoto, Estreito, and Jaguara. *Source:* Brasil, Ministério das Minas e Energia, "O suprimento de energia elétrica à região centro-sul do Brasil no período 1962/1970," *Relatório do Grupo de Trabalho,* printed in *Engenharia* (São Paulo, April and May 1962).

because of its rich bauxite deposits. The aluminum industry, needless to say, is a most desirable consumer for an electric utility. Because aluminum is an electricity-intensive product, the industry buys large blocks of power at high voltage and on a continuous basis. Poços de Caldas, as shown by Figure 4.3, is in a very pre-emptive location: it is one of the few points touching the areas of three companies—CHERP, CEMIG, and the Furnas-São Paulo transmission line of Furnas. It lies, as well, almost on a state border, presenting the possibility of São Paulo-vs.-Minas Gerais claims, as well as federal government interest in state border projects. Indeed, the three state companies represent these three political divisions— CHERP of São Paulo, CEMIG of Minas Gerais, and Furnas of the federal government.

When Furnas projected its high tension line to São Paulo, CEMIG was already insisting on building a substation at Poços de Caldas, which lay on the route of the Furnas-São Paulo line. At that time aluminum still had not come to Poços.[12] But in the meantime, as the joke goes at Furnas, Poços de Caldas became the only town in Brazil in possession of a brand new substation whose only function was to nest birds. As it turned out, the substation at Poços represented a wise technical decision from the standpoint of the stability of power transmission along the Furnas-São Paulo line. These considerations, however, were not a part of CEMIG's argument.

The pre-emptive timing of CEMIG's insistence at Poços was determined by Furnas' decision about the line to São Paulo. The fact that the Furnas-São Paulo line passed by Poços de Caldas put on the map a very likely and powerful contender for the market of the anticipated aluminum company—that is, Furnas itself. CEMIG, moreover, was forced to be somewhat pre-emptive by nature. Its combination of the richest hydro potential in Brazil and a power demand relatively weak in comparison to deficit-ridden Rio and São Paulo meant that the power-starved states that neighbored Minas Gerais were anxious to exploit for themselves immediately the sites that Minas preferred to save for its own future. Minas had already lost three important sites on the Grande River: Peixoto had been developed by AMFORP to supply north-central São Paulo state; the Furnas site, although pondered by CEMIG, had gone to the federal government for a project that in its initial years would also benefit the state of São Paulo; and Estreito,

12. In early 1967 ALCOMINAS was formed by the ALCOA Company, the Hanna Company, and local interests to build an aluminum plant at Poços. The initiation of production is planned for late 1969.

located downstream from the other two sites, had also been taken over by the federal government through Furnas. Although the Rio Grande forms a considerable portion of the state border between São Paulo and Minas, two of the three sites (Furnas and Peixoto) fall on a stretch of the river that lies inside the Minas border (see Figure 4.3). Minas, then, had learned from its experience with Peixoto, Furnas, and Estreito that the only way to keep a hydro site was to develop it—if at all justifiable by prospective power demand—before anyone else did. This factor probably had some influence in CEMIG's current construction of the 400-mw Jaguara Plant on the Rio Grande. Minas had at first resisted Furnas' takeover of the Estreito concession, but Furnas apparently overcame that resistance by guaranteeing Minas' right to develop Jaguara instead.

Minas' power development, in addition to being a purposeful effort to create infrastructural appeal, was to some extent pre-emptively determined, in that it was a reaction to expected raiding by other regions rather than to a felt need for infrastructure. This tendency toward pre-emption in hydroelectric power—or in any similar situation involving a state's natural resources—may result in the generation of an autonomous development impulse in stagnant areas bordered by richer regions. As the richer state dips into the natural wealth of the more backward state, the latter is impelled to develop the resources involved, perhaps before the need or inclination for them exists. The less developed state wants to prevent the permanent appropriation of its resources by the richer region. This mechanism could be placed alongside other beneficial effects, in contrast to those considered harmful, of the development of richer regions on their poorer neighbors. Minas itself was not particularly poor or stagnant, but it had great difficulty in breaking the vicious cycle of Rio and São Paulo's lure: the more industry located there, the richer became their unique combination of factors favoring industrial location.

The cushion of power capacity that is developing in Minas Gerais, in contrast to Rio and São Paulo, may now be counterbalancing somewhat the absence of other important features in the state—principally skilled labor and a seacoast. Because pre-emptive power development contributed to abundant power capacity, Minas is now attracting industry with cheap as well as abundant power. CEMIG reported in 1964 that even with a new rate schedule, its rates were still among the lowest in the country. Furthermore, it stated proudly, "The rationing that affected almost all the central-south region of Brazil did not touch the areas served by [CEMIG] at any moment. In face of the company's availability of power, CEMIG was even able to cede its statutory right to Furnas power to other regions that were in greater need of it. This quota, ceded provisionally, will be returned to the company's area progressively as the capacity of absorption of the consuming market requires it." [13]

The proclivity of electric power for pre-emptive maneuvering was behind much of the conflict that occurred between state and foreign utility. The most clear-cut case of the once-and-for-all nature of locational decisions in power was the granting of distribution concessions contiguous with already existing concessions. Such a situation is well illustrated in the wrangling that went on between the CHEVAP Company and Rio Light. During the time that CHEVAP was constructing its two plants (Funil and Santa Cruz) and planning the location of its transmission lines and substations, it was still uncertain about its future plans as a distributing company. It knew, however, where it wanted to locate the substations at which it would hand over power to Rio Light—locations and conditions to which the Light objected. CHEVAP wanted to have enough control so as to use these stations as a possible future base for distribution to the surrounding area. This surrounding region was the periphery of the Rio Light concession and, at points, fell within it (see Figure 4.4).

Rio Light at that moment was not equipped to serve this market and could barely meet the demands of its own customers. If the company acceded control to CHEVAP over this

13. CEMIG, *Relatório Geral*, 1964.

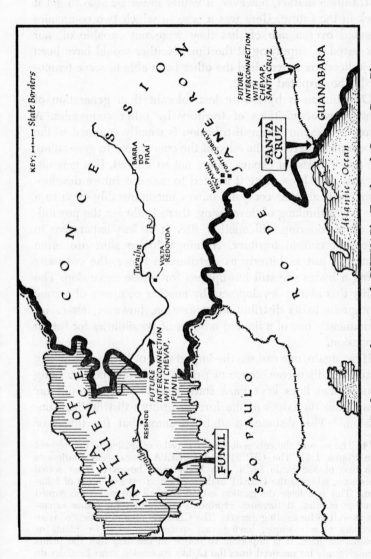

Figure 4.4. Rio Light zone: location of CHEVAP's Funil and Santa Cruz Plants. *Source:* International Engineering.

distribution market, however, it would never be able to get it back in the future. Here was a case in which two companies haggled over a market that they were not capable of, nor interested in, supplying at the time. Neither would have been prejudiced, moreover, had the other been able to serve temporarily the disputed market.

Distribution is by nature less tolerant than generation of contiguous acquisitions of territory by other companies. A company's expansion in distribution is usually confined to the unoccupied spaces at the edge of the concession. In generation, the possibilities for expansion are not so limited. If a generating company loses a site it wanted to save for future development, or if another company moves uncomfortably close to a site it was thinking of developing, there is always the possibility of considering still another site. It is less imperative to defend a certain territory. Although hydro sites are often contested just as bitterly as distribution zones, the company losing a hydro site still has options for future expansion. The utility that allows development by another company of a zone contiguous to its distribution concession, however, closes off permanently one of a limited number of possibilities for future expansion.

Here, again, one can see the importance of hydro technology to the Brazilian coexistence of private and state power. Long transmission lines kept most state generation companies far away from the edges of the foreign utility's distributing concession.[14] This distance diminished somewhat the threat of

14. The map of the concession areas may be confusing in this respect (see Figure 1.4). The CHERP and USELPA zones seem contiguous with that of São Paulo Light. The Light zone, however, is an actual concession, whereas the CHERP and USELPA zones are "areas of influence." This is a loose designation extended to all the areas unoccupied by other utilities. It therefore represents possibilities for future expansion as well as for existing markets. The CEMIG "area of influence" is an especially clear example, having vast spaces unmarked by plants or transmission lines. It is important to notice on the map that the plants themselves are far removed from the Light's concession area: Euclides da Cunha, Limoeiro, and Graminha on the Pardo; Barra Bonita and Bariri on the Tietê; and Salto Grande, Chavantes, and Jurumirim on the Paranapanema.

state power to the open-endedness of the private utility's future. Or perhaps more accurately, it reduced the foreign company's expectation of that threat, and therefore its resistance to state activity in the power sector.

Distance and De-escalation

It may seem strange that cases of conflict have been described here in order to explain an atmosphere in which conflict was not ruinous, and at times remarkably minimal. But it is precisely in trying to understand the presence of conflict in the above cases that one comes upon a possible explanation of its absence in others.

Each state company sold, or was planning to sell, a considerable block of power to the foreign utility. At the same time, each company, with the exception of CHEVAP, was involved in its own developmental task, unrelated to the distributing zone of the Light. Furnas was building the key plant for a future interconnected south-central realm, with three principal objectives: "to create a large source of power in the middle of the south-central region, in the position of serving simultaneously several consuming markets; to regulate the streamflow of the Rio Grande; and to become the axis for interconnection of the principal electric systems of the region, with a view toward creation of an integrated regional supergrid." That Furnas would be selling all its initial power to São Paulo Light could not detract from the dignity of this grander scheme. It would, moreover, provide the company with the certainty of revenues for financing its future plans for the Grande River.[15]

CELUSA, in turn, was busy constructing the four-million-

15. Central Elétrica de Furnas, "A usina de Furnas," public relations brochure. The Grande River is one of the largest rivers in Brazil. Government power officials who did not approve of the Furnas Company and its president, John Cotrim, often referred to the Grande as "Cotrim's little river" (o riozinho do Cotrim). This somewhat playful association of the company president with the river illustrates nicely the complete absorption of the company in an area 316 kilometers removed from the edge of the concession zone to which it would supply bulk power.

kilowatt Urubupungá complex on the Paraná River, and was
not in any way disturbed that it was to hand over all of its
power, at least initially, to São Paulo Light. Indeed, CELUSA
officials considered their project too grandiose a scheme to
become involved with the "small" problems of distribution.
Their revenues from the Light would serve as a stepping stone
to their projected development program for the sparsely inhab-
ited area in which the plant was located. CELUSA had to
some extent adopted a Brasília-type image. It considered itself
engaged in one of those dramatic conquests of the interior that
would cast a spell on coastal populations and draw them in-
ward toward it. "Urubupungá of Brazil is larger than the
renowned Aswan Dam of Egypt," proclaimed the company.
"Located right in the middle of Central Brazil, it will draw out
all the buried potential of that region . . . The capacity for
expansion of its industry is immeasurable, the land is good for
agriculture, and the fields are propitious for cattle-raising. Its
inhabitants are living on soils among the most fertile of this
earth; they are, nevertheless, millionaires dressed in rags.
Urubupungá will mean the development of all this unexploited
wealth, the liberation of this potential. It will be work, progress, development, and a better life—for you, for your children
and your grandchildren—for all Brazil in the years to come." [16]
    Would CELUSA actually promote movement toward the
interior by implanting distribution systems along the path of
its transmission lines? These lines, going west from metropolitan São Paulo toward the interior, suggested a natural
avenue for decentralizing the extreme industrial concentration
of São Paulo (see Figure 4.2). Yet such development-
promotion through distribution was exactly the type of activity
that would have brought the company perilously close to the
western edge of the São Paulo Light concession. CELUSA
did not seem interested, however, in exploiting the location
of its transmission lines by implanting distribution systems.[17]

16. Centrais Elétricas de Urubupungá, S.A., "O que é a CELUSA,"
public relations brochure.
17. In the conflict between the Light and CELUSA over the place-

This was precisely because of the far-away involvement that its hydro complex provided. "The industrial concentration in São Paulo has reached extremes and caused severe problems," an official of the company said. "The Light is to blame because it did not expand or let others introduce power supply to the outlying areas, but it's not our job to worry about that. After all, we're in the business of putting up a huge hydroelectric plant and selling power." [18]

USELPA and CHERP were both too involved in their own regions to feel constrained by their dependence on the Light as a buyer, or to have any design on the Light's distribution zone. Indeed, they were to a certain extent using the Light to their advantage. Each wanted to concentrate on a power-neglected area of the state of São Paulo—USELPA in the south, with plants on the Paranapanema River, and CHERP in the northeast, developing the potential of the Pardo River and later the middle reaches of the Tietê. Their interconnection with the Light provided a solid underpinning of expected sales, which gave the companies confidence to experiment free-handedly in the lesser known regions around the plants they were building.

Both companies projected plants with admittedly excess capacity, counting on the deficit-ridden Light area to absorb the surplus. In 1960, the construction programs of USELPA and CHERP were expected to result by 1966 in a capacity 50 percent greater than the needs of the local market for the Pardo plants, 70 percent greater for the Tietê plants, and 68 percent greater for the Paranapanema plants. The excess would be no problem, USELPA claimed in its loan application to the BNDE, for it could all go to São Paulo Light. [19]

---

ment of a substation outside the periphery of the former's concession, discussed above, CELUSA wanted the outside location more on the principle of an open-ended future than on the basis of any specific plans. It also considered the location socially desirable in that it would facilitate the servicing of the area by *any* future non-Light contender for it.

18. CELUSA official to the author.

19. Letter from President of USELPA to President of the BNDE, June 3, 1960, BNDE Files, p. 16. The BNDE's own study of a USELPA

The World Bank, as a condition for lending to USELPA, actually required that São Paulo Light commit itself to buy any excess power that might exist in the systems of USELPA and CHERP.[20] The importance of this market certainty for the fledgling state companies appears again in the BNDE loan feasibility study for the financing of an expansion of two CHERP plants, Limoeiro and Euclides da Cunha. If the market studies for these plants turned out to be too optimistic, the bank's technical report stated, the neighboring zones (especially São Paulo Light) could take up the excess. There was no reason to have doubts about demand in the justification of this expansion.[21]

CHERP and USELPA were thus able to dispel some demand uncertainties through their connections with the Light. Their role as marginal supplier to that company helped obtain financial and political support for their programs. Contrary to what one would expect from nationalistic state power undertakings, they did not object to publicizing their supplier relation to the foreign utility. It was a means to their end of providing power to their regions; it was *they* who were "using" the Light. In sum, their willingness to integrate partially with the foreign utility was facilitated by the identification of each company with a particular region, distinct from the Light's domain.

That the two companies' supplier relationship with the foreign utility was protected somewhat from conflict because of geographical separation was illustrated by their later attitudes about interconnection with the Light. After the initiation of its interconnection with São Paulo Light in 1962, USELPA found that its "exploitation" of the Light connection was back-

loan application expressed the same considerations. The company's installations were expected to generate 960,000 mwh in 1961, 420,000 of which would be surplus that would be totally absorbed by São Paulo Light, via the projected transmission line connecting USELPA's Jurumirim Plant with the Light system.

20. Official of USELPA to the author.

21. "Financiamento de Cr$1.010.000.000,00 à CHERP—Parecer do Grupo de Trabalho," DPE-5/58, Aug. 5, 1958, BNDE Files, pp. 2–3.

firing. After the state company had built up a solid local market for its power, the Light network continued experiencing chronic crises in power supply. When crisis threatened in the Light zone, the São Paulo state government sometimes ordered USELPA to supply the Light with the maximum amount of power that the interconnection permitted. The state, of course, preferred to avoid power crises in its metropolitan complex, even if that meant resulting power problems in its less developed regions. CHERP's interconnection with the Light, however, was of a smaller capacity than that of USELPA, and turned out to be inadequate for crisis situations. Although they had not planned it this way, CHERP managers considered this limitation a blessing in disguise. In view of USELPA's experience, the limited CHERP-Light interconnection protected the state company's locally cultivated market from the voracious power appetite of metropolitan São Paulo.

CHEVAP, A Case of Proximity

The argument for geographical separation of private and state power as an important ingredient of coexistence may appear more convincing when seen in contrast to a case where this ingredient was conspicuously and disastrously missing. The CHEVAP company was not geographically removed from the Light, nor did the two ever achieve coexistence. Founded in 1961, CHEVAP immediately began construction of the Funil hydroelectric project, and started work a few months later on the Santa Cruz Thermal Plant. There was constant controversy among the various shareholders of the company—the states of Rio de Janeiro, Guanabara, Minas Gerais, and São Paulo, and the Ministry of War—which contributed, among other things, to considerable delay in the completion of these projects. In July 1965, the Minister of Mines and Energy announced to the press that the company's Funil project on the Paraíba River "is still just getting started, and is beset with grave technical problems. During the period that Funil has been in construction, other state power companies have started,

completed and operated plants of considerable size, like Três
Marias and Furnas, which amount to three and six times, respectively, the capacity of Funil. In 1961, CHEVAP was given
responsibility for construction of the Santa Cruz Thermal
Plant, and until today, the company doesn't know whether the
plant will burn oil or coal . . . What interests the government
is the supply of electric power. As far as that is concerned,
whoever depended on CHEVAP would be completely lost.
In existence for twelve years, it still has not produced a single
kilowatt hour nor is there any chance of its doing so before
1967." [22]

On the same day the president of CHEVAP told the press
that his Board of Directors could not be held responsible for
the twenty-month delay in the construction schedule of the
Funil Plant. "We've only been with the company for fourteen
months," he explained, thereby revealing another symptom
of the company's sickness: its frequent changes of managing
officers, usually caused by changes in politics. A few days
later the *Jornal do Brasil* totaled up CHEVAP's problems: "In
little more than four years, CHEVAP has had three Boards of
Directors, one intervention, and, after the March [1964] revolution, two investigating commissions, formed to examine
charges of subversion and corruption in the firm." [23]

In August 1965, the problem-ridden CHEVAP finally came
under federal intervention. The government took over the
four-year-old company and administered its activities for two
years. In 1967 the company was dissolved, and its projects
were placed under the jurisdiction of Furnas.

There were various reasons for CHEVAP's problems, one of

22. "Thibau acha que CHEVAP não tem sido eficiente," *Jornal do
Brasil,* July 29, 1965. The Minister of Mines and Energy was being a
little unfair to CHEVAP: the company was not twelve years old but
only four. He was probably including the length of time that the Funil
project had been studied on a preliminary basis, before construction had
begun in earnest.
23. "ELETROBRÁS inicia estudos para fusão da CHEVAP com
antiga emprêsa da AMFORP," *Jornal do Brasil,* July 29, 1965; "Obra
difícil e diretórias sucessivas atrasaram Funil," *Jornal do Brasil,* Aug.
1, 1965.

the most important being the representation of the four share-holding states on the Board of Directors. The federal government's first move against the company in 1965 was therefore an attempt to "unpack" the Board of Directors by reducing its statutory number from six to three. Another factor, however, contributed significantly to the company's difficulties. The Funil and Santa Cruz projects were not merely close to the Light's distribution zone; they were actually inside it (see Figure 4.4). The Funil Plant was within the Light's "area of influence," while the Santa Cruz Plant lay inside the concession area itself. It was this geographical superposition of CHEVAP on the Light that induced the state company to snipe at the foreign utility. By taking on such a powerful company, the fledgling CHEVAP contributed to its own demise. At first sight, it appears that CHEVAP was in the same position as USELPA and CHERP: by relying on the foreign utility to take its excess power, it would be free to concentrate on power development for the region in which it was interested. CHEVAP's original idea was to distribute power in the energy-poor area around its plants and to sell any excess to the Light. In a summary of its plans, presented to the BNDE in 1961, the company reported that it was not at the moment thinking of distribution and planned to deliver energy at high tension to the existing distributing firms. Perhaps in the future it would organize a distributing company.[24]

But unlike USELPA and CHERP, the area around CHEVAP's plants was Light territory. One could almost have predicted from the company's description of its plans that it would tangle with the Light. In the report to the BNDE on the Santa Cruz Plant, CHEVAP said that the thermal plant would reinforce power supply to Guanabara and some counties of the state of Rio, "absorbing part of the market of Rio Light, and thus releasing a considerable part of Rio Light power for other sectors." CHEVAP's area of influence, the report continued, would be the regions of Santa Cruz, Campo

24. "Sinopse do mercado consumidor e sistema energético da Central Termo-elétrica de Santa Cruz," n.d., BNDE Files, p. 5.

Grande, and the area along the Avenida das Bandeiras, "where all the new industries of Guanabara will be locating." In the state of Rio, the company noted, it would supply the counties of Itaguaí, Nilópolis, Nova Iguaçu, and Mangaratiba—"almost all in the Rio Light zone." By 1963, CHEVAP was taking steps to create a subsidiary company to construct and expand existing distribution facilities. The purpose of this measure was to coordinate expansion of Rio de Janeiro's new industrial region (Avenida das Bandeiras) with the distribution and supply of additional electric power, as well as to ameliorate "the inadequate capacity of the Rio Light Company system." [25]

CHEVAP, in sum, was going to "release" the Light of some of its excess load of retail customers. It would "absorb" part of the Rio Light market, and its area of influence would extend to future industrial consumers, whom it would supply because of the "inadequate capacity" of the Light system. Yet the last thing that a distributing utility would want is to be liberated of its future market.

In direct contrast to the other state companies, CHEVAP's mission was to rescue the inhabitants of the Rio Light concession from the difficulties of inadequate power supply. [26] To act as the Light's wholesale supplier, therefore, was somewhat in contradiction with the state company's conceptions of its reason for being. The events leading up to federal intervention in CHEVAP illustrate the development of this contradiction.

CHEVAP planned to deliver Santa Cruz power to Rio Light at the substation of Acari Nôvo (see Figure 4.5). Conflict

25. "Sinopse do mercado consumidor," BNDE Files, p. 1; AID, "Brazil —Santa Cruz Thermal Plant (CHEVAP)," Capital Assistance Paper: Proposal and Recommendations for the Review of the Development Loan Committee, Document #AID-DLC/P-138 (June 17, 1964), Annex III, p. 3.

26. During highly nationalistic periods, CHEVAP represented the threat not only of liberating the Light of some of its consumers, but also of liberating the consumers from the Light. In a speech given in 1960 by the governor of the state of Rio de Janeiro (Roberto Silveira), CHEVAP was praised as "the instrument for liberating the people of Guanabara, Rio de Janeiro, and São Paulo from a thirty-year domination by foreign capital." "Usina de Funil vai ser concluida em 5 anos," *Jornal Carioca*, Sept. 11, 1960.

arose over ownership of the station: each company wanted absolute control for itself. If the Light were to own the station, CHEVAP would have to sell all the power on the line to the Light, in high tension. But CHEVAP wanted to distribute retail power in the areas served inadequately by the Light, especially in those expected to give rise to future industrial demand. If it owned the substation, it would have the option to pursue these markets itself, besides the security of being able to sell any surplus to the Light. The Light adamantly opposed an arrangement that would make so insecure an important supply of its power and that would threaten its dominion over the concession area.

A related conflict between the two companies arose over an important new consumer. In 1963 the state of Guanabara was constructing a large water pumping station, Lameirão, for the expansion of a major aqueduct, Guandu. Lameirão lay somewhat north of a direct line between the Santa Cruz Plant and the projected substation where Furnas would deliver power to Rio Light (see Figure 4.5). It would have been

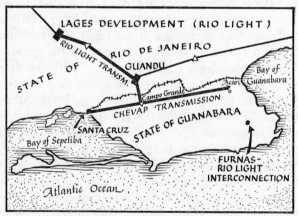

Figure 4.5 Guandu water-pumping station and transmission lines of CHEVAP and Rio Light. *Source:* "Central Termelétrica de Santa Cruz: Solução para a Guanabara," *Revista Brasileira de Energia Elétrica,* II (May-October 1964), 21.

natural for CHEVAP to interconnect with Furnas and Rio Light at the Furnas substation. But CHEVAP wanted the Lameirão station as its own consumer, instead of routing its power directly to the substation for bulk sale to the Light. It wanted the transmission line from its Santa Cruz Plant to the Furnas substation to bend upward in order to include Lameirão in its trajectory.

Inasmuch as a water pumping station is a desirable and dependable consumer for a power utility, CHEVAP simply wanted to make a firm power contract directly with the pumping station. Although the Light was at that time suffering critical shortages of power owing to a particularly severe dry season in 1964, it expected the situation to be regularized as soon as the rains began. The Light would not accept CHEVAP's arrangement, therefore, because Lameirão was in its concession area. The problem was finally resolved, to CHEVAP's dissatisfaction, by letting the transmission line bend upward, but having CHEVAP hand over the power to Light before the line reached the Lameirão station.

The federal government's intervention in the CHEVAP case was to a certain extent an attempt to force CHEVAP to accept its function as supplier of the Light. The resistance to this function was most vocally expressed by the governor of the state of Guanabara, Carlos Lacerda: "With the financial resources of our government we are going to generate electricity in order to hand it over in bulk to the Light. All this so that the Light can resell the power retail without having to make any investment other than wires and posts, which the company, needless to say, is installing with great haste." [27]

When the minister of mines and energy took exception to the governor, arguing that electric power distribution was a natural monopoly and that it would be inefficient to have two utilities distributing power in the same area, the governor replied, "Nobody is talking about several utilities putting posts on the same street. What we are dealing with here is posts in

27. "Lacerda manda Mandim agir para anular decisão da ELETRO-BRÁS sôbre CHEVAP," *Jornal do Brasil,* July 23, 1965.

zones where the concessionaire never went before—zones the concessionaire is not going into now, except to sell retail the power that with government credit, government capital, and government talent, Your Excellency is going to generate for the purpose of handing over to the Light." On the next day the governor made a clear, concise statement of his conception of CHEVAP's functions. "We must demand the presence of our [state power] companies," he said, "in the areas which the Light is not capable of serving, or where it is capable only of serving poorly."[28]

In sum, CHEVAP's geographical interweaving with the Light made a functional separation between the two companies difficult. Coexistence between state and foreign utility was therefore almost impossible. The geographical fusion of the two companies' interests meant that CHEVAP, in its normal pursuits as a power utility, inadvertently committed constant aggressions against the established domain of the foreign utility. As early as 1961 the Light reported that many of the substations in CHEVAP's plans duplicated substations that the Light had already projected.[29] The more trespassing that CHEVAP attempted on Light property, the more resistance it was bound to evoke from the Light. Even those officers of CHEVAP who complained most strongly about being victimized by the Light sensed that their problem was geographically determined. When asked why the Light did not victimize Furnas, a past president of CHEVAP replied that Furnas represented no threat to the Light. "Furnas is too far away," he said. "It is nowhere near the Light's concession area."[30]

The CHEVAP-Light conflict developed into a situation where each side was induced by technological factors to live

28. "Do Governador da Guanabara ao Ministro de Minas e Energia" and "Lacerda quer emprêsas nacionais nas áreas onde 'Light se mostra incapaz,'" *Jornal do Brasil*, Aug. 19, 1965.

29. Alexandre Henriques Leal, of the Light, in José Varonil de Albuquerque Lima, "Mudança de freqüência," in Clube de Engenharia, "Semana de debates sôbre o problema de energia elétrica no estado da Guanabara; relatórios parciais" (processed, Rio de Janeiro, 1962), p. 11.

30. President of CHEVAP to the author.

up to its political stereotype. The foreign utility used its overbearing influence to undermine a local, state-operated undertaking, and the state utility, highly politicized because of its constant bickering with foreign capital, became weak and incompetent. Geographical closeness brought out the worst in each.[31]

The CHEVAP story shows that the possibility of coexistence between competing power companies is to some extent a positive function of transmission mileage. Yet the cost of hydropower is also a positive function of, among other things, the length of the transmission lines. For example, one of the principal justifications of CHEVAP's Funil Plant was that it lay relatively near the city of Rio and therefore required almost no transmission.[32] The company's Santa Cruz Plant, being thermal, was also close to its consuming center. A major criticism of CELUSA's Urubupungá complex, as a contrasting example, was that it represented a considerable diseconomy to transmit power over 572 kilometers to metropolitan São Paulo, when other feasible developments existed closer to the consuming market. Yet CELUSA's diseconomy may have contributed to its evolution into a strong and active enterprise. And the economy of CHEVAP's transmission-less plants may have been canceled out by the political diseconomy of its closeness to the Light. Expensive transmission distance, that is, yielded some important benefits.

In view of the evolving division of labor in south-central Brazil between foreign company and state enterprise, both

31. The problems of the Caraguatatuba project, discussed above, grew out of similar circumstances. Caraguatatuba was beset with the same difficulties and delays that characterized CHEVAP. It, too, was very close to its potential consumer market, São Paulo Light. Its realization would have meant imminent state involvement in an area bordering the Light's distribution concession, or even within it, if the utility were to handle a part of its own distribution.

32. A BNDE report stated: "Transmission is insignificant in this project. This constitutes one of its major advantages. It is exceptionally well located in relation to the consuming market." "Pronunciamento preliminar sôbre o seu esquema de financiamento [i.e., Funil]," Parecer DP-83/58, Aug. 22, 1958, BNDE Files, p. 5.

the CHEVAP plants and Caraguatatuba seemed strangely out of tune with the times. The development of hydro sites in the south-central region which were close to their consuming centers belonged to Brazil's dramatic power past, when the Light had conquered the coastal scarp by turning back the region's interior-flowing rivers. This feat was matched by the less dramatic but equally unusual accomplishment of eliminating hydro's transmission distance, thus doing away with a major component of hydro cost. The scarp developments were nevertheless undertaken when distribution and generation were a function of only one utility, the Light. Any method of lessening the distance between the two was an unmixed economy. But by the time the transmission-less Funil and Caraguatatuba sites were developed, things had changed. It was not that nearby hydro sites no longer represented an economy. Rather, closeness had begun to breed an institutional diseconomy because of the vertical deintegration of the industry. The pecuniary economy of minimum transmission distance now had to be balanced against its institutional-political diseconomy.

If Funil and Caraguatatuba could be considered exceptions, or throwbacks to pre-state-enterprise days, one might say that there was an inherent logic in the way the Rio-São Paulo power industry evolved. In most hydro systems, the sites closest to the consuming centers are developed first. One then moves to successively remoter sites, somewhat compensating the greater transmission costs with the economies of a larger, more diversified market and an integrated system. During a power system's early phase of nearby plants, it is difficult to conceive of two potentially antagonistic companies in the same system. That essential minimum of transmission distance does not yet exist, and the two companies are too close for comfort. But as the system reaches toward ever-further hydro sites— as was happening in south-central Brazil during the postwar period—it gradually develops an increasing tolerance for containing antagonistic components.

The emergence of the state as power manager may in itself

have changed somewhat the atmosphere in which government and foreign utility dealt with each other. To move government-foreign utility relations from the sphere of government to that of business was to transfer the two parties to a setting where conflict, while not necessarily minimized, was not so destructive. The state, as power producer, loses its regulatory superiority to the foreign company and moves into a world where it is perfectly legitimate for one company to drive a hard bargain with another. In regulatory government-private enterprise relations, there is not so much place for this competitive form of behavior. The state-sponsored Furnas Company, for example, was very proud of the hard bargain it had driven with São Paulo Light in drawing up the contract for the wholesale purchase of its power. After buying power under the contract for a while, the Light decided it had been "taken" by the state company's unexpected cunning, but was angry only at itself for not having been more astute. Toward Furnas, the Light expressed admiration at such shrewd tactics.[33]

In contrast to the relation between regulatory government and foreign utility, the state company-foreign company relation may have a further beneficial effect. In regulatory or policy-making functions, pro-foreign-company government officials may be bribed by the foreign company or simply ignore it. In a business relationship with the foreign company, however, the success of the state manager's venture will depend in part on his agility at fending off the foreign company's business maneuvers, on his ability to "one up" the foreign company. Government power managers will thus have to put some distance between themselves and the foreign utility in order to make their companies perform well.

One government power official, in discussing the Light's extra-legal methods of exerting pressure on regulatory agencies, said to me, "It is not the Light's fault for trying to bribe us. The fault is ours—that we could be bribed." By having the

33. São Paulo Light's version of the incident, from an official of the Light to the author; Furnas' version, from an official of Furnas to the author.

state interact with the foreign company as coproducer rather
than as regulatory authority, one lessens considerably the gain
to be achieved by the state power official from bribery. The
cost of the bribe to him is no longer the remote "national
interest," but the concrete business venture for which he is
directly responsible. Put in another way, the state power manager's private interest comes much closer to the actual "national
interest" than does the private interest of the pro-foreign-
company government official.

5. Geographical Separation: The State Companies

The technology of hydropower not only accommodated the existence of potentially antagonistic companies looking after the two distinct branches of the industry, generation and distribution, but it also allowed the proliferation of various companies *within* one of the two branches—generation. Several state generating companies, that is, could supply the same consuming market in an industry in which competitive supply is not normally thought to be feasible. In distribution, however, the supply to one market can not very well accommodate more than one company.

It will be shown in this chapter that certain benefits could be gained from having several companies in the state generation business. Some of the benefits arose from the conflict of interest between state companies in the power sector. Others had more to do with the resulting smallness of the companies and the local nature of their task. It will not be argued that conflict was necessarily a good thing, but rather, that the existence of several state companies was good for getting generation facilities built in the power sector. In addition, the geographical distance separating hydro installations kept the inevitable antagonisms among these various entities from overwhelming the benefits of multicompany development.

Manyness and Rivalry

In the spring of 1959 the Special Commission to Study the Funil Rapids on the Paraíba River approached the BNDE about the possibility of financing a hydro plant at Funil. The BNDE indicated that a loan to Funil would result in an over-proportionate commitment of federal electrification appropriations to the south-central region. Furnas, the bank explained, was already absorbing roughly eighty percent of the resources of the bank-administered Federal Electrification Fund (Fundo Federal de Eletrificação—FFE). It would be politically difficult, the bank told Funil's promoters, to assign FFE resources to Funil in light of this conspicuous commitment to the Furnas project. A decision to support one project, in other words, could mean the failure of another to locate financing.

A few years later the state of Guanabara had an experience similar to that of the Funil Commission. In 1963–1964, when the power supply of Rio Light was curtailed because of a particularly severe dry period, the governor of the state, Carlos Lacerda, announced an emergency plan to buy two gas turbine plants with a capacity of 22 mw each. He applied to AID for a loan to finance the purchase of the plants from an American manufacturer. AID officials were already worried about the power crisis: they thought that it might, among other things, weaken the Guanabara governor politically, and they had already committed themselves to his support with considerable financing for urban development.

AID assigned the governor's loan request to its power advisers, who recommended that the crisis be met by the emergency construction of a transmission line from Furnas to Guanabara, instead of by the governor's gas turbines. It was suggested that a Furnas-Guanabara line would be more economical, in addition to being more justifiable as part of the long-range program for power supply to the south-central region. Moreover, the Furnas Plant would already be in operation when the new line was completed (1965). The urgency of the situation could be met by having the line pass by CEMIG's Itutinga Plant, which was expected to have available capacity. The Itutinga-Guanabara stretch of the line could be constructed first, so as to shorten the time required to bring into operation this emergency source of power for Guanabara.

AID took up the suggestion of its power advisers and decided
to finance construction of the Furnas-Guanabara line. Thus,
Lacerda's loan request resulted in AID financing for Furnas
rather than for the state of Guanabara. Guanabara bought the
gas turbines anyway, without the help of AID. "Lacerda was
furious with AID," was the comment made by an AID official.

Here was another case, like Funil and Furnas, where the
project of one state power entity failed to receive financing
because another state company's project had obtained it
instead. Power projects thus came to be considered by their
promoters as mutually exclusive in terms of financial support
from federal or state governments, even when there was no
evidence that one project would actually cancel the possibilities of another. Proponents of a power project would often
oppose any other proposed plant on the assumption that government support of the two projects was an impossibility. This
was the reasoning behind much of the opposition of the state
of Minas Gerais to Furnas.

Minas, in addition to some northeastern states, thought that
the government's decision to support Furnas in 1956 meant that
the Três Marias hydro project would be dropped by the way-
side. This fear was voiced in the Congress in 1956, when both
projects were just being started. "[Três Marias] is being aban-
doned," said a Minas deputy, "while [Furnas] is now in favor.
Três Marias is of national interest because of the stream
regularization it will provide on the São Francisco River . . .
But with the support of the president of the republic and the
president of the BNDE, the capitalist groups [i.e., the Light
and government power officials sympathetic to it] are trying
to construct Furnas, which is going to inundate the most fertile
zone of southern Minas . . . Minas Gerais is being sacrificed to
the federal government's support of international trusts." [1] The
fears of Minas turned out to be unfounded. Not only was Três
Marias undertaken, but the project was completed before

1. Brasil, Congresso, *Diário do Congresso Nacional*, Sec. I (Dec. 7,
1956), p. 12,241. The deputy was Oscar Corrêa, National Democratic
Union Party (UDN) of the state of Minas Gerais.

Furnas, in 1960, and even set a construction record for power plants of that size in Brazil. Its start and completion fit within a five-year presidential term of office: 1956–1961.

Disbelief in the possibility of simultaneous government support of two power projects, and the resultant opposition to certain projects, was not limited to state companies. At the same time that Minas was campaigning in the Congress against Furnas, the AMFORP subsidiary of São Paulo was campaigning against the same project at the Export-Import Bank in Washington, where Furnas had originally requested financing. "There appears to be a danger," an AMFORP official said at a company meeting, "that in deciding to go ahead with the Furnas project, the [Brazilian] Government may also decide that no financing will be available from the Development Bank for [our] Praia or Estreito developments until after the Furnas development is completed." AMFORP was worried as well that the installation of the second stage of its Peixoto Plant (units three to ten) would be postponed in deference to Furnas, and that it would therefore "have no energy for sale to the Light." [2]

2. "Abstract from Minutes of Meeting held in Rio on May 14, 1957," in American and Foreign Power Company, Inc., Files of AMFORP: Companhia Paulista de Fôrça e Luz (subsidiary in São Paulo), p. 1— cited hereafter as AMFORP Files; "Brazil: The Power Problem in the South-central Zone—Comparative Advantages of 'Furnas' and other Hydro-electric Projects," July 12, 1956, AMFORP Files, p. 6. Praia and Estreito were included in the plans of AMFORP's São Paulo subsidiary to develop the Grande River. The BNDE granted financing to AMFORP for Peixoto, the first project, in 1955 and 1957. In the summer of 1956 the Brazilian government requested foreign financing for Furnas from the Export-Import Bank. While that request was being considered, AMFORP presented a memorandum to the bank entitled, "Brazil: The Power Problem in the South-central zone—Comparative Advantages of 'Furnas' and other Hydro-electric Projects," July 12, 1956, AMFORP Files. The memo attempted to demonstrate that AMFORP's Estreito was at that time a much more feasible project than Furnas. AMFORP did not let the Brazilian officials know of the memo, because "to have done so . . . would very likely have created antagonism towards the Company [AMFORP] in the mistaken belief that we were trying to block the construction of the Furnas project." Letter from F. F. Vaughan to John D. Fitch, Aug. 10, 1956, AMFORP Files, p. 2. The Export-Import Bank granted financing to Brazil for several projects, but Furnas was not included among them.

The result of this real or imagined exclusiveness of public financing of power projects was that state power companies often engaged in a somewhat novel form of competition. Each carried on a perpetual campaign for its project, a good part of which included debunking all other state companies' past and intended feats. Furnas scorned the extravagance and brashness of CELUSA; CELUSA charged that Furnas served foreign interests by buying as much equipment as possible abroad ("Even the nails in the Furnas plant are imported"); Caraguatatuba proponents criticized CELUSA, CHERP, and USELPA for being "dam-happy" and not worrying about more "responsible" multipurpose approaches to power developments;[3] CELUSA criticized Caraguatatuba supporters for childlike insistence on having their own coastal scarp development; CELUSA scornfully referred to USELPA's and CHERP's plants as "playthings" *(usinas pequeninas)* in comparison to the much more adult size of their own project; and USELPA and CHERP, in turn, called CELUSA's Urubupungá complex a political white elephant, in view of the existence of closer, more economical sites.

In short, one finds no camaraderie among state power interests, based on the common cause of state capitalism or dislike of the foreign utility. The lack of experience at cooperation among the south-central region's state power companies manifested itself in the intercompany controversies that flared up during the Furnas-sponsored planning for integrated power supply in the south-central region. The frequent unwillingness to cooperate on the part of one of the companies, CELUSA, led an international power consultant to comment in a memorandum on the Brazilian power situation, "the boundless ambition of the CELUSA Company must be curbed." [4]

3. These critics also suggested—in probably a closer approximation to the truth behind their rivalry with the other companies—that CHERP, USELPA, and CELUSA were "ganging up" against multipurpose Paraíba Valley development because they wanted for themselves the appropriations set aside for that purpose. Officials of the Water and Power Department of the state of São Paulo to the author.
4. Official of CANAMBRA to the author.

Because the state companies depended on a common, limited supply of financing, there was actually more basis for conflict of interest among them than between them and a foreign utility in distribution. In many cases there were specific reasons for these rivalries. Two companies might be vying for the concession to the same site (as in the CEMIG-Furnas conflicts over the Furnas and Estreito sites); or two companies might tangle with each other when interconnection put them in the same grid (as in a Furnas-CELUSA controversy over CELUSA's use of a transmission voltage different from that of the Furnas lines). But in these cases, conflict arose where the companies brushed each other geographically. What is of more interest is the rivalry that existed even when companies were far apart. Geographical separation of hydro plants, in other words, minimized one kind of rivalry between state companies—that having to do with physical proximity—but left still another—that concerning the struggle for financing.

An important aspect of the rivalry between state companies was the standards that each used to proclaim its superiority. In this respect such rivalry seemed to exhibit characteristics of market competition. The questions the companies would ask and answer about themselves and other companies were, "Who can be a less corrupt company? Who can get more international financing? Who can get the most from the Ministry of Finance? Who can amortize his foreign loan the quickest? Who can build the biggest dam? Who can survive important political crises? Whose construction schedule has the least delays?"

Each company dreaded a failure in one of these areas, because of the possible loss of financial support that could result. The public press was an important link in this mechanism. For example, newspaper reports that the Furnas project was running behind schedule, whether confirmed or not, could be as damaging to the company as could be an exposé of scandal to a city government. Public indignation would be expressed at the possibility of failure in such an important project, and the company would make painstaking denials. Indeed, the state company itself often manipulated this kind of indignation to mobilize action on delayed financing. It would let newspapers or legislators know that a certain politician or financial institution's delay was threatening the completion of its project. For instance, Furnas used this tactic when the BNDE took considerable time to process a loan application from the company. In August 1962 the president of Furnas told the press that the BNDE had promised financing for two tie-lines 25 kilometers in length, but still had not granted the funds. A power crisis would ensue, the Furnas president warned, if the BNDE did not grant financing in time to allow completion of the lines before commissioning of the plant itself.[5]

The newspaper announcement set off a wave of criticism of the BNDE. "I appeal to the BNDE," said the director of the National Confederation of Commerce (Confederação Nacional de Comércio), "to release without further delay the funds necessary for construction of the [Furnas tie-lines] in order to avoid a power collapse of incalculable proportions, with great damage to the entire country." [6] The BNDE delay became the subject of meetings of the various federations of industry and commerce, who issued a warning to the President of the country. If the federal government did not release the funds for Furnas through the BNDE, they stated, there would be a total collapse in the supply of electric power to the states of Guanabara and São Paulo.[7]

The CELUSA Company also resorted to this tactic. In 1960 a new governor took office in São Paulo, Adhemar de Barros, who did not exhibit the same enthusiasm for CELUSA's Urubupungá complex as had the previous governor, Carvalho Pinto. "We laid our camp well," said an official of the company "in preparation for this change in government. We made friends in the top echelons of the military. If the new governor

5. "Rio ameaçado de racionamento de energia elétrica em 1963," *Jornal do Brasil*, Aug. 31, 1962.
6. "Colapso de energia ameaça à Guanabara," *Jornal do Comércio*, Sept. 20, 1962.
7. "Colapso na indústria: BNDE prejudica Furnas," *Tribuna da Imprensa*, Oct. 6, 1962; "Furnas: Assunto de debates na FIESP," *O Estado de São Paulo*, Oct. 5, 1962.

threatened to slow down outlays to CELUSA, we just tele-
phoned an important general; another telephone call from him
to the governor, and things were settled. We made friends
with journalists—we made ourselves known among congressmen. All we'd have to do would be to spread it around that
the governor was making it hard for CELUSA. That was
enough to control things." [8] It was also not unusual to hear
accusations such as the following in Congress: "The Governor
of São Paulo has impeded the commencement of construction
of the Jurumirim Hydroelectric Plant. The project has been
ready for initiation since the beginning of his term . . . It is
well known . . . that pressures and suggestions have been
made to 'take it slow.' "[9]

Such accusations were based on the same measure of performance that were an important element in the rivalries of
state companies. The term "competition" is used here to char-
acterize such rivalry even though it occurred in a noncompeti-
tive industry—in order to describe its efficiency-inducing
aspects. It might be argued that state company competition
occurs in the factor, rather than the product, market, for the
various companies are competing for limited supplies of the
input, financing. It would be more apt, however, to argue
that state company competition is like competition in the product market, in that the product sold by the company is not
power but a power project. Each company strives for efficiency
in its "product" so that the financier or politician will be more
apt to "buy" its project rather than that of the rival company.
A BNDE manager, in a report favoring the concession of
financing to Furnas, cited the company's performance in one
of these competitive areas. "In spite of all the snags that the
company ran into, Furnas is one of the few firms that has
met almost all its construction deadlines." [10]

8. Official of CELUSA to the author.
9. Brasil, Congresso, *Diário do Congresso Nacional*, Sec. I (April 5,
1956), p. 1956. The speaker was São Paulo Deputy Dagoberto Sales, of
the Social Democratic Party (PSD).
10. "Parecer do Diretor-Relator," Dir. I-51/62, Sept. 20, 1962, BNDE
Files, p. 14.

Crucial to this efficiency-invoking aspect of state company competition is the fact that the project must seek financial support *all the way through* its period of construction. This results from a combination of inflation, and variations in the intensity of political support. Projects of long gestation, like hydro plants, are always victim to inflationary cost increases during construction. As a result, considerable finance-hunting must be conducted during the course of the project's construction, in order to meet these unforeseen costs. Even foreseen costs are not always provided for by the time construction has begun. This is because of both the difficulty of arranging public financing so far in advance and the changes in official support for projects in midstream—changes that may even cut off earmarked revenues. The consequent perennial worry over a project's financing by its manager was described by the president of Furnas, in recounting his experience as technical director of CEMIG: "Whoever has lived through—as we did in CEMIG—the execution of an investment program, is well acquainted with the nights of insomnia, when one lies awake worrying about the possibilities of an abrupt change in the politics of the state. A new secretary of finance may arrive on the scene who does not have the same understanding as his predecessor of the importance of one's program." [11]

Inflation, on top of these variations in political support, simply increases a project's vulnerability to politics. It turns once-and-for-all legislative and executive approvals into temporary authorizations that require periodic and difficult reaffirmation. New appropriations must be authorized again and again throughout the project's construction in order to make up for the depreciation of the currency. These appropriations adjustments are not necessarily granted without using the occasion to make a new and often political judgment of the project, its proponents, and its managers. The decision by a new finance secretary, governor, or president to allow the continuation of a project in construction thus becomes a political proc-

11. Instituto de Engenharia, *Semana de debates sôbre energia elétrica* (São Paulo: Imprensa Oficial do Estado, 1956), p. 264.

lamation of strong support. Hence, lukewarmness on the part of a new government official toward a project in construction can be equivalent, in an inflation-ridden country, to opposition. In a country without inflation, in contrast, a public works project in execution is more capable of withstanding lukewarmness on the part of a new secretary of finance, for the degree of support required of him is not nearly so great. Instead of having to authorize new appropriations to meet inflationary cost increases, he has only to feed previously earmarked revenues to the project.

A perception of this problem was well illustrated by the action of the Furnas Board of Directors following the first national change in government after the company's founding. When Jânio Quadros took over from Juscelino Kubitschek in 1961—with Furnas half-completed—the three top managers of Furnas submitted their resignations to the new President. The resignations were not accepted by Quadros, "to the great satisfaction of the management of Furnas." [12] It would not have been sufficient, in other words, that the new President leave the project alone. To the contrary, Furnas required that Quadros take explicit and favorable notice.

In sum, projects in execution that might be left alone by a new crop of government leaders in an inflation-absent country will have to struggle continuously to survive inflation's requirement of periodic feedings of strong support. For this reason, the hard battles won by project managers for approval of their undertakings must be fought again and again. So it was that Furnas proudly reported its survival of the period of turmoil following President Quadros' resignation in August 1961: "The crisis of August-September obliged the company to take certain financial precautions, causing the postponement of various tasks scheduled for this period . . . Fortunately, however, the impact of such a major national crisis on a project as important as Furnas was less than had been feared. The completion deadline was not altered, and the company did not

12. Central Elétrica de Furnas, S.A., *Relatório da Diretoria—Exercício de 1960*, p. 19.

become involved in the political turmoil. Thanks to this firm
orientation—removed from partisan politicking and wholly
directed toward rapid and efficient realization of the project—
we report with great pride that the management of Furnas
was preserved intact . . . by the two governments that during
this past year presided over the nation." [13]

The prejudicial effects of such financial and political uncertainties are well known and become highly visible in projects
that suffer long delays or complete failure, but there may be
beneficial effects as well. By forcing the project's promoter to
"sell his product" many times, financial uncertainties necessi-
tate the invocation of performance standards throughout the
whole period of construction—precisely the period when the
discipline of these standards is most needed. These standards
of performance, it should be noted, are not as applicable to a
company performing *both* generation and distribution, or only
distribution. A generation-distribution or strictly distribution
operation has much less clear-cut measures of performance
than does a simple generation construction program. Because
generation-distribution is an ongoing activity, it is more difficult
to point to single achievements—such as meeting construction
deadlines—as measures of performance.

There is one more reason why state company rivalry might
be characterized as competition. When many government
companies, rather than one, participate in the power sector,
the "friendship" between government and state company is,
to a certain extent, sundered. Never certain of its sponsor's
continued support, the company may seek to get out from
under the government's protective wing. Instead of relying
on subsidy, it may feel safer finishing up its project in a hurry
so as to start earning its own revenues. In addition, it may
pursue a more zealous rate policy, in its desire to end the
precarious dependence on government favor. "You hold your
breath until your plant starts selling power," said one of the
directors of CELUSA. "Then you won't have to depend on
state budgets any longer."

13. Central Elétrica de Furnas, S.A., *Relatório da Diretoria—1961*, p. 1.

The Brazilian state power generating companies thus demonstrated a novel way of spurring performance in state enterprise. A traditional argument against state production is that such ventures are not exposed to the rigors of market competition—either because they operate in an industry with natural monopoly (e.g., electric power), or because the state imposes its own monopoly (e.g., petroleum refining in Brazil). In the Brazilian electric power sector, the government went into a naturally monopolistic industry, but left alone the branch of the industry (distribution) that required supply by only one company. By taking on generation only, state power production could contain many companies. In lieu of competition in the product market, competition for financing could stimulate state enterprise to behave like competitive private enterprise. Although the performance of the Brazilian state power companies in many cases, and at many points, fell below the standards of efficiency suggested here, there is no doubt that the successful cases can be explained in part by the competitive atmosphere in which they had to exist.

That the foreign company remained in distribution may therefore have had advantages, even though it involved a severe deterioration of distribution facilities. To have a strong company in the common distribution market of the state companies was in effect to create a "buffer zone" between groups in rivalry. If São Paulo Light had been weak or anxious to give up its concession, there would probably have been a serious struggle between CELUSA and Furnas for that distribution market. Not that the two companies were interested in shouldering in on the São Paulo retail market; but if a vacuum had ever developed there, they might have been impelled to seek the market in order to maintain the strength of their respective realms.

That the Light was already firmly entrenched in distribution kept state enterprises busy out in the open spaces, where their competitiveness worked to build a power system. The foreign company occupied the branch of the industry in which such competitiveness was intolerable. The presence of Light in distribution was thus a basic part of a delicate mechanism that made competing state companies contribute to the same market without making them cooperate.

Another favorable aspect of the development of generating sites by several state companies was that each company started with a specific or local task to perform. Considerable benefit may have been gained from the consequent harnessing of strong local interests to incipient power projects—interests that were perhaps more compelling in getting power plants built than the more general appeal of a national power program.

The imminent power crisis in the industrial heart of São Paulo (the original focus of the Furnas project); the power-neglected areas of São Paulo state, ready with infrastructure for development but left out of the concession area of São Paulo Light (CHERP and USELPA); the desire of Minas to have adequate power and to free its economic growth from the constraints of the stagnant AMFORP subsidiary (CEMIG); the concern of Rio to free itself from power dependence on São Paulo (CHEVAP); the challenge to the state of São Paulo to build a large hydro complex, as well as to show the world's uninterested lending institutions that it could do without them (CELUSA)—all these separate drives and vivid appeals were more effective than a generalized plea to provide Brazil with increased power supply in order to free and stimulate its development. Through this specificity, the state companies drew up local interests in support of them. At the same time, their scaled-down and simultaneous development thrusts did not remain forever at the local level. Every state power enterprise in Brazil's south-central region started out as a limited venture and later grew, sometimes inadvertently, into a more comprehensive undertaking.

I am suggesting that multicompany development of electric power had important benefits. It may seem strange to advocate disaggregation in an industry that often is beset with the problems of piecemeal development. The proliferation of equipment standards can be a considerable obstacle to interconnection and to growth of the local electrical equipment industry. Varying standards multiply the requirements for servicing skills and training as well as for spare parts. Disaggregated development of power supply nevertheless harnesses the growth of power to the virulence of local drives and personal ambitions. A more unified approach to power development, such as one federal company undertaking several projects, might neutralize rather than utilize this push of local interests.

There was another sense in which multicompany development of electric power may have represented an adaptation to existing opportunities. Many Brazilian power managers received years of training and experience with the two foreign utilities, the Light and AMFORP. The president of Furnas, for example, had worked with AMFORP for fourteen years. The power technician who leaves the foreign company usually does so because he has become competent enough to take on more complex tasks but can rise no further in the organization. This failure to secure promotion can be the result either of discrimination against natives in upper positions or simply of a limited number of managerial positions in an industry occupied almost solely by two companies. Regardless of the reason, the foreign company ends up releasing a heavily weighted proportion of technicians who are ready and eager to take on managerial positions. Those who stay with the company are most likely to be middle-level people who either have not yet come up against the ceiling imposed by the limited number of managerial positions or are uninterested in taking on more complex tasks. They tend to prefer foreign over state enterprise, for in the former, working conditions and salaries are generally more secure than in the state companies.

By this interesting process of natural selection, the state sector finds available to it a fair proportion of high-level talent. State enterprise may be better able to absorb this released talent through many companies rather than one, for the engineer up against the ceiling in his foreign utility may not leave if the alternative is to work under another ceiling in a state utility; or he may go into another activity altogether, in order to be his own boss. The success of Brazil's power growth, in other words, may have been related to the fact that multicompany development allowed the state sector to capture several somewhat frustrated technicians on the verge of doing something important.

One final factor may have made multicompany development particularly well suited to Brazilian aptitudes. Foreign power consultants—both North and South American—often remark upon the independence and inventiveness of the Brazilians whom they encounter in their work. At the same time they criticize the indiscriminate assertion of this independence in circumstances that require only routine responses. They marvel at the Brazilian engineer's ability to resolve quickly and imaginatively a problem never before encountered, but they become annoyed at his unwillingness to master the more pedestrian routine. One state company had to fire one of its most inventive engineers because he insisted on novel and intricate solutions in circumstances that dictated a more direct, traditional, and less costly alternative.

That Brazil's power sector contained many companies meant that it did not lose this hyper-inventive engineer. He went to another state company, whose work was in a more pioneering stage than the first, and where he was able to take on a position of at least equal rank. If managerial positions in fact give greater scope to, and benefit more from, the exercise of indiscriminate independence, then multicompany state power development in Brazil was a way of utilizing and benefiting from that independence.

The trouble with encouraging independence and giving concrete expression to personal ambition, is that it becomes more and more difficult to achieve cooperation in circumstances where that is desirable. The power companies of the state of São Paulo were an obvious example. Of the six state power companies in the south-central region, three were involved solely in the state of São Paulo (CELUSA, CHERP, and USELPA), and one more (Furnas) initially sold all its power in that state. One state's power problems were being attacked by four highly independent state-sponsored companies, in addition to the state's vigorous Water and Power Department. Several São Paulo politicians and power managers began to believe in the late 1950's that allowing the creation of so many state power companies had been a mistake —not because the specific projects would have been better executed by a single state company, but because by the time it was institutionally desirable to unify and coordinate the state's disparate power programs, it had become politically impossible. Each company had grown into the fief of various local groups, perhaps cultivated by the power manager who had made his career with the company and therefore wanted to prevent its submersion in a state-wide power enterprise. To cut down the number of state companies, moreover, would mean a limitation of the state governor's opportunities to repay political favors with appointments to the boards of directors. For various politicians, jobholders, and power managers interested in preserving their achievements there was no particularly compelling benefit to be gained from merging the several state power companies into one.

When the São Paulo state companies finally did merge in October 1966, there was a compelling reason for doing so. These companies had been finding it more and more difficult to obtain federal and international financing because of the growing criticism that too much power financing was going to São Paulo in relation to the rest of Brazil. Any further lending to that state for power, according to the financing institutions, would have to be justified as part of an efficiently organized and unified state power program. What turned the tide in favor of merger, in short, was not an appreciation of how inefficient it was to build the state's power supply with several independent companies; it was, rather, the threat of losing out on financing. The political benefits of maintaining several power companies had suddenly been superceded by the financing costs.

A Digression on Interconnection

The resistance of state companies to submersion in a larger entity where each would have to compromise is the same problem encountered when an attempt is made to form an interconnected power system. "There is . . . a growing interdependence among these companies," noted AID in its observations on the south-central region's power situation. "The many problems arising from this interdependence have not yet been settled; nor has a completely satisfactory mechanism been established to reconcile the conflicting interests." [14]

Multicompany development and its concomitant uncooperative behavior may further complicate the problems of interconnection. The technological desirability of interconnection for stubborn independent companies, however, is a more compelling force than the need to unify state expenditures in power, which would be the justification for merging several state companies. Power technology, that is, may begin to *force* cooperation at a certain stage of growth of the independent systems. The more interconnection is resisted and postponed, the greater will be the pressure that is exerted on its recalcitrant future components. For as power systems grow toward each other, the effort to interconnect becomes less and less, and the benefits foregone in not interconnecting become greater and greater. This may be especially true in hydro systems, where lines from the plant to its consuming center are likely to pass close by the lines of other systems.

I have suggested that the untrammeled independence allowed the Brazilian power manager may have helped to bring about significant growth in the country's power supply. Because a component of this process was the considerable distrust that existed among the various state companies, cooperative action would have represented a significant constraint on their way of doing things. To introduce interconnection under such

14. AID, "Brazil—Rio Light S/A and São Paulo Light S/A," Capital Assistance Paper: Proposal and Recommendations for the Review of the Development Loan Committee, Document #AID-DLC/P338 (June 9, 1965), p. 15.

circumstances is to undo, in effect, what geographical distance
has accomplished; it makes the companies close neighbors
again. Interconnection is a kind of social contract, which com-
mits a company to take a certain amount of power from others,
and to supply it to them when they need it. The company is
obligated to construct and operate its installations according
to standards considered desirable for the interconnected
whole. One of the major conflicts between the state companies
of the south-central region, for example, had to do with the
transmission voltage chosen by CELUSA for its high-tension
line to São Paulo. This voltage was different from that which
would have been in keeping with the standards of the Furnas
system, thereby creating some problems for the projected
interconnection of the system and the future standardization
of equipment for local production. CELUSA's choice of voltage, however, was determined in great part by the equipment-
tied foreign financing it had obtained in Italy. Although Furnas
and The Steering Committee exerted great pressure on
CELUSA to change its decision, it was to no avail.[15] Some
Furnas officials admitted in private that had they been faced
with the same situation ($63 million of guaranteed foreign
financing on the condition that a certain voltage be used),
they would have made the same choice as CELUSA.[16] Conflict over CELUSA's transmission voltage became so acute and
drawn out that the transmission line in question came to be
referred to as "o linhão"—the big (problem) line.

Interconnection, then, circumscribes somewhat the power
manager's room for maneuver. It requires a damping down of
managerial independence—a progressive "domestication" of the
power manager. With complete interconnection the power

15. Furnas had used 345-kv lines and CELUSA was planning 400 kv.
"Because the international voltage standards adopted by the International
Electrotechnical Commission specify 345 and 500 KV," CANAMBRA
reported, "it would be desirable to select one of these in order to take
take advantage of international standardization . . . It is recommended
that serious consideration be given to the 500-KV voltage." CANAMBRA,
I, pp. III-22, IX-35.
16. Furnas officials to the author.

managers of the hitherto isolated systems are fused into one super-power manager who is master of the grid. This final stage of the super-manager is highly sophisticated technologically and very difficult to achieve politically. The natural candidate for the controller of the grid is somebody who does not rise out of any of the contributing systems. If he is associated with one of the component companies, he will be accused by the others of helping his old company to get the best deal from the interconnected operation, because the exercise of his authority bears directly on the revenues of the component systems. It will be difficult, therefore, for him to achieve the compliance necessary to make interconnection work.

This difficulty was one of the sources of conflict in the regional planning for power in south-central Brazil. Because Furnas was the champion of the cause of interconnection, the other state companies were less inclined to cooperate. They believed that interconnection was a device by which Furnas would further its own position, at the cost of the other participating companies. That such conflicts occur suggests that interconnecting systems, technologically ready for the stage of one super-manager, may encounter great difficulty in surmounting the political problem of establishing centralized decision-making. Even though they are already interconnected and are technically ready for unified operation, they continue running themselves separately. They bicker intensively, for they have been brought within the same grid without yet having agreed to submit to a master law.

This administrative lag in the growth of the system can result in continuing instability, in which the power sector benefits neither from unified operation nor from the strong growth impulses of independent managers in full control of their systems. This very lag was an important factor in one of the major accidents in electric power history: the blackout of November 1965 in the northeastern United States. From the Federal Power Commission's (FPC) study of the power failure, it appeared that the interconnection of the northeastern power systems (the CANUSE group) was lopsided; the degree of technical interdependence was not matched by a corresponding level of administrative unity. The FPC report is an excellent illustration of this point, and has considerable relevance for the Brazilian situation: "The power companies in the northeastern United States were interconnected on November 9, but it is apparent that the systems were not operating as a true power pool, that is, a fully integrated network . . . With the physical interconnection of adjoining companies, there arises an important responsibility of the management of these companies to assure that there is some group which can coordinate administratively the planning of the systems involved. There must be a recognition by the CANUSE group of the interdependence of each upon the actions of the other." [17] In view of the consequent need for a "neutral" master of the grid, perhaps the Federal Power Commission itself was responsible for the Northeast blackout, for it failed to impose a unification which the companies could never have been expected to enforce upon themselves.

These points are not to be taken as an argument against interconnection. Failure to interconnect would mean the foregoing of opportunities to increase the capacity and efficiency of the system at a low cost, and would miss a rare opportunity provided by technology to draw out cooperative behavior in a highly individualistic society. It can be argued, however, that to postpone interconnection may sometimes be desirable, whether or not the systems are technologically ready for it. More generally, the "political" timing of interconnection may be as important as the technological timing.

State companies compete with each other for political and financial support. An important component in their struggle for financing—this selling of their power projects—is that each company keeps separate from and even speaks disparagingly of the others. There is, in short, a built-in resistance to "collusion" in the state power sector that is probably much more effective than any legal measure against oligopoly in the

17. From excerpts of recommendations made by the FPC on December 6, 1965, on the Northeast power failure, *New York Times*, Dec. 7, 1965.

private sector. This competition between state companies, however, may diminish considerably as each company begins to sell power and to acquire the ability to finance its future projects internally. With this diminution of the necessity to compete for outside financing, the resistance to "combining" with other state companies may begin to lessen. The more successful the company, in other words, the more likely that interconnection will serve it well. Maybe this transition from competition to oligopoly provides an indicator for when a group of power companies is "politically" ready for interconnection.

There was one other important force promoting interconnection in Brazil's south-central region: the possibility of international financing for projects that had the blessing of the CANAMBRA program. For instance, CEMIG received a handsome reward for giving up the Estreito concession to Furnas in exchange for Jaguara, in that the World Bank granted the company a $49 million loan for construction of the Jaguara Plant. "The Jaguara project," the bank announced, "has been given highest priority in an integrated program of power expansion for the south-central region, prepared by CANAMBRA.[18]

Unlike the FPC in the Northeast blackout, the World Bank, in administering CANAMBRA's studies and always encouraging the most general approach possible, was fulfilling the need for a strong neutral force to surmount the political problems of interconnection. It was, of course, a major breach of that neutrality to name the president of Furnas as Brazilian coordinator for the planning group. This circumstance helps explain the conflicts that occurred despite the ostensibly neutral position of the World Bank as master unifier, because the other companies often believed that the bank's interests were really those of Furnas.

The timing of present interconnection efforts in Brazil may

18. International Bank for Reconstruction and Development, "$49 Million Power Loan in Brazil," Press Release No. 66/7 (mimeo), March 9, 1966, Washington, D.C.

actually be very close to our idea of *perfect* timing with respect to the competitive stage of growth of the companies involved. Of the six state companies comprising the projected south-central grid, four have already begun earning revenue through power sales—CEMIG, CHERP, USELPA, and Furnas. Two—CELUSA and CHEVAP—have not yet completed construction of their first plants and are therefore not earning revenue. Of these two, CHEVAP has been taken over by Furnas, and CELUSA has turned out to be the most obstreperous participant in the attempts to unify the power planning of the region. CELUSA, who won't start selling power until at least 1968, is still competing in the "project" market because it is completely dependent on outside financial support. The collusion that interconnection requires may therefore be out of phase with its stage of development.[19]

The Trouble with Distance

In spite of the advantages of distance and the problems which arise when that distance is violated—as in the case of interconnection—a qualification must be made to the general case for keeping various power companies separated territorially. If the transmission path from plant to consuming center has to cross state boundaries, there is less chance that geographical distance will be able to perform its mediating functions. The existence of state boundaries may introduce major problems based on overlapping jurisdictions and the distrust of states for one another.

The growth of a hydropower system is beset with interstate as well as international rivalries. These conflicts will occur less in a predominantly thermal system, where plants usually stand next to their consuming centers. Since state borders are so often rivers, antagonisms arise over which state will ex-

19. CELUSA, CHERP, AND USELPA were merged into CESP in late 1966. CELUSA may have been able to be more obstreperous than the other state companies because it was the only such company that could match Furnas in the size and cost of its hydro project, as well as in the affluence of its major financial backer, the state of São Paulo.

ploit and benefit from the development of sites along that river.[20] Minas objections to the use of Grande River hydro potential for the benefit of São Paulo are a case in point. There is a related and even more intractable interstate power problem than common rivers. A state whose borders are rivers has a fighting chance of getting that hydro potential for itself, or it may be able to develop sites on its interior rivers. But a state that has no hydro sites of its own, and which can not turn to the thermal alternative because of relative costliness, is forced to be utterly dependent on other states for its hydro supply. It is impossible, that is, for a state to build a hydro project for itself in another state. The smaller the state, moreover, the more likely that it will not have hydro sites within its boundaries.

Such a state is Guanabara, the old Federal District before the move to Brasília. Guanabara is an extreme example of a small state: it comprises only metropolitan Rio de Janeiro. But even within the broader area of the Rio system, which straddles Guanabara and the relatively small state of Rio de Janeiro, an abundance of distrust is still displayed over the dependence on other areas for supply. The small state, in short, neither can provide its own power nor wants to let others provide for it.

Distrust related to out-of-state power supply characterized even the limited interconnection (150 mw) between the Rio Light and São Paulo Light systems, even though that tie united the supplies of the same company. During the severe dry season of 1953, 1954, and 1955 both systems were in short supply. In 1954 São Paulo in particular was in need of relief. It wanted assurance of assistance from the Rio System, which was based on the power complex diverting the Paraíba River. At a meeting of the São Paulo State Electric Power Council (CEEE), the representative of the state's Federation

20. Of the five rivers with major power developments in south-central Brazil, three constitute state boundaries (Paranapanema, Paraná, and Grande). There has been interstate rivalry, however, only over the Grande River projects, probably because that was the only boundary where *both* sides were vigorously pursuing power development.

of Industries expressed his concern over the matter to the president of the National Water and Electric Power Council (CNAEE), since Rio power supply questions were dealt with by the federal government through the CNAEE. "As brothers of the Cariocas, can we expect," asked the São Paulo representative, "that São Paulo will be able to count on assistance from Rio de Janeiro?" "Of course," the CNAEE president responded. "We all know that São Paulo is Brazil. It's the Federal District that is dependent on the industry of São Paulo, and not vice versa. But one can not give what one does not have. The members of the São Paulo Council can rest assured that our good will is sincere and infinite; the only thing that could make it finite is the Paraíba River." [21]

Insecurity about power supply from other states was based on various factors. Out-of-state power, first of all, was many times shared with the supplying state, as in the case of São Paulo's assistance from Rio. A state dependent on outside power believed that the supplying state would not hesitate during a shortage to consider its own needs first. Furthermore, orderly contractual arrangements for the supply of power were not common in Brazil. A state might therefore not feel certain about a promised supply of outside power. When contracts and regulations were actually made, they were often vulnerable to modification under the pressure of shortage conditions and the political influence of power companies. A case in point was the Furnas statute guaranteeing a fifty-fifty division of power between São Paulo and Minas.[22] After Furnas had been in operation for a year and a half, the state legislature of Minas Gerais requested an explanation from CEMIG as to why all Furnas power was being sent to São Paulo. "Aside from the fact that Minas will never be able to get back this power that is being sent to São Paulo . . .," a state legislator complained, "our state is not even receiving compensation for the fifty percent to which it has a contractual right." [23]

21. CEEE Minutes, March 19, 1954, p. 10.
22. *Capítulo VII, Disposições Finais, Estatutos da CEF, S.A.—Furnas.*
23. "Assembléia pede à CEMIG que explique desvio de energia gerada em Furnas," *Jornal do Brasil,* May 23, 1965.

The president of CEMIG explained that Minas had excess power at the moment, and did not yet have the installations necessary for receiving its fifty-percent share of Furnas power. Such an argument was to no great avail, for in an atmosphere of rivalry and competition among states, electric power was not something to be shared with a neighbor in distress—especially if the neighbor was wealthy and strong, like São Paulo. On the contrary, it was something a state kept to itself, in order to get ahead of the other states. "The chronic scarcity of power in our state . . ." said the governor of Minas Gerais to his legislature in 1953, "is in direct contrast to the neighboring states. They have had an ample supply of electricity, principally in the region encompassing Rio and São Paulo . . . The creation of a strongly based electric power system in the major industrial areas [of Minas Gerais] . . . will coincide with a period of serious crisis in the power supply of [Rio and São Paulo]. There, in a nutshell, is Minas' opportunity to recapture her competitive position in the industrial development of the country." [24]

The Governor's words reveal a glimmer of delight at the prospect of a power shortage in Rio and São Paulo. It is difficult to imagine those two states depending with confidence on a power supply from Minas, or vice versa.

Another example of distrust about out-of-state power supply is the comment of a Rio-Guanabara power official concerning future federally-sponsored sources of generation for that area. "Even though the large Furnas and Três Marias projects, as well as those in construction by the state of São Paulo, are supposed to serve indirectly the Rio de Janeiro system, it is nevertheless obvious that we will always be dependent on excess power that these plants may or may not have available." [25] At the same time that Rio and Guanabara were expressing skepticism about out-of-state power supply, they were complaining about being left out of federal power programs. "There is no

24. Juscelino Kubitschek, in *Águas e Energia Elétrica* (Rio de Janeiro, Jan. 1954), V, 23.

25. Amaury Alves Menezes, "Informações sôbre um plano de eletrificação do estado do Rio de Janeiro," *Revista do Clube de Engenharia* (Jan. 1960), p. 21.

long-range plant that serves the needs of our state," said a
Guanabara deputy, "and that gives us access to the large
sources of power in the south-central region, especially the
sites of the Rio Grande . . . Guanabara is the largest contributor to the Federal Electrification Fund, and yet it is the only
state not benefited by the enormous federal investments in
large hydro plants made recently in the south-central region." [26]

A state, in other words, did not feel secure with control over
one of its basic resources resting in the hands of another state.
In the view of a small state, the distrusted "foreigner" could
just as well be a native neighboring Brazilian as it could be a
foreign company. This was the dilemma of Guanabara-Rio
state power policy. To free itself from dependence on the
foreign company's nearby generating sources meant to fall
into dependence on yet another outsider: the Furnas company. The attempt of Guanabara to squeeze in between the
foreign Light and the out-of-state Furnas was represented by
the two gas turbine plants of Governor Lacerda, and later the
two plants undertaken by CHEVAP. These plants, occurring
as they did within the Rio-Guanabara territorial limits, filled
uniquely a specific function: providing this small region with
its own source of power. Even the largest of power plants
situated outside the area's borders could not have served the
same purpose.[27]

It was not only distrust that dampened enthusiasm for
power projects outside the state. The power situation was
always an important political lever for state governors. To
witness a major alleviation of power shortage without being
able to take credit for it was for a state government a costly

26. "Estreito—um teste para a ELETROBRÁS," *O Globo*, Feb. 2,
1963.

27. This problem aspect of Guanabara power supply was noted by
one of Brazil's distinguished economists. A certain difficulty, he said,
limits the state of Guanabara's liberty of action in matters of power: any
hydro project for the area has to be outside the state. The undertaking
of such projects, therefore, always involves political understandings with
other governments. Antonio Dias Leite, "Problema financeiro dos serviços
de eletricidade da Guanabara," file document of the Federação das
Indústrias do Estado da Guanabara (mimeo), Nov. 1962, p. 16.

missed opportunity. This was the reason for the Guanabara governor's fury when AID decided to finance the Furnas-Guanabara transmission link instead of his two gas turbine plants. Though the connection with Furnas was more economic and would provide greater alleviation to the system than the gas turbines, it would bring no political credit to the governor of Guanabara. This political handicap also explains the governor's diatribe against the federal government when it took over CHEVAP in 1965. Inasmuch as this event placed CHEVAP in the hands of power interests sympathetic to Furnas and terminated the representation of each state on its Board of Directors, the governor of Guanabara was deprived of the chance to take credit for a future addition to Rio's power supply.

Multicompany development of power was beneficial to the extent that the highly local nature of each company appealed to specific interest groups, which in turn generated pressures in favor of project completion. One of the most important specific interests that could be served by locally executed projects was precisely that of the state governor. This was illustrated by the tumult caused when his political fortunes were being robbed — that is, when Furnas and the federal government would not allow the Guanabara state government to deliver Rio from its power crisis. Only through the experience of this exceptionally small state can one guess at the importance of the political drives of the governors of Minas and São Paulo in seeing through the projects of CEMIG, CELUSA, USELPA, and CHERP.

Rio's smallness not only forced that state to seek distrusted supply from outside its borders, but it also meant a proliferation of groups dealing with power questions, which may have made more difficult the resolution of such questions. The Rio power supply encompassed geographically three political jurisdictions: the state government of Rio de Janeiro, the federal government, and the municipal government of the city of Rio (later the state of Guanabara). In 1960, when the state of Guanabara was created to replace the old Federal District, the federal government, although officially giving up Rio for Brasília, continued to operate out of that city in questions of power. Thus, even though a strong new jurisdiction with its own ideas about power had come into being, the federal handling of municipal power questions continued to some extent as if the new state of Guanabara were still the old Federal District. As a result, one state was occupied by two political jurisdictions regarding questions of power. The one jurisdiction (Guanabara) was anxious to exert its new statehood in the matter; the other (the federal govrnment) was sluggish to let go of its customary handling of the city's power supply. This geographical superposition of two political jurisdictions—as well as the juxtaposition of a third, the state of Rio—eliminated an important ingredient of foreign company-government coexistence. The significance of this lack can be more readily perceived by comparison with São Paulo, where the ingredient did exist.

In São Paulo only one government jurisdiction dealt with the Light: the state, whose power arm was the Water and Power Department (DAEE). Relations between the Light and the state government were better there than in Rio. They were marked by informal agreements and adjustments. The most important meeting ground between foreign utility and state government, in fact, appeared most clearly during crisis when the political interests of the state government were endangered, for power shortages could cause unemployment and slowdowns in the rate of industrial growth. Thus it was that during the worst rationing of the postwar period the governor of São Paulo asked the Light to continue granting new connections for requested expansions in priority industries.[28] His request meant a relatively greater burden of rationing on the non-industrial consumer as well as on the already-existing industrial consumer, who would have to tolerate an even more stringent quota. The result of this coddling of industrial growth in São Paulo was that the consumption of commercial and residential

28. The Governor to the author.

classes remained constant during rationing, while that of the industrial consumers increased progressively.[29]

The agreements between São Paulo Light and the governor as to the policy toward new connections had to be made with considerable discretion. It would have been politically impossible to formalize such arrangements, for public disclosure would have raised the cries of the consumer. It was important, in short, that the two parties be able to enter into private league with each other in order to work out solutions that, from the point of view of the consumer, were "conspiratorial." Indeed, the perpetual shortages of the Light system over so many years created two somewhat opposite phenomena: virulent public hostility to the company when the power shortage was most critical, at the same time that cooperation between the company and the state in working out emergency makeshift measures was at its greatest. During shortages of power it was to the state's political interest to work with rather than against the company.

In addition to the state's concern over maintaining employment and indusrtial growth, there was another reason for the community of interest between foreign company and state government during shortage. When power is in short supply, the shortage becomes an avenue for granting or withholding political favors. Increases in consumption or size of installation are no longer decisions of the individual consumer; they must be passed upon by the power company or the state. The company, beleaguered with complaints about power shortage, delegates to the state the responsibility for much of this sensitive decision-making. This was done by São Paulo Light during the 1952–1955 crisis when it requested that the DAEE process

29. CEEE Minutes, Sept. 28, 1954, p. 4. This phenomenon was also remarked upon at a meeting of the Administrative Council of São Paulo Light in late 1958. Despite restrictions on the granting of new connections, the growth of load had not been affected. Most of this growth was accounted for by the industrial category. "Atas da sessão do Conselho de Administração [da São Paulo Light]," Dec. 18, 1958, BNDE Files, p. 4.

all requests for new connections above 100 horsepower.[30] State rather than company organs also dealt with requests by consumers for increases in their quotas. In Rio, as well, such decisions were made not by the company but by the federal government's Power Rationing Office (Coordenação de Racionamento).

The state, of course, attempted to dole out the rationed power according to some system of objective priorities. In São Paulo, requests for new concessions during rationing were filled according to criteria favoring basic industries. But these criteria were never spelled out in a system of priorities, even though the State Power Council suggested repeatedly that this be done. In 1953, for example, the representative of the São Paulo Federation of Industries, proposed a regulation that would establish a scale of priorities for new power connections, "keeping in mind the degree of essentiality of the industrial activity." The suggestion was apparently never implemented, for the director of the DAEE later expressed his dissatisfaction with the system under which new connections were authorized during the 1952–1955 crisis. "The system [of priorities in rationing and for granting new connections] previously adopted was not very satisfactory," he said, "especially with regard to industry. Those of good faith were prejudiced in benefit of those who were less responsible." [31]

Priorities, in short, were applied on an *ad hoc* basis. This did not mean that such decisions were always politically determined; rather, the urgency of the situation did not often allow time for a careful definition and administration of priorities. Set up in this informal way, however, the apportioning of rationed power supplies was bound to become somewhat politicized. Politicians are usually in short supply of ways to return political favors, and those who have favors due and difficulty in obtaining electric power would naturally consider a power connection just repayment.

With an abundant supply of electricity, the power sector is

30. Head of the Rationing Section, DAEE, to the author.
31. CEEE Minutes, July 31, 1953, p. 11; June 18, 1957, p. 2.

shut off as an avenue of political favor-exchanging. During
short supply, in contrast, even the politician who is determined
to impose objective priorities must submit somewhat to the
sudden politization of increases in consumption. He must
work closely and informally with the company to carry out his
"enforced" favor-granting. He must work "conspiratorially"
as well, for the time of shortage, when he is most subject to
favor-granting pressures, is the time when public hostility to
the company is the greatest.

Power crisis, in sum, meant the bypassing of formal and
open procedure between the Light and the government, because of the politization of increases in power consumption
and because of the rapid responses required in such emergency
situations. That the system was hydro, moreover, meant that
unforeseen improvements or deteriorations in supply were frequent and sudden, which made highly responsive and flexible
administrative arrangements for dealing with power crises
even more necessary. These circumstances turned the public
authority into a coconspirator with the company against the
consumer. Though this friendliness between state and company may not have helped to promote long-range solutions to
the power problem, it must have facilitated somewhat the
interim coexistence between the two.

Only after observing the Rio situation does one realize the
importance of the ability to conspire in São Paulo. Whereas
two antagonistic parties can make bargains with each other,
the existence of a third on the scene will make it difficult for
the other two. One of the three will always be accusing the
other two of making deals behind his back; the party with the
left-out feeling will always want to expose the other two's
conspiracy to the public. In Rio, there were three parties
instead of São Paulo's two: the Light was dealt with by the
state of Guanabara and the federal government. Guanabara
constituted the third party because of the longer association
of the federal government with Rio power supply. It was not
surprising, then, to see Guanabara publicly accusing the federal government of conspiring with the Light. "Starting with

our administration," said the Guanabara secretary of public services, "the traffic of influence between the government and the Light has been ended definitively and, we hope, irreversibly. The Light is not going to receive any more notes like this: 'Install electricity in my country home and I'll arrange for the government to take care of some of its unpaid light and power bills.' " [32]

The state of Guanabara continually haggled publicly with the Light instead of negotiating with it behind the scenes, as was happening in São Paulo. The same secretary of public services told of his first day as chief of Guanabara's Department of Light and Gas, when he found on his desk a file of unpaid bills owed by the state government to the Light. With the bills was the following message from the governor: "I will not pay! I want to be informed with the greatest urgency and detail why the Light serves the population so poorly . . . All the company has to do is get together laborers in quantity, present us with a list of what is going to be done, and we will pay our bills as the company completes its improvements. Outside of this, not one penny. Maybe the state owes money to the concessionaire, but the concessionaire is in debt to the people. We are simply bringing about a balancing of accounts." [33]

Guanabara, as third party, considered itself a victim of both the Light and the federal government. After the governor had applied for an import license and foreign exchange to purchase the gas turbine plant, he accused the federal government of purposely delaying action and of not letting him solve the power crisis of his state. [34] When the government's

32. "Guanabara nada deve à Light—ela que está devendo ao povo," *Diário de Notícias,* April 30, 1963.
33. "Guanabara nada deve à Light." The Guanabara governor of these passages, Carlos Lacerda, is a unique and fiery politician. His electric power diatribes against the Light and the federal government were as much a product of his general political strategy as of Guanabara's small-state, many-jurisdiction circumstances. These circumstances, of course, created the situation that was handy for the governor's political exploitation.
34. "Lacerda culpa União por crise de energia que aflige Guanabara,"

foreign exchange department (SUMOC) finally released the exchange necessary to import the turbines, the Guanabara state government placed the following advertisement in the papers: "Attention, electricity consumers: The Secretary of Public Services of the state of Guanabara informs the people that SUMOC has just released the exchange necessary for a 20 percent down payment on the purchase of the generators ordered abroad. This authorization occurs *five months after it was requested from the federal government.* The application to import, however, still has to traverse other federal organs, from CACEX and FIBAN to Customs . . . In consequence, the Secretary of Public Services regrets to inform you that the generators will not arrive on time to help out Guanabara in the present power crisis. It is clear that the darkness is due not only to the drought but to a bad government that neither works nor lets others work." [35]

Guanabara complained, not so much because deals were being made between the federal government and the Light, but because it was not the party with whom the deals were being made. It was being deprived of that important instrument for serving its political interests: distributing the rationed supply of power and alleviating the power shortage. The federal government's political fortunes, after all, were much less

Correio da Manhã, April 24, 1963. The 44-mw generating capacity of the governor's proposed gas turbine plant would represent an insignificant proportion of the installed capacity of the power system. The generators would produce power, moreover, at an uneconomic cost. When the foreign exchange department of the federal government received the governor's request for exchange, it asked the BNDE's electric power technicians for an opinion on the purchase. The BNDE was strongly negative, emphasizing the uneconomic nature of the installation. The governor's political strength, however, overrode the BNDE's opinion, and the foreign exchange was eventually authorized. That the governor's attempt to make an exclusive Guanabara contribution to power supply was so expensive and insignificant is an apt illustration of the small state's frustrations in electric power.

35. *Tribuna da Imprensa*, Oct. 21, 1963. SUMOC stands for the Superintendency of Money and Credit (Superintendência da Moeda e Crédito); CACEX, for the Foreign Trade Desk of the Bank of Brazil (Carteira de Comércio Exterior) and FIBAN, for the Department of Bank Inspection (Fiscalização Bancária).

crucially concentrated in Guanabara than those of the governor of that state. A bargaining friendship with the Light was much more essential for the state government's political survival.

The greater problems of the Rio system in comparison with São Paulo and the greater enmity between company and government seem to have had much to do with the continued and inefficient presence in Rio of three parties. This situation was a result not only of the size of the state of Guanabara but of its unique position as former Federal District. Since the problem was caused by too many jurisdictions dealing with power, it could just as likely exist in any small state where hydro power supply would involve more than one state in power policy decisions. The existence of the state of Rio as the source of Guanabara supply could only have made more problematical the already difficult informal cooperation between company and government in Guanabara.

Geographical distance, in conclusion, may not perform its functions if the path of the transmission lines is cut by interstate boundaries. Hydro, that is, needs lots of space if it is to generate certain institutional benefits. If the state is to go into electric power and the foreign utility is to remain, their coexistence will be easier if the country is big enough to contain long transmission lines. If power growth is to benefit from competing companies, it will be helpful to have considerable distance between rivers and between plants on the same river. And if all this is to work properly, a state may have to be large enough to fit a hydro system within it. If the above conditions are not met, hydro's benefits may turn into costs: the state generating company tangles with the foreign distributor: the state companies' enthusiastic drives degenerate into vitiating squabbles with other state enterprises; and a state's distrust of other states over the use of natural resources becomes a hindrance to the out-of-state hydro power supply necessary for small states. It might be concluded, therefore, that underlying Brazil's interesting experience in power is a unique triple resource endowment: a big country, big states, and lots of water power within each state.

6. Functional Separation

In Brazilian power circles there was one point on which opposing sides always agreed. The Light and the anti-foreign-company nationalists, the *privatistas* and the *estatistas* (those against and in favor of state-sponsored power), the World Bank and the Brazilian Development Bank—all said that Minas Gerais' state power company, CEMIG, was one of the best run enterprises in Brazil.

Thirteen years after CEMIG's creation in 1952, most of the company's founding team had risen to important positions in the power sector, and its founding president, Lucas Lopes, had served a term as Juscelino Kubitschek's Minister of Finance.[1] CEMIG managers had played important roles in the governmental committees and study groups concerned with the modification of power legislation and coordinated planning for the south-central region. Yet thirteen years before, when they were organizing CEMIG in order to build hydro plants for Minas Gerais, they had called in a foreign consultant on power. "We need your help very much," they said. "We're underdeveloped."[2]

1. John Cotrim, CEMIG's technical director until 1956, became president of Furnas; Flávio Lyra, another CEMIG director, became technical director of Furnas and acquired an international reputation as a construction engineer; Benedicto Dutra, the company's commercial director, became deputy (Chefe do Gabinete) in 1964 to the Minister of Mines and Energy, Mauro Thibau, also a director of CEMIG; Mário Bhering, vice president of CEMIG, was appointed president of ELETROBRÁS in 1967.
2. Official of CEMIG to the author.

In light of this uncertainty about their abilities, what made CEMIG's founders take on such a task? If their self-appraisal was accurate, what helped them to succeed? These questions lead to the nature of the task that CEMIG and other state companies undertook, and its effect on their ability to make a significant contribution to the growth of power supply in the south-central region. Whereas in the last chapters the role of geographical separation in keeping rival interests at arm's length was emphasized, focus will here shift to the actual nature of the task assigned by this division of labor to the companies of the state.

It is now possible to make a more positive statement about the role of the foreign company. Up to this point it has been claimed merely that things did not turn out too badly in the power sector, given the fact that the foreign company remained. Only once was it noted that the foreign company's presence was desirable, as a kind of buffer state to keep the competing state companies from coming together in the distribution market. Now, the premise is advanced that the Light's occupation of distribution was essential for the success of the state companies. Its occupation impeded the state, in effect, from going into distribution and left to it a limited and special task—generation. I earlier suggested that distribution was well suited to the disposition of the foreign utility. Here I will argue that generation was well adapted to the abilities and weaknesses of the state sector.

The technical and financial flexibility of distribution, in comparison to generation, has already been described. In distribution expansion one can take small, short-range steps and alternate operation with expansion with a certain facility. In hydro generation, however, this fluidity does not exist. One must take comparatively giant steps, and if there is waiting time between the steps, the nature and scale of the firm's activities fluctuate considerably. Generation, one could say, is "construction-intensive," while distribution is "operation-intensive."

Generation, if separate from distribution, is a task that one undertakes; distribution, in contrast, is an activity that one carries on. If the two are merged in the same enterprise, the construction-intensity of generation is diffused by the operation-intensity of distribution: after building the plants, the company gets involved in the business of selling power. Even the construction tasks of distribution have an "operations" quality about them. Because they are more divisible than generation expansions, they can occur at an ongoing pace, in contrast to the sporadic jumps of construction in generation. Distribution construction, moreover, is probably more interchangeable with another ongoing operations activity—maintenance. In generation, substitutability between construction and maintenance is zero.

Finally, there were two areas in which the distinct nature of hydro generation in Brazil had important effects. One was the attraction of talent to the state power sector and the quality of its subsequent achievements. The other concerns the general attitudes that prevailed about state enterprise in the power sector.

The Skill Intensity of Generation

CEMIG ultimately went into distribution as well as generation. In fact, it took on distribution soon after its founding, forced by the financial problems of the distributing utilities buying CEMIG power. The company's founding managers, however, had resisted distribution from the start, even against the advice of the foreign consultant they called in. Given the precarious conditions of the local utilities, the consultant had argued, the new company would eventually be forced to go into distribution if only to market its power. Since this was the case, he said, CEMIG might as well plan an integrated program from the start. But the company did not want distribution and would not accept its consultant's advice. Though CEMIG was shortly forced into that part of the business, its founders organized the state company on the premise that they were going to construct hydro plants.

The idea that the state should limit its electric power activ-

ities to generation is not uncommon, especially in Brazil. One
of its best expressions appeared in the Presidential message of
Getúlio Vargas to his Congress, accompanying the bill for a
national electrification plan: "The study of the electric power
industry reveals that we can divide it into two distinctly different branches. The one branch is generation—the other distribution . . . Although the whole industry is characterized by a
remarkable degree of mechanization, resulting in a fixed cost
disproportionately large in relation to total cost, generation
possesses all these characteristics in an even greater degree,
especially in the case of hydroelectric power. These features
result in an extremely limited requirement for personnel in
generation, considerable simplicity of operation, and great
facility therefore in inspection and control. The latter is an
indispensable prerequisite for the satisfactory performance of
public enterprise. The homogeneous final product—power at
high voltage—is easily measured and normally sold in bulk.

"Distribution, in contrast, is an activity more suited to the
qualities of private initiative. One operates with a considerably
smaller fixed capital in relation to value added, and with more
rapid turnover of capital. Technologically, distribution is characterized by a considerably lower level of mechanization and
a relatively numerous amount of personnel, including the large
staff necessary to deal with the public." [3]

This passage, though introducing the state to the power
sector, seems like a testimony of lack of faith in its managerial-
administrative abilities. Vargas considered state enterprise
suitable for generation because that activity offered the least
opportunity to misbehave, by virtue of its greater facility for
inspection and control; and it allowed the least latitude for
autonomous decision-making, by virtue of its high degree of

3. Quoted in São Paulo, Secretaria de Viação e Óbras Públicas, Departamento de Águas e Energia Elétrica, "Plano de eletrificação do estado
de São Paulo," *Mensagem encaminhada à Assembléia Legislativa do
Estado em 7 de novembro de 1955* (processed, São Paulo, 1955), p. 19.
This National Electrification Plan (Plano Nacional de Eletrificação) was
sent to the Congress on April 10, 1954 (Bill No. 4,277). It was never
enacted into law.

mechanization, limited requirements for personnel, and simplicity of operation.

The preference of state power managers for generation was
based on a quite different and almost opposite characterization of generation's attributes. State managers liked generation
precisely because of the *un*inspectability of the activity. They
favored it because of the distance that the technical complexity of the business imposed between the power enterprise and
the sponsoring state. Generation is not so much technologically
complex as it is technology-intensive, in comparison to distribution. Decisions in the generation branch can be more out
of reach of the irresponsible politician's or policy-maker's
understanding than in distribution, where the percentage of
nonengineering activities is much higher. Because of the
technology-intensive nature of their business, power managers
in generation feel somewhat protected from the interference
of the state that sponsors their enterprises.

Brazil's state power enterprises often did what they could
to increase their technological insulation from the politician,
to make even greater the lack of communication. One of
CEMIG's managers, for example, specifically wanted *not* to
be president of the company. He preferred to see a politician
as company president, that is, to have the state governor assign the position as political spoils. According to the preferences of the CEMIG manager, the less this politician-president
knew about engineering, the better.[4] Having a politician in
the company who knew nothing about electric power and at
the same time occupied the managerial position most sensitive
to political pressure was a kind of pre-emptive maneuver. The
company became politically well-connected and at the same
time ensured that it would not be meddled with. The new
enterprise might feel safer with the politician in its midst
rather than on the outside.

Both the state power manager and the responsible policy-
maker, in other words, preferred generation because of the
concern of each about the access of incompetent persons to

4. Official of CEMIG to the author.

the other's position. For the policy-maker, the simplicity and inspectability of generation granted the least latitude to an irresponsible state power manager. For the responsible state entrepreneur, the technological nature of the generation business kept the irresponsible politician at a distance.

There was truth on both sides. Power generation *is* a simpler undertaking than distribution or distribution-generation, for it makes less demands on administration and management. "To build plants is relatively easy," said the president of the São Paulo Electric Power Council, in a statement *opposing* state enterprise in electric power. "But to administer transmission, distribution, maintenance, bill collection, renewal of equipment, and expansion of the industry—this is considerably more difficult." [5] For the engineer, generation construction was simple in relation to management and the coordination of different types of activities about which he knew little. For the layman policy-maker, it was precisely this predominance of the engineering component that put generation out of his reach.

Generation is a highly specialized activity in comparison to distribution, whose functions range from purely engineering to bill collecting and dealing with the public. The generating company—selling all its power at high voltage to a few consumers—can do almost completely without the latter functions, and therefore without the administrative organization needed to coordinate them. The generating company's working force is smaller than in distribution, more highly skilled, and homogeneous.

There is also great latitude in generation construction for contracting out work—another factor that lessens the essentiality of complex management. Indeed, Brazilian state power firms were eventually urged by AID to make more use of this latitude by contracting out the more familiar tasks in order to learn the complicated tasks of management. "Brazilian state power organizations," the agency said, "are top-heavy in con-

5. CEEE Minutes, Dec. 16, 1955, Annex No. 2, p. 13.

struction and design engineering people with little or no operating and managing experience. By proceeding from one project to another they have developed a high degree of skill and know-how. This works counter to the AID preference for projects where design, procurement, and construction supervision are delegated to an engineering firm, and construction performed under a construction contract is let out on the basis of competitive bids. The owner should devote himself to the full time requirements of managing, operating, and maintaining the system . . . There is a need to 'sell' the Brazilian utility organizations on contracting for a greater portion of their engineering and construction services while they prepare to take on the problems of operations and management." [6]

The "top-heaviness" of the Brazilian state power companies, which was considered a weakness by AID, had in effect been an important source of these companies' strength. The underdevelopment of management and operation was no doubt accommodated and perpetuated by the technology-intensity of the business, which could be run, if necessary, by engineers. At the same time, this very predominance of engineering in generation-construction provided some insulation from political interference during a period when the new companies were trying to get established. Generation's potential for protection was important in attracting capable technicians to the state power sector. The simultaneous occurrence of talent and political insulation was considered basic by the Joint Commission, when explaining the competence of CEMIG. "The progress of CEMIG . . ." the commission reported, "reflects predominantly two factors: the effective performance of a number of outstanding Brazilian engineers and administrators and the fact that they are able to operate within an organizational framework that protects them reasonably well from undue political pressures." [7]

6. AID, "Brazil—Sector and Program Review: Power," File Document (processed), May 13, 1965, pp. 11–12, 18–19.
7. Joint Brazil-United States Economic Development Commission,

The Political Intensity of Distribution

The importance of generation's insulation from state interference is best revealed by contrasting to it the situation in distribution. One area in which distribution is subject to political pressures is the granting of new connections when the supply of power is scarce, which has already been discussed. There are three other such areas: the employment of personnel, the collection of accounts, and the raising of rates.

Hiring in distribution is more subject to favoritism than in generation because of the greater quantity of labor employed and the more extensive use of nonprofessional labor. This is the reason often cited by state power companies for avoiding distribution. They want to shield themselves from political pressures and from their own propensity, as they admit, to submit to these pressures. A past president of CHERP and USELPA, when asked why he did not want his companies to expand into distribution, said, "I'm an engineer, not a politician!" [8]

Rate-raising also means political problems for a distribution company. It must shoulder the public resistance to increases in the rate, even if they result from an increase in the price of power purchased from a generating company. "Let the Light have distribution," a CELUSA official said, "because if your electricity bill goes up, who are you going to complain to? CELUSA? No, the Light!" [9]

Antipathy for the distribution business was not the only reason that the state went into generation. If a generating company was to go into distribution, it would have to at least double its organization. Furthermore, policy-makers and power managers believed that, given the scarcity of public funds to commit to the power sector, distribution could look after itself more easily than could generation. Because of its spatial location amid the population that used it, distribution, it was

The Development of Brazil, (Washington, D.C.: Institute of Inter-American Affairs, 1954), pp. 167–168.
8. President of CHERP to the author.
9. CELUSA official to the author.

thought, could rely more on local authorities and interests for financing. It was the massive capital requirements for hydro construction, as pointed out in Vargas' Electrification Plan message, which led the state to believe that its presence in generation was indispensable.

One further aspect of distribution explains the state power manager's preference for generation. AID noted the weakness in the financial management of the state power companies, "especially in the preparation and use of financial statements, planning, accounting and rate analysis." [10] It was not simply that the power companies were inexperienced in financial management; they were often completely uninterested. They wanted to build things, not to be bothered with the money-making aspects of their ventures. Distribution meant going into and running a business, which was considered unexciting and almost undignified because of its details and routine. Distribution, in short, was "intensive" in aspects uninteresting to the state power engineer-manager.

The "a-financial" aspects of generation made it possible for the state power sector to attract into its service an important and responsible segment of the Brazilian elite—the engineer. In generation, engineering talent could serve for managerial positions because the presence of experienced financial management was not absolutely essential to the undertaking, at least in its initial stages. At the same time, the centrality of engineering in generation, as opposed to distribution, made it rather difficult to fill managerial posts in hydro construction companies with businessmen or politicians. It was not that the engineer was guaranteed to be a more able administrator than the businessman. Rather, his strangeness to the world of political nuance and jockeying—and often an absolute distaste for it—was important in helping the fledgling enterprise to acquire an initial distance between it and the government that had created it.

The business of generation could draw for its managerial positions on a class of talent likely to be more immune than

10. AID, "Brazil—Sector and Program Review," p. 11.

others to politization. It was, or could be, very low in the activities out of which arose the politization of state enterprises —or of any enterprise. Distribution, in contrast, was more intensive in these politization-prone functions. The competent engineer and potential power manager, usually convinced of the inefficiency of state enterprise, might nevertheless join the state power sector precisely because of generation's low propensity for such politization. Some of the most important contributors to the state power sector in Brazil were those who often expressed the greatest scorn for state enterprise. "It has been a constant of the Brazilian scene," said a prominent contributor to state power, "that state companies, after a certain period of time, become bureaucratized. This happens even when they get off to a good start. By 'bureaucratization' we mean the loss of efficiency and the absence of enthusiasm for the project. This results from the climate of insecurity— or too much security—that reigns within the company and pervades its existence . . . To my mind, that which we in Brazil call a 'mixed company' is nothing more than a government office. Through its majority stockholding participation, the government holds *de facto* control of the state company. Because of its power to hire and fire directors at will, the government exerts pressures on the management, generally impeding the company's proper functioning." [11]

Such disapproval of state enterprise is common among capable technicians in Brazil, who believe their integrity will be compromised by its built-in demands for inefficiency and dishonesty. This is true even among those technicians anxious to enlist in their government's devleopment efforts. The prejudice against state enterprise, however, is not based on strong ideological convictions, but rather on the general sentiment that state undertakings, like politicians, usually turn out badly.

11. Statement by Octávio Marcondes Ferraz, ELETROBRÁS Interviews. The speaker had been chief engineer of CHESF (Companhia Hidroelétrica do São Francisco), which built the first state-sponsored power plant of significant size in Brazil: Paulo Affonso in the Northeast. In 1964 he was appointed president of the federal power company, ELETROBRÁS.

A Brazilian engineer, skeptical of state enterprise but convinced that a specific undertaking is honest and efficient, will therefore have no ideological qualms about working for it or leading it. In so doing, he is not violating personal principles but is simply acting on the conviction that this project will be an *exception* to his general experience with the state. Perhaps it is also easier for the Brazilian technician to cross the line from private to public sector because he often believes that private enterprise in his country is afflicted with the same inefficiencies as public enterprise. He is likely to consider incompetence a weakness as much of his whole society as of its economic organization. He casts a plague on both sectors, and considers success on either side an exceptional event, based on a unique factor, such as the character of the firm's manager.

In sum, the dedicated Brazilian power manager who builds an efficient company, acquires no corresponding ideological beliefs about state capitalism but considers his undertaking to be an exception to the common path taken by most state companies. The ex-technical director of CEMIG, for example, referred in a symposium to the "accidental, circumstantial success" of the company. Regarding the success of Furnas, which he founded, and the unusual long-range survival of its Board of Directors, he later said, "Whoever is familiar with our milieu and knows the situation from the inside, realizes that this lack of political interference in the Board of Directors is due not to the system, but to fortuitous circumstances." [12]

12. John Cotrim in Instituto de Engenharia, *Semana de debates sôbre energia elétrica* (São Paulo: Imprensa Oficial do Estado, 1956), p. 262; John Cotrim, "O problema da energia elétrica no Brasil," *Revista do Conselho Nacional de Economia,* IX (May-June 1960), 110. Cotrim sounded more optimistic about state enterprise at the beginning of his experience with it. During the same symposium cited above (p. 121), he commented that the institution of *jeito* was "the peril of Brazil. [*Jeito* is the well-known Brazilian word that describes the knack of getting around the usual obstacles to a particular course of action. The word can be used in either a complimentary or pejorative sense; for example, it can mean inventiveness at cutting the red tape for a worthwhile project, or inventiveness at arranging employment for an unworthy candidate. Cotrim is using it in the latter sense.] There is no law, no rule—no matter how strict—that resists the institution of *jeitinho* [diminu-

Even outsiders considered successful state enterprise an exception to the rule. The president of the São Paulo Federation of Industries, after visiting the Furnas construction site four months before the project's completion, said, "This is an undertaking that, *although* government-sponsored, had a strong stamp of private enterprise. It stayed within the limits of responsibility and sobriety . . . Furnas was not interrupted, nor did it undergo changes in its management; it was not the target of political spoils nor petty politics." [13]

Hydro generation was important in that the technology promised skeptical but competent potential power managers that, in the case of power, state enterprise might prove an exception. Hence, because the government's initial participation in the power sector was limited to generation, an ingenious mechanism of natural selection was brought into play. Generation was uninteresting to those who might want to work for government enterprise because of the opportunities to earn more by serving various political interests (as may have been possible in distribution), but it attracted the competent technicians who would otherwise be suspicious of government enterprise on grounds of its fabled dishonesty and inefficiency.

Limited Commitment and Unlimited Appeal

Competent talent, as well as public support, may have been drawn to the power sector by other aspects of hydro generation. Each state power company started with the purpose of constructing a specific plant or complex. For such a massive introduction of government capital into the power sector,

tive form] . . . And it is precisely this *jeitinho* that has been responsible for the mishandling of public funds in the past. Political spoils, nepotism, patronage, and general political interference in public enterprise have always prevailed above everything . . . But . . . I am an optimist about Brazil. I have noticed that the postwar generation—or at least the present generation—is changing considerably. [Take, for example, CHESF, CEMIG and Volta Redonda, the government-owned steel complex]. They are irreproachable in the question of administration."

13. "Dentro de três mêses Furnas fornecerá à GB," *Última Hora,* May 15, 1963. Italics mine.

there was extremely little talk of nationalization of power or state production on a continuing basis. Large plants like Três Marias and Furnas seemed to have been promoted by the government because of their impressiveness as development projects. Hydro construction lent itself to this single-project emphasis, for it was a task with a definite beginning and an imposing end.

According to the skeptical state power manager, what happened after the initial enthusiasm of the first task was precisely what doomed state companies to a certain degeneracy. This judgment of state enterprise, commonly held in Latin America, was expressed in typical form by a Brazilian industrialist. When asked if he was in favor of state intervention in the economy, he answered, "Yes. But when *pionerismo* [the pioneering task and spirit] ends, so does the justification for the intervention of the government—for as an administrator, it is a miserable failure." [14]

Building a hydro plant was much more *pioneirismo* than administration, whereas in distribution or distribution-generation, the case was the contrary. In generation, it was possible to attract power managers to the state sector who might be willing to join government enterprise to undertake a single project, but would never consider associating themselves with a state venture on a more committed basis. This aspect of hydro generation is, in effect, a significant "divisibility." It is a divisibility of commitment, in contrast and as counterpart to the well-known indivisibility of hydro investment with respect to capital requirements. One can build power plants, that is, without committing oneself to the power business. The first steps of a government in distribution, however, require simultaneous commitment to the business—to becoming an administrator in the power sector.

Given the lack of faith in state enterprise, it might not have been possible to attract the talent or popular support that

14. Richers, Bouzan, Machline, Carvalho, Bariani, *Impacto da ação do govêrno sôbre as emprêsas brasileiras* (Rio de Janeiro: Fundação Getúlio Vargas, 1963), p. 62.

actually gravitated to the state power sector if the Brazilian government's first steps in electric power had required a massive investment of commitment as well as of capital. In these circumstances, divisibility of commitment may have had a more important impact on thresholds of entry into the power sector than indivisibility of capital requirements.

The most striking example of the process of attraction by limited commitment was the Furnas company. At its start that company bore the least possible mark of "administration." The Furnas Plant was so large that it was necessary to pour all effort into the task of just designing and executing it. The venture was more of an economic development project of the Kubitschek administration than a sign of state entry into the power sector. And its management was composed of some of the most ardent opponents of state enterprise in the power sector. The Furnas company, however, continued with the efficiency and enthusiasm of *pioneirismo* long after the completion of its original pioneering task. Its anti-state-enterprise managers stayed on and themselves guided the company into its more administrative phase. Indeed, AID criticized Brazil's state power managers for being *too* committed to their companies—that is, for not making their talent available to the economy at large. "Such engineering talent as there is, resides primarily in the large public utilities. They are thus unavailable to either the smaller utilities, or the engineering firms which could be used to assist them." [15]

Hydro's promise of limited involvement has other ramifications. It has been seen that the founders of Brazil's most successful state power company, CEMIG, started out with a considerable lack of confidence. "We're underdeveloped," they said to the foreign consultant from whom they were asking help. Although beginning with the purpose of constructing specific plants, CEMIG and the other Brazilian state power companies ended up in the power business. Had they known in advance what they were getting into, these future power managers might have shied away from the specific tasks they

15. "Brazil—Sector and Program Review," p. 12.

set out to undertake. Because of a lack of confidence in their own abilities, they might have been scared off by accurate foresight.[16] That their commitment was to build only a few plants was important in an atmosphere charged with uncertainty about their own capabilities, as well as those of their backers.

Given this double lack of confidence on the part of the power manager—in state enterprise and in his own ability to succeed—opportunities to increase generation's limited-task characteristics become important. For example, if there is a choice between a large power project and a number of smaller plants adding up to the same capacity, it might be easier to lure competent talent from the nongovernment sphere into power by undertaking the one large project. Several smaller plants will not hold the same attraction because of their resemblance to an overall government power *program*—smacking of administration instead of *pioneirismo*. The mechanics of an unusually large hydro plant, moreover, will be less understandable to nonengineers and might therefore appear to future power managers as being better insulated from outside interference. Controversy along these lines arose at the time that the Furnas Plant was projected. Many felt that the same addition to installed capacity should have been achieved with several smaller plants, more within the range of Brazilian experience and based on the development of unexploited hydro sites closer than Furnas to the consuming centers. Furnas defended itself with various arguments, but observers later remarked that one element in the company's political perseverance was the incapability, or even fear, of politicians to meddle in something so complex and large as a 1.2-million-kilowatt hydroelectric project.

16. The idea that ignorance could be important in such circumstances was suggested to me by Albert O. Hirschman, *Development Projects Observed* (Washington, D.C.: Brookings Institution, 1967), Ch. I, p. 13: "Since we necessarily underestimate our creativity, it is desirable that we underestimate to a roughly similar extent the difficulties of the tasks we face so as to be tricked by these two offsetting underestimates into undertaking tasks that we can, but otherwise would not dare, tackle."

Actually, hydro generation was uniquely endowed politically. Although, like any development project, it was hardly
immune to political interference, it ranked high in built-in
protection against such interference. It ranked high at the
same time in political appeal—in the ability to muster political
support. Hydro generation, in short, possessed a fortunate
combination of attributes: it attracted political support and
repelled the meddling consequent upon that support. Distribution, however, seemed uniquely unfortunate: it was not
politically attractive and was defenseless against political
meddling.

For a politician, the greater appeal of hydro generation over
distribution or distribution-generation is related to these distinctions between the two types of activities. The hydro plant
is a single task, a well-defined achievement with high visibility
in time and space. Its construction spans certain years, and its
location occupies a certain space. Distribution, in contrast, is
spread out indefinitely through time and space and mixed up
with other activities. Because of its ongoing quality, it can not
be cited so effectively as a material, finished achievement. The
political "mileage" gained from an economic development
project, moreover, is usually measured in terms of certain
standards of performance. In distribution or distribution-
generation, these measures are less clear-cut and give less
compelling evidence of achievement.

The political attractions of hydro plants are familiar to
observers of the process of economic development.[17] It was
precisely this catholic appeal of hydro that overshadowed the
less interesting and less politically agreeable fact that the
Brazilian government, in building a few hydro plants, was
becoming an entrepreneur in the power sector. With its
first steps in power construction, that is, the state was choos-
ing from a whole range of possible development projects. To
build power plants was one of the most impressive ways to

17. For an elaboration of this point, see my article "Technology and
Economic Development: The Case of Hydro vs. Thermal Power,"
Political Science Quarterly, 80:236–253 (June 1965).

carry out its new role as promoter of industrial development in general.

The developmental aura surrounding the government's power projects was always reflected in the ceremonies celebrating their commencement or termination. "Inaugurating this monumental construction task of Três Marias," President Kubitschek said at the project site, "I cast out a challenge to the Brazil that is negative, unproductive, and dragging its feet —to the Brazil that is incapable of believing in its own greatness. I make this challenge in the name of a Brazil that wants to grow, that wants to become great." [18]

The best illustration of the development mystique that carried along the government's power projects, and was in turn enhanced by them, is a journalistic account of the day preceding the Furnas inauguration. "The first stage of Furnas— diversion of the Rio Grande to the tunnels—was completed. Everything in order for the inauguration . . . The program all planned. The timing set. But the waters of the Grande, like the spirit of Brazilian development, were in too much of a hurry. The river, perhaps eager for its new destiny, refused to wait. At ten o'clock of the night preceding the inauguration . . . the workers grew worried and informed the management that the waters were rising rapidly. (There had been fifteen days of uninterrupted rainfall.) Around midnight, the impetuous and impatient waters overran the dike and invaded the diversion tunnels. The river, in short, simply put an end to the climax of the ceremony planned for the following day—the dynamiting of the dike—and the whole program had to be reorganized. When President Kubitschek learned the next morning of what had happened, he laughed and laughed. 'The river,' he exclaimed, 'inaugurated itself!' " [19]

The state, in sum, seems to have built a few, impressive power plants before it ever started thinking of power as its

18. "A barragem de Três Marias assinala um programa do Govêrno," *Eletricidade* (Lisbon, July-September 1960), p. 259.
19. "Furnas: Ação substituiu palavras." *O Cruzeiro*, April 16, 1960. *O Cruzeiro* is a weekly photo-newsmagazine in Brazil, similar to *Life* in the United States.

business, let alone of purposely dividing the task between itself and the foreign utility. Hence, the division of labor between the state as generator and the foreign utility as distributor was not necessarily the result of determined policy objectives. In a sense, the state found out first that it was capable of building the plants, before it ventured into something so committed and permanent as promoting the whole generation end of the business.

One last factor was of considerable importance in mobilizing support, or lessening resistance, to the state's ventures into hydro construction. Brazil is uniquely endowed with water resources. Its sixteen and a half million kilowatts of hydro potential place it sixth among the countries of the world.[20] Because hydropower was one of its great potentials as a nation, Brazil felt destined to develop that potential, quite aside from questions of choice between sectors or within the power sector. Hydropower was one area where the country could achieve a "first"—the largest hydro plants in the world—while still being underdeveloped.

The importance of this factor was magnified by Brazil's conspicuous lack of fuel resources, which are the only possible substitutes for water in the conventional generation of electricity. Hydro development meant not only the utilization of one of the country's greatest endowments but also a way to lessen its excruciating dependence on imported fuel. "We are, and we will continue to be," wrote the federal government's Water Division in 1935, "a country that must import coal and petroleum . . . Water is the only source of energy that we can

20. Canada has 44,751 mw of hydro potential; India, 31,400 mw; United States, 28,955 mw; Norway, 18,400 mw. The Soviet Union ranks among the highest in hydro potential, but no figure is available according to the measurement used. The figures here express the full potential output of power sites at 100 percent efficiency (streamflow per second multiplied by gross head); streamflow, natural or modified, is assumed available 95 percent of the time. World Power Conference, *Survey of Energy Resources, 1962* (London: The Central Office, World Power Conference, 1962), Table 8. These figures and rankings are only approximate. Brazilians generally ranked themselves fourth, rather than sixth, in hydro potential.

draw upon for massive industrial development. Our duty, therefore, is to safeguard it against improper exploitation and profiteers, as well as to intensify its use in every way possible." [21]

This theme was so dominant in the Brazilian literature on development that it is not surprising to see it expressed similarly in an article written twenty-four years later by a Brazilian journalist of political sentiments diametrically opposed to those of the government Water Division. "Until today," he wrote, "neither coal nor petroleum have come to represent national wealth for our country. Our rivers are the only key to industrialization that we possess . . . The purchase of petroleum with the dollars that we earn from coffee and cocoa represents an immense bloodletting. Either it ceases, or we will come to be a people who vegetate—a people without *élan*. If petroleum is not discovered to the extent that we hoped, then the only source of power that we have is water . . . Furnas, Três Marias, and Paulo Affonso are three parts of an achievement that in other countries would have been possible only on the basis of coal and petroleum." [22]

Because of Brazil's lack of fuel resources, decision-making in the power sector was less complex than if the country had possessed a more equally balanced mix of water and fuel resources. Fuel scarcity made thermal power expensive for Brazil: the heat-conversion rate and supply of domestic coal were low, and the cost to the economy of importing fuel for thermal plants was high because it would tie up permanently a considerable portion of the country's scarce foreign exchange. [23] Owing to the expensiveness of thermal, an important

21. Brasil, Ministério da Agricultura, Departamento Nacional de Produção Mineral, Divisão de Águas, *Utilização de energia elétrica no Brasil* (Rio de Janeiro: Papelaria Mendes, 1935), pp. 5, 7.
22. Assis Chateaubriand, "A razão de espera," *O Jornal*, Sept. 24, 1959.
23. Because of the relative expensiveness of thermal, the CANAMBRA program did not include thermal among its recommended projects: "No additional major thermal power plant construction (400 MW or larger) is recommended because of its high annual cost relative to hydro . . . A 400 megawatt (380 MW net) oil-fired plant located on the coast of

area of choice—hydro vs. thermal—was almost eliminated from the investment process. In an economic feasibility study of its projected Estreito Plant, for example, Furnas pointed out that because of the high cost of any equivalent thermal alternative, it would be senseless to make a hydro-thermal cost-benefit comparison. The company suggested as a more realistic comparison the prevailing cost of power in the region to be served by the new plant.[24]

If the case for hydro had been less clear-cut, power investment decisions would have been complicated by the presence of different interest groups backing each alternative, which would perhaps have subjected such decisions to considerable delay. Thermal was, in fact, pressured for by groups wanting to stimulate fuel consumption, namely, the coal interests of Brazil's southern states, who were searching for a market for their by-product steam coal ("carvão vapor"). Hydro projects were promoted by those already involved in hydro construction programs, as well as by the domestic construction and equipment companies, who had more to gain from hydro than from thermal construction. Although the southern coal interests struggled tirelessly to obtain coal-based thermal plants, they never had a chance of winning out over hydro supporters in

---

South Central Brazil would cost an estimated US$140.50/KW net capacity. The estimated comparative annual cost, including carrying charges, operation, maintenance and imported Bunker "C" fuel oil to produce power at system load factor would be US$41.59 per KW per annum, or 8.05 mills per kilowatt hour. A similar coal-fired plant burning Brazilian coal is estimated to cost US$189.60/KW net. Its comparative annual cost would be US$64.22/KW per annum, or 12.42 mills per kilowatt hour operating at system load factor. These annual costs per kilowatt may be compared with those for new hydro projects [in Brazil], shown . . . to vary between $12.70/KW and $42.22/KW . . . A reference to the costs of thermal power . . . and to the capital cost of nuclear power . . . illustrates conclusively, *that there are no other sources of power available to Brazil that can compete with these hydro costs.*" CANAMBRA, I, pp. 7, IX–6.

24. Central Elétrica de Furnas, S.A. "Plano de desenvolvimento do Rio Grande; segundo estágio: Projecto de Estreito, sistema de transmissão, Furnas unidades 7 & 8," File document (processed), Aug. 1962, p. 78.

the Rio-São Paulo area.[25] The costliness of thermal, in other words, considerably diminished a potential source of project-blocking controversy in the power programs of the government.[26]

To sum up, the power sector was privileged to be in charge of a natural resource that the country was determined to develop, both in order to exploit its comparative advantage and to escape its comparative disadvantage. On the grounds of fuel shortage and the presence of great hydro potential, state-sponsored activities were thus able to gain almost unquestioning support. That the state's first efforts in power were restricted to generation meant that its power program received the full impact of this privileged position.

Hydro Generation and Conflict Alleviation

So far features of hydro generation have been noted which helped muster support for the state's ventures in power, or

25. They did obtain some mine-mouth thermal plants for supply of power to the surrounding areas, a meager victory because of the relatively small power market in the southern states.

26. Thermal costliness may at the same time have eliminated, or at least delayed, the development of modern techniques of project evaluation. The idea that the absence or presence of choice partially explains the degree of sophistication of a country's project-evaluation techniques was suggested by Ronald L. Meek: "It is no accident that the most interesting contemporary ideas on the subject of criteria of choice in the electricity supply industry should be those put forward by the economists of countries like France and the USSR, where the choice between thermal and hydro-electric power is of great significance . . . Nor is it any accident that the British electricity authorities have as yet put forward scarcely any interesting ideas at all on the subject. In England and the south of Scotland, the possibilities of developing hydro power are extremely limited, so that until recently there was virtually only one method of producing electricity which it was physically possible for the industry to adopt . . . Thus neither in England nor in Scotland . . . have the relevant electricity authorities ever really regarded themselves as being faced with any serious problem of choice between basic methods of producing power and as a result they have for a long time been satisfied to rub along with the traditional easy answers." Ronald L. Meek, "The Allocation of Expenditures in the Electricity Supply Industry: Some Methodological Problems," in Alan T. Peacock and D. J. Robertson, eds., *Public Expenditures: Appraisal and Control* (Edinburgh and London: Oliver & Boyd, 1963), p. 38.

lessened popular resistance to state power programs. However, the most damaging source of possible resistance was the foreign company, the Light. One has only to remember the strong opposition of privately owned utilities in the United States to the idea of public power in order to appreciate the type of opposition the Brazilian government was courting by deciding to enter the power sector. On the basis of similar private-public conflicts in the power sectors of other countries—and the tradition of antagonism between foreign utility and government in Brazil—one would expect to find more extreme and deleterious conflict than existed. Given the superior financial, technological, and sometimes political power of the foreign utility, any strong opposition from that utility to the state's new presence in its sector would have been disruptive. Crucial importance must therefore be ascribed to certain factors, relating to hydro generation, which softened the acuteness of this public-private antagonism.

The state was less likely to oppose foreign company expansion in distribution than in generation, for distribution expansion did not require the appropriation of territory and natural resources. By the same token, the foreign company was more sensitive to the intrusions of the state into distribution than into generation. To give up customers on the periphery of one's distribution concession could easily result in a ring of other distributors around one's concession zone. By agreeing to mix its own generation with state supplies, however, the Light was not restricting access to any future distribution market it might want to seek. It could even look upon government power as a way of shoring up its position rather than threatening it.

The Light, for example, instead of opposing the state-sponsored Furnas Plant, promoted it in order to reap the greatest possible benefit from its construction. Furnas planned initially to sell all its power in a simple and profitable arrangement to São Paulo Light. The Light, in return, took a stockholding participation in Furnas and championed the state company's cause at the World Bank.[27] As a result, the bank

27. Official of the Light to the author. The Light originally held 50.6

granted a $73 million loan to Furnas in 1958, at a time when it was making a point of not lending to Brazil because, among other reasons, of inflationary policies. The bank had in fact just canceled a $25 million loan to the State Power Commission of Rio Grande do Sul (Comissão Estadual de Energia Elétrica), because of antagonism between the commission and the bank, and the consequent delay in use of the funds. The loan to Furnas thus followed on the heels of an unsuccessful contact by the bank with state power in Brazil.

In view of these adverse circumstances for international financing of state power in Brazil, the Light's backing of Furnas at the World Bank no doubt played a significant role in the bank's consideration. This support was remarkable in view of the atmosphere of continuing tension that had prevailed between the government and the foreign utility. But because the Light was guaranteed to be rescued by Furnas power—in an agreement that was somewhat unfaithful to the regional-interest image that Furnas had projected of itself—the foreign utility went to bat for the fledgling state enterprise.

An important element of the Light's acceptance of Furnas, strangely enough, was the threat of expropriation. Had the foreign-utility been secure of its future, it would probably have had its own plans for generation expansion, and may have been less amenable to the idea of state generation. Under the threat of expropriation, however, the Light was interested in earning what it could without risking the long-term investments necessary for expansion in generation. To be able to buy state-generated power would serve that end. Faced with the prospect of Furnas in the middle 1950's and a growing presentiment of increasing difficulties in the future, the Light made a definite decision to cultivate relations with state-sponsored generating companies, so as to obtain their power on the most

percent of the preferred stock of Furnas, carried in company accounts as $3,825,700, representing 30.3 percent of total equity capital. Brazilian Traction, Light and Power Co., *Annual Report, 1961*, p. 10. Because of the Light's failure to subscribe to new increases in Furnas capital, its percentage share of total equity capital had dwindled to 7 percent by 1963.

favorable terms.[28] Indeed, Light officials often joked about
their wholehearted acceptance of state-sponsored Furnas. Referring to their representation on the Furnas Board of Directors, Light would say, "While the government was busy trying
to infiltrate us through equity participation of the BNDE, we
succeeded in infiltrating *them!* We got onto the Furnas Board
of Directors. They never got onto ours." [29]

The Light's acceptance of state power may seem to display
some traces of bearhugging. But it makes an impressive contrast to the resistance put up by AMFORP when Furnas
applied for financing from the Ex-Im Bank. The difference
between the two foreign companies' reaction to state power
is understandable. AMFORP was not going to buy power
from Furnas in any significant proportion; there was no
supplier-consumer interdependence between the two that
could forge a common business interest. AMFORP comments
on relations among Furnas, themselves, and the Light reveal
this difference clearly. "Our basic data on Furnas . . . is negligi-
ble," wrote a company official in 1956. "We have been forced
to guess and assume." [30]

AMFORP, in short, was kept in the dark about Furnas,
partially because there was no functional interdependence that
required their working together. The company felt uncomfortable about Furnas, even though it would benefit from the
project's stream regularization, which would "make possible
a substantial increase in the capacity of our Peixoto Plant"
one hundred kilometers downstream.[31] Despite its acknowled-
ment of the benefit to be reaped from Furnas, AMFORP acted
out of a greater belief in the potential threat of the state company. "The major disadvantage of Furnas," asserted a company
memo, "is the disruption or at best interference with Peixoto
operation, caused by the initial filling of the Furnas reser-

28. Official of Rio Light to the author.
29. Official of the Light to the author.
30. Letter from John F. Pett to Emprêsas Elétricas Brasileiras, Aug.
27, 1956, AMFORP Files.
31. John F. Pett letter.

voir."[32] Though Furnas would bestow new capacity on
AMFORP's Peixoto, there did not exist the ongoing dependence of each company on the other that marked the cooperation between Furnas and São Paulo Light.

The importance of this technologically determined temper-
ing of public-private antagonisms is illustrated by the progress
currently being made on planning an interconnected system in
the south-central region. The Light is an important participant
in the discussions and preparations for this development. In
the United States, however, it has often been difficult to get
private power companies to plan with public companies for
the interconnection of their systems. This difference between
the two countries is easily explained. The resisted interconnection in the United States involved private and public
companies, each with its own generating-distributing facilities,
and *none* in supplier-consumer interdependence with the
other. In Brazil, on the contrary, the private utility had already
bought power from the state generating company; it had already mingled with state power. For the Light, interconnection—or for that matter, any other cooperative undertaking
with state power—did not represent the severe violation of
preference that it did for the integrated private utilities in the
United States. Indeed, among the power enterprises of south-
central Brazil it was often the foreign utility who showed the
least resistance to interconnection.[33] The state companies were
distrustful of having to pool their realms with each other.

One other factor tended to reduce antagonism between
private and public enterprise in the power sector. During the
construction of CELUSA's 1.2-million-kilowatt Jupiá Plant, a

32. "Brazil: The Power Problem in the South-central Zone—Comparative Advantages of 'Furnas' and Other Hydro-electric Projects,"
July 12, 1956, AMFORP Files, p. 5.
33. Official of Furnas to the author. At the often stormy meetings on
interconnection sponsored by Furnas, the Light frequently sought out
the Furnas representatives afterward. "You don't have to convince us
about the benefits of interconnection," the Light official would say.
"We're all for it!"

group of American congressmen toured the project site as guests of the company. After the day-long inspection, one congressman expressed his admiration for the project and asked of his host, "Now why couldn't this have been built by private enterprise?" "For the same reason," replied the CELUSA official, "that private enterprise didn't build TVA." [34]

TVA could not have interested private enterprise, he implied, because of its massive requirements for capital, its multipurpose features, and the consequent discrepancy between private and social benefits. "The law that created the Tennessee Valley Authority," said the governor of São Paulo in a message to the State Legislative Assembly, "stipulated that irrigation, agriculture, and fluvial control would be of primary importance, whereas the production of power would be secondary. It is this condition that causes diametrically opposed points of view as between the planning made by private firms, which must depend on earnings made from the sale of power, and that done by the state, whose function is to resolve problems of national interest." [35] The message went on to describe a "national interest" plan for multipurpose development of the eroded and flood-plagued Paraíba Valley.

An ironic aspect of this often-heard explanation was that public enterprise undertook hydro construction in Brazil in circumstances quite contrary to those surrounding the United States government's initiation of TVA and other multipurpose power projects. In Brazil, it was *private* enterprise that in the 1920's had built the daring hydro developments of the coastal scarp. The Light made massive capital commitments for the developments at Lages and Cubatão at a time when demand was much less strong or certain than it was when Furnas was undertaken, or when CELUSA was building Jupiá. As to the

34. Official of CELUSA to the author. The congressmen's interest in Jupiá was a result of United States participation in the Inter-American Development Bank, which granted a $13 million loan to CELUSA.

35. São Paulo, Secretaria de Viação e Óbras Públicas, Departamento de Águas e Energia Elétrica, "Plano de eletrificação do estado de São Paulo," *Mensagem encaminhada à Assembléia Legislativa do Estado em 7 de novembro de 1955* (processed, São Paulo, 1955), pp. 4–5.

multipurpose social benefits that were the assumed justification of state enterprise, the Jupiá and Furnas Plants were anything but multipurpose. They were concerned exclusively with power, and would sell their products in the simplest way—delivering almost all of it to a single customer, São Paulo Light. This was true of most government power undertakings in the south-central region, which narrowed considerably, of course, the gap between private and social benefits that was alleged to justify state power development.

Although the Brazilian allusion to TVA may have been inaccurate, it shows how the nature of hydro generation gave the state a remarkably nonantagonistic way of rationalizing its entry into the power sector—a justification that was repeated by *estatista* nationalists and *privatista* industrialists alike. It was not that the private company had failed to meet its obligations, according to this explanation, or that the state had failed to allow the company a living income. Rather, the construction of hydro plants was too financially grandiose a scheme to fall within the capabilities of private enterprise.

This characterization of hydro was imported straight from the United States. In contrast to Brazil, the history of government-sponsored power construction in the United States was truly multipurpose—causing the aforementioned divergence between private and public benefits. The American government's activities in the power sector, moreover, originated in the *nonpaying* aspects of hydro development.[36] Power was later integrated into the government's water development programs as the breadwinner for the nonrevenue-yielding features. The initially subordinate role of power was to a certain extent a result of the chronological sequence of

36. Indeed, the government's first interest in hydropower development was aroused in the late ninteenth century by the construction by private enterprise of hydro plants on rivers being improved by the government for fluvial navigation. The government could not leave unnoticed the construction of barriers on rivers it was improving for the sake of commerce. Joseph Sirera Ransmeier, *The Tennessee Valley Authority: A Case Study in the Economics of Multiple Purpose Stream Planning* (Nashville: Vanderbilt University Press, 1942), pp. 8–12.

technological developments in the United States. The government's interest in fluvial navigation, and later flood control, *antedated* the commercial development of electricity as a form of energy. With time, of course, power came into its own in American water resource projects. But the distinctly multipurpose, nonpaying origins of the government's involvement in power production created a strong association between hydropower development and government enterprise.

Hydropower was considered a justifiable sphere of activity for the state because private enterprise could not be expected to undertake projects in which a significant percentage of the return would accrue to society rather than to the company. To this day, for example, long-established and proven government power entities, such as the Bonneville Power Administration, find it difficult to secure congressional approval of appropriations to construct thermal plants. Even if the purpose of the plant is to "firm up" an existing hydro system, Congress objects that a thermal plant is a paying proposition, in contrast to hydro, and should therefore be undertaken only by private enterprise. Hydropower is a perfectly justifiable government project, they say, because its large capital requirements and multipurpose benefits make it an unlikely candidate for private backing.[37]

In Brazil, the sequence of government development of water resources was reversed. Power came first, and the other aspects might, or might not, follow. This sequence is bound to occur with greater difficulty than the other. In the United States, that is, the emergence of a technology (power) that would finance the nonpaying features of water development almost automatically insured the integration of that technology into water resource projects. Promoters of state-sponsored water development were naturally eager to introduce hydropower into their schemes as an opportunity to increase their financial viability. In Brazil, however, the introduction of new features in current water developments will *lessen* the monetary yield of these projects, for the aspects yet to be introduced

37. Official of the Bonneville Power Administration to the author.

are the nonpaying ones. The power managers themselves, therefore, are likely to be uninterested in, and may even oppose, the introduction of multipurpose features. This may explain the prevalence of single-purpose plants in the state-sponsored hydro developments of Latin America.

The planning of locks for fluvial navigation in the Jupiá dam illustrates the possible difficulty of introducing nonpaying features into hydro projects conceived by those interested in electric power. CELUSA decided to assign construction and financing of its multipurpose feature to another entity, the São Paulo state department concerned with fluvial navigation. In so doing, it went counter to the logic of integrated water development, for it relegated the task of financing the non-paying feature to a government agency without access to the power revenues of the project. It reaped the benefit of having a multipurpose "image," without having to pay for it.

In general, the state power sector benefited uniquely from the multipurpose image of water-based power. It eased the way among potential opponents to state power, while in reality the state was undertaking highly single-purpose and profitable projects. State power revenues, in short, were not diluted by the nonpaying features on which the popular justi-fication for state enterprise in this sector was based. Hydro generation provided an amicable justification for the state's participation in the power sector, even though the justification did not fit the case.

The administration of Juscelino Kubitschek, President of Brazil from 1956 to 1961, provides an appropriate closing for this section on the conflict-avoiding aspect of hydro generation. If there was one political figure especially associated with state power development in Brazil, it was Kubitschek. In 1952 he campaigned for governor of Minas Gerais on the promise of power and transport for his state. He followed up his promise with the creation of CEMIG, the highly successful state power company. As President of the nation, Kubitschek drew up a Target Program (Programa de Metas) for economic development that placed major emphasis on state-financed

electric power construction. He vigorously promoted construction of two of the country's most important hydroelectric plants
—Três Marias and Furnas. With the exception of Paulo Affonso
in the Northeast, these were the first hydro projects of considerable size to be undertaken by state enterprise in Brazil.
Furnas itself was the largest hydroelectric plant in Latin
America.

Although Kubitschek was Brazil's most consistently ardent
backer of the state's venture into the power sector, he was considered by the Light to be the *least* antagonistic of Brazil's
four Presidents from 1950 to 1964.[38] Indeed, the first two years
of Kubitschek's term—1956 and 1957—were considered by the
Light as its "golden years" with the Brazilian government.
What made them golden was the fact that the President was
sympathetic enough to sponsor in the Congress a bill proposing
legislative reform of the basic rate.[39] Although the company
gained this legislative victory only by executive decree nine
years later, the willingness of the Kubitschek government to
back such an unpopular measure in the Congress was a sign
that relations between it and the utility went remarkably well
during this brief period. "The legislation concerning electric
power concessions has been discouraging to private initiative,"
wrote President Kubitschek in the message accompanying the
bill. "Theoretically, it guarantees a reasonable margin of profit,
but it does not provide for a mechanism to correct for the effects
of the depreciation of the currency ... We should not nurse the
illusion that these government power organizations, in their

38. Official of the Light to the author. The three other Presidents were
Getúlio Vargas, 1950–1954; Jânio Quadros, 1961; and João Goulart,
1961–1964. The Castelo Branco regime, 1964–1967, was the most popular with the Light because of its reform of the basic rate legislation. The
Dutra government of 1946–1950 was nonantagonistic, and spanned a
period when the Light had less acute problems and was therefore less
interested in making basic changes in the rate situation. During that
period, moreover, the Light had considerable informal access to the
government. As a result, the basic problems of the power sector's legislative and regulatory mechanisms never really emerged then.

39. Bill No. 1,898 of 1956, published in *Diário Oficial*, Sept. 28, pp.
8,807–8,809.

early stages, will be able to attend to all the necessities of the country by themselves." [40]

The President's bill was in essence an escalator clause that would make electric power rates keep up with inflation. Economic indices reflecting the rate of inflation would be applied to the original cost of the company's assets; rate increases consequent upon this monetary correction of capital would be automatic.[41] The bill did not come to a vote in the Congress because of an unexpectedly intense wave of nationalist opposition and a later waning of the President's enthusiasm and effort to push it through—a result, probably, of the unexpected degree of popular resistance.[42] The point is that the President who gave such strong impetus to the state power sector was the same President who sponsored a legislative reform that would have conceded to the foreign company what it wanted most— the modification of the concept of historic cost as a base for calculating the power rate.

Such a dual stand would not necessarily evoke comment if it were not for the antagonism customary between public and private sectors in this particular industry. Because the state enterprise that Kubitschek encouraged was hydro generation, however, his support of both sectors may have been less problematical, or inconsistent, than it seems. Since the foreign company was less opposed to state intrusion in generation than in distribution, Kubitschek's support of state hydro construction was not necessarily an affront to the company, or a betrayal of his sympathy toward it. Although hydro generation

40. Presidential Message No. 476, Sept. 19, 1956, published in *Diário Oficial*, Sept. 21, 1956, p. 7999.
41. Another important feature of the bill was an increase of the legal rate of remuneration for electric power companies from ten to twelve percent.
42. Kubitschek's subsequent actions regarding power legislation demonstrated that he had not changed his sympathies; he merely chose to express them in a less politically explosive form. He issued Federal Decree No. 41,019, which granted automaticity to the additionals increases. He also vetoed a nationalist amendment to an income tax law (Art. 57, Par. 20, of Federal Law No. 3,470, November 28, 1958), which would have prohibited power utilities from raising rates consequent upon the monetary correction of a company's capital provided for in that law.

was "not a task for private enterprise," still another area was—distribution. The state's power ventures, in other words, did not have to be undermined by rendering to the foreign company what it requested in order to function in its own domain.

I have suggested that the performance of Brazilian state enterprise in power was strongly influenced by the nature of the task it undertook—generation rather than distribution or distribution-generation, and hydro rather than thermal generation. The distinct character of hydro generation was described by way of its marked contrast with distribution. I would like, in conclusion, to add one more dimension to the description of hydro by drawing a further contrast with thermal power.

A hydro system (generation and distribution) contains important functional divisibilities that a thermal one does not. The financial divisibility of thermal investment is considered more desirable in a developing country with scarce supplies of capital and considerable uncertainty over demand and supply conditions. By adding to power facilities in the thermal way, one makes more limited demands on these scarce resources. Mistakes in estimating cost and demand will be less serious than with hydro, since a thermal system can be built more mincingly.

In a system with predominantly thermal capacity, however, generating facilities are considerably closer to the consuming center. There is no transmission distance to interpose a clear-cut boundary between the functions of generation and distribution. Functional division of the two activities between different companies, therefore, is not as likely to occur. Within a thermal system, moreover, generation is not as interesting and self-contained an activity as it is in a hydro system; state enterprise in a thermal region is thus less likely to take on only one branch of the business. Thermal, in other words, has a kind of functional indivisibility in contrast to its financial divisibility. By making total takeover of both generation and distribution the minimum level of the state's first move in electric power, thermal sets too high the "institutional" threshold for this move—in the sense of political and administrative complexity as much as of engineering difficulty.

Because of this institutional "lumpiness" of thermal power, a thermally-based power industry is less able to contain more than one company supplying the same market, whereas a hydro system allows the separation of generation from distribution and hence the proliferation of various suppliers. Thermal power, therefore, may leave underemployed an abundant resource in developing countries: the strength and capabilities that emerge when vigorous entrepreneurial talents are allowed to run relatively rampant about certain limited tasks of development.

Hydro divisibilities offered two advantages in these circumstances. Functional divisibility set a more attainable threshold for entrance of the state into the power sector. Geographical divisibility allowed the coexistence of several antagonistic entities, both private and public, all making significant contributions to power supply. A somewhat analogous mechanism was described by Albert Fishlow in a study of American railroad history. Fishlow showed how a large number of local railroad-building projects were, in effect, substituted for a single coordinated enterprise which, though more efficient, would have required a much more concentrated commitment of capital. Although this piecemeal development may have reduced overall efficiency of the transport system, it eased considerably the access to funds in an imperfect and fragmented capital market.[43]

The mechanism described here is similar. A large number of separate hydro-generation projects were substituted (in theory) for an integrated power program with more concentrated, or rather more difficult-to-satisfy, requirements for talent and popular support as well as financial resources. Although this fragmented development may have been more costly and less efficient than integrated power development, it eased considerably the access to managerial talent and political support in circumstances where these resources were hard to come by.

43. Albert Fishlow, *American Railroads and the Transformation of the Ante-Bellum Economy* (Cambridge: Harvard University Press, 1965), p. 308.

7. Generation: The Pampered Sector

Throughout this study I have suggested that the way the power industry was divided up between private and public enterprise may have been important in relieving the problems of power supply in Brazil's south-central region. Distribution was suited to the foreign utility and its conservative approach to expansion, while generation went well with the new state enterprises. The task of hydro generation drew vigorous development enthusiasms into the power sector and, in turn, commanded a surprisingly impressive performance from the new state managers. Did not this separation of public and private enterprise, however, only perpetuate two basic problems of the power sector—the neglect of distribution and the inadequacy of rates?

When cut adrift from generation, the foreign distributing utility in a developing country may feel more secure in its non-expansionary position, for a distribution system can limp along for quite some time under the management of a risk-averting company, whereas generation facilities can not. By the same token, the distribution system may miss out on the pressures for remedial action emanating from the conditions of shortage throughout the power system. The public sense of urgency over the shortage is reduced somewhat by the relief already being provided by the state in generation, the more worrisome branch of the business. The division of labor between state and private enterprise, in short, does not seem to do anything for the problem of distribution: it cuts off this sector from the branch of the industry most capable of mobilizing remedial action. The deintegration of the industry may thus stabilize the shortage in distribution.

By dividing up the industry into domestic-led generation and foreign-owned distribution, furthermore, an opportunity may be missed to solve the power sector's other basic problem —the inadequacy of rates. The distributor is the one who fights the battles for rate increases and the public resistance to them. The generator, selling power in bulk to a few customers, can ride the coattails of the distributor's rate increases. Since a considerably smaller share of the generator's activity has to do with rates, he can run his business without being very conversant with these problems. For state companies, moreover, there is always the alternative of public subsidy or financing if an adequate return is not received through the rate.

On the one hand, the state company is the most capable, politically, of imposing rate increases. Yet it takes over the branch of the business least involved in problems of rate policy. The private company, on the other hand, is the most likely to arouse public resistance to rational rate policy. Yet it is left with the sector whose business is to pursue that policy. The power sector, in other words, may miss out on one of the major advantages of the nationalization of public services: the greater ability of the state, in contrast to the foreign utility, to impose increases in the price of the service. It would seem, then, that by introducing the state into power via generation, one courts the danger of stabilizing the rate problem as well as the chronic shortage in distribution.

The rate problem is not the proximate subject of this chapter, nor is the question of chronic shortage in the distribution system. I shall approach these topics indirectly by discussing the possibility of excess capacity in generation arising from the deintegration of the industry. This excess capacity—or rather, the imminence of it—has an important effect on the two problems of neglected distribution and rate stalemate.

The Tendency to Excess

Inasmuch as expansionary drives in the power sector were devoted almost exclusively to generation, a relative surfeit of installed generating capacity would be expected as an outcome of this unevenly spread enthusiasm. Indeed, almost all government development programs contained a passage such as the following, expressing concern over the bias toward generation. "For several years," it was reported in the economic program of the Goulart government, "complete emphasis has been placed on generation and transmission projects, while the construction of distribution and subtransmission lines has been relegated to second place . . . The deficiencies of transmission and distribution . . . constitute one of the most serious problems in the country's electric power industry."[1]

Several factors explain this tendency to excess in generation. The competition of state companies may result in additions to generating capacity without regard for the capacity of corresponding distribution systems. The structure of the generation-construction company also contributes to this tendency, since radical changes in company administration are necessary if the company's construction activity is not continuous. Another factor working toward excess in generation, relative to distribution, is that in hydro generation, overexpansion is a lesser error, within limits, than underexpansion. Because of the long construction period, underexpansion in generation is a mistake that will take years to correct, or it may result in expensive emergency deviations from long-run programs. One might expect, therefore, to find less concern among power managers about the risk of overemphasizing generation than about the neglect of distribution. The willingness to risk, within limits, overoptimistic forecasts as bases for generation construction appears in a re-evaluation made by CANAMBRA of one of its previous forecasts. "In submitting this revised forecast . . ."

1. Brasil, Conselho de Ministros, *Programa de Govêrno: Bases* (Brasília: Departamento da Imprensa Nacional, 1961), pp. 54–55.

CANAMBRA reported, "we are aware that a low level of economic activity has continued in South-Central Brazil beyond mid-1964, and that the revised power demand we show for 1964 will not be realized. Moreover, it is unlikely that the demand we show for 1965 will be fully realized. However, Brazil has in past years demonstrated such a remarkable capacity for a high rate of recovery following periods of depression, that we are now reluctant to lower our forecast for 1970 before 1964 has run its course. As was stated in our December 1963 Report, *'To meet power demands in 1970, there must be confidence in 1964.'* We believe this is still a sound principle to follow." [2]

The importance of "confidence" during the year in which the forecast is made was also stressed by one of Brazil's most competent and influential state power managers. When faced with two independent power demand forecasts on which to base his proposed program for construction of hydro generating plants, this manager preferred the more optimistic forecast, although admitting that the conservative one might have more validity.[3] In order to push through a long-range investment program, he believed, he had to forecast both buoyantly and with a show of great certainty. With a more conservative, perhaps more accurate forecast, he would run the risk of not being able to convince those government officials and politicians who would argue that demand could be met with smaller, short-run additions to capacity. Moreover, if the level of uncertainty surrounding any such forecast were admitted, these officials would be likely to object that it was better to wait and see just how demand did develop. Short-run increments could then be made as needed, instead of initiating a massive investment program on the basis of uncertain forecasts. In the case of Brazil, these short-range detractors were especially threatening because they coincided with a particular

2. CANAMBRA, "Revised Forecast of the Market for Power through 1970" (mimeo), May 1964.
3. Official of the engineering firm contracted to make the power forecast to the author.

interest group—the coal interests of the southern states. Although these interests may not have been effective enough to
get coal plants substituted for hydro in the Rio-São Paulo area,
their general aims certainly would have been served by obstruction of long-range power programs. The ensuing need
for rapid solutions would have given their uneconomical but
rapidly-constructed coal-fired plants a chance.

Slight overestimates of power demand, reasoned the same
power manager, also kept him on the safe side because any
power construction program was certain to be fraught with
unforeseeable delays in financing and execution. If demand
did not happen to materialize by the year for which the
project's completion was scheduled, he could safely figure that
it would certainly materialize by the year the project, with all
its delays, was actually completed.

This power manager preferred the risk of some excess
capacity for his system to what he considered the risk of no
capacity—that is, with a less optimistic forecast he might not
secure any support at all for his program. He therefore told
the group who had produced the less optimistic forecast that
he did not disagree with their results; he merely asked that
they not be made public until *after* he had received government authorization for his construction program. In distribution, on the contrary, if a power manager leaned toward the
high side of a demand forecast in order to help push through
his expansion program, he would be on more dangerous
ground, because of the relatively rapid time in which he could
correct an underexpansion.

The general tendency to concentrate on generation facilities
was also a function of the political appeal of hydro projects.
The glamor of hydro construction was often singled out when
criticism was being made of the neglect of distribution. "The
use of 'publicity' criteria in the selection of priorities," wrote
a Brazilian economist, "tends to create bottlenecks. Complementary investments, that is, do not always have the same
capacity to dazzle public opinion. An interesting example is
what has happened to many electrification programs in Brazil.

Investment in distribution is not very good at captivating
public opinion and has therefore been more or less neglected.
At the same time, investments in generation are promoted with
great fanfare and, no doubt, with great 'publicity' effects." [4]

Distribution seems destined to suffer from chronic neglect,
in comparison to its complement, generation. With the state
in generation and the foreign utility in distribution, one would
expect to see this imbalance grow. The most dynamic enterprises are being put to work in the sector most endowed with
expansionary attractions. The nonexpanding company is left
with distribution—the activity least capable, on its own merits,
of inducing expansion.

Distribution and Transmission: Derived Investment

Distribution, it turns out, may not be as neglected as it
appears. To illustrate, I return to the history of the Furnas
project. During the eight years of projection and execution
of this largest hydroelectric plant in Latin America, the greatest outcry about a possible delay arose not over completion of
the plant itself, but over two tie-lines of São Paulo Light,
twenty-five kilometers in length. The episode occurred one
year before the plant went into operation.

In the early 1960's São Paulo Light imported equipment to
build the tie-lines that would enable the company's distribution system to receive Furnas power (see Figure 7.1). The
230-kv lines would connect the Guarulhos substation, where
Furnas power would be received, to São Paulo Light's substations of Anhanguera and Terminal Norte. The Anhanguera-
Guarulhos-Terminal Norte link was a construction job that at
a normal pace should have taken one year to complete.[5] In
September 1961—a year and a half before the scheduled com-

4. Mário Henrique Simonsen, "Tensões em países subdesenvolvidos:
O papel da economia nos setores público e privado e as tensões surgidas
da administração de uma economia mista," *Desenvolvimento e Conjuntura*
(October 1962), p. 106.

5. John Cotrim in "Rio ameaçado de racionamento de energia elétrica
em 1963," *Jornal do Brasil,* Aug. 31, 1962.

Figure 7.1 São Paulo Light tie-lines with Furnas and the substations of Anhanguera, Guarulhos, and Terminal Norte. *Source:* Central Elétrica de Furnas, *Relatório da Diretoria* (1962), p. 5.

pletion of Furnas in early 1963—São Paulo Light requested supplementary financing from the BNDE for the cruzeiro expenditures necessary to complete construction of the lines.[6] Without this financing, the Light maintained, it could not carry out the construction program, which had already been

6. Letter from São Paulo Light to BNDE, VP-SPL-13, Sept. 15, 1961, BNDE Files. The Light was also requesting funds for the Guarulhos-São José dos Campos transmission lines, whose construction was subsequently delegated to Furnas. The Light considered its financial request a supplement for the construction program financed in part by a BNDE stockholding participation of Cr$1.3 billion (about US$7.5 million), authorized in May 1959. (The cruzeiro figure is converted at an average of the free market exchange rates prevailing at the beginning and end of 1959—Cr$146.50 and Cr$203.00 to the dollar, respectively. The free market rate applied to most invisibles and all capital transactions not made at preferential rates.)

suspended because of inflationary increases in costs and the inability of the company to recoup these cost increases through the power rate.[7]

The Light's loan request became embroiled in controversy at the bank, owing in part to the threat of imminent nationalization, but primarily because precedent had already been set for financing foreign utilities such as the Light only in the form of equity participation.[8] The Light insisted on either a loan or else equity participation on its own terms: that is, no corresponding bank control on the Board of Directors.[9] Neither party would concede enough to facilitate a solution, nor did the urgency of the matter allow time for the delicate negotiations necessary. By May 1962—less than a year and a half before Furnas's completion in September 1963—a decision still had not been made.[10] The Light's construction work on the tie-lines had been suspended and was awaiting the BNDE's word about financing.

The Furnas company was the least culpable in this impasse. Neither the tie-lines nor the financing were within its jurisdiction. But it was Furnas that would suffer the greatest financial and "prestige" loss if the tie-lines failed to materialize. The company would have to postpone its schedule of debt amortization and interest payments, and hence the moment when it could escape from dependence on shaky government appropriations procedures and gain the more solid footing of its own power revenues.

Furnas protested strongly to both the BNDE and São Paulo Light. "The current phase of Furnas construction," the company wrote to São Paulo Light, "allows us to predict that the plant will start functioning within the year. The time available

7. Letter from São Paulo Light to BNDE, VP-SPL-49, March 28, 1962, BNDE Files.
8. Parecer DP-41/62, Aug. 17, 1962, BNDE Files, p. 8.
9. Parecer do Diretor-Relator, Dir 1-51/62, Sept. 20, 1962, BNDE Files, p. 12.
10. Such a delay in processing BNDE loan requests was no longer than average. It was significant because on it hinged the functioning of the almost completed Furnas project.

to you for construction of the tie-lines seems quite limited, therefore, in view of the amount of work that has to be done ... It is unnecessary to point out the unfavorable repercussions that would occur here and abroad if Furnas were not able to honor its financial obligations with [the BNDE and the IBRD]. Default will be unavoidable if we are not able to earn the revenues projected within the scheduled period, owing to the inability to sell our power. If this complementary work of irrelevant magnitude is not completed in time, a financial and technical investment that has taken years to mobilize will be seriously jeopardized. The crucial nature of this complementary tie-line construction was known and recognized by you ever since the beginning of Furnas construction." [11]

Furnas exerted equal pressure on the BNDE. "Conclusion of [the tie-lines] in proper time," the company wrote to the bank, "is indispensable in enabling Furnas to supply metropolitan São Paulo. All this is based on plans that were laid well in advance and announced to the public. Tie-line completion is fundamental if Furnas is to market the power necessary to meet its financial obligations to the BNDE and the World Bank." [12]

Furnas arranged for as much pressure as possible to be exerted on the two parties whose delay was threatening its existence. Letters were sent to the World Bank, the major creditor of the company ($73 million) and of the Light. "As has been brought to your attention for some time ... " Furnas wrote to the World Bank, "we are extremely concerned with the prospects that São Paulo Light may not be able to complete in time the 230-kv tie-lines between our Guarulhos substation and the São Paulo Light's Anhanguera and Terminal Norte substations, necessary to supply the city of São Paulo with Furnas power." [13] The World Bank, in turn, made its concern felt at the BNDE. "I am sure," the bank wrote to the

11. Furnas to São Paulo Light (carbon copy), DPE.030.62, March 12, 1962, BNDE Files, p. 2.
12. Furnas to BNDE, DPE.035.62, March 29, 1962, BNDE Files.
13. Furnas to IBRD (photostat), DPE.036.62, March 29, 1962, BNDE Files.

president of the BNDE, "that when you have completed your deliberations, you will conclude that this transmission line is of vital urgency in order to avoid a power shortage both in São Paulo and Rio de Janeiro and that you will be able to contrive a solution to the financing problem, without which the work cannot proceed." [14]

In May 1962, less than a year before Furnas' scheduled completion, a solution was finally found. Furnas, in desperation, offered to construct the lines and enlarge the substations itself. "In the eventuality," Furnas wrote to the BNDE, "that the bank finds it impossible to grant the financing requested by São Paulo Light, we would like to be allowed to replace the latter, in order to receive the financing." [15]

The Furnas solution would be cumbersome technically and financially. The tie-lines were within the Light's distribution area, and the substations Anhanguera and Terminal Norte were the property of the company. Even if constructed by Furnas, therefore, the lines would have to be operated by the Light, requiring a leasing arrangement between the latter and Furnas. "Because power will be transmitted in both directions along the tie-lines," the BNDE Working Group reported, "it would be very difficult for any company other than the Light to operate, meter and maintain them. The President of Furnas himself, with good reason, considers that the operation of this line by his company would be quite out of the ordinary. He suggests that if Furnas receives BNDE financing to build the lines, it is imperative that they be leased afterwards to the Light." [16] This solution would be more expensive for the BNDE than if Light were to build the lines, for the bank would have to finance Furnas' purchase of equipment that the Light had already acquired for the project. The equipment,

14. IBRD to BNDE, April 13, 1962, BNDE Files.
15. Furnas to BNDE, DPE.041.62, June 4, 1962, BNDE Files, p. 3. Furnas had already suggested this solution to São Paulo Light, which wrote that it "would not oppose such a decision." São Paulo Light to BNDE, VP-SPL-68, May 30, 1962.
16. Parecer DP-41/62, Aug. 17, 1962, BNDE Files, p. 5.

moreover, would have to be purchased at a price that corrected for the intervening depreciation of the cruzeiro after the original purchase.[17]

Three months after the Furnas proposal, the BNDE was still deliberating the problem, this time with the bank staff divided between pro-Furnas and pro-Light people. The bank's technical departments were strongly against the Furnas solution, because of its awkwardness. "After all," stated a memo of the Project Department, "if the technical problems involved mean that São Paulo Light will have *de facto* ownership of the installations, then it is fitting that it have *de jure* ownership as well. The Bank, therefore, should make possible direct financial collaboration with São Paulo Light, because the Anhanguera-Guarulhos-Terminal Norte line is an inherent part of their system." [18] This group also objected to the greater cost for the bank of financing Furnas instead of São Paulo Light.[19]

Furnas exerted more pressure. It told the story to the press a half-year before scheduled completion of the plant. In August 1962, the president of the company told the Rio press that the first unit of Furnas (150 mw) was to go into operation between January and March of 1963. Rio was in danger of not receiving power from São Paulo in a year expected to be critical: if the tie-lines were not constructed in time for Furnas completion, São Paulo would not have electric power to release to Rio. The BNDE had promised financing but had not done anything about it up to the present. Failure to complete the tie-lines, the president warned, would mean drastic rationing

17. Financing the Light's construction of the tie-lines would have cost the bank Cr$1,300 million (about US$2.7 million). If Furnas executed the same task, it would cost the bank Cr$2,000 million (about US$4.2 million). The Cr$700 million difference (about US$1.5 million) represented the Furnas purchase of the equipment from São Paulo Light and inflationary cost increases. (Cruzeiro figures converted to dollars at the unified rate of Cr$475.00, which prevailed at the end of 1962.)
18. Parecer DP-41/62, Aug. 17, 1962, BNDE Files, p. 4.
19. "Any [inflationary] cost increases could be covered by São Paulo Light itself. This would not be true if Furnas built the lines, because the company has no other source of funds." Exposição DS-179/62, Sept. 5, 1962, BNDE Files, p. 2.

for Rio as well as São Paulo.[20] At the same time, Furnas sent a telegram to the BNDE: "Regarding financing for interconnection substation Furnas in Guarulhos with São Paulo Light system, without which Furnas power not able reach Paulista consumers: we stress urgent need pronouncement by bank because deadline arrived for placing orders material and equipment. Further postponement these steps will cause unavoidable rationing."[21]

In September the National Confederation of Commerce made a public appeal to the BNDE to release funds for the tie-lines, "in order to avoid a collapse of incalculable proportions, affecting the whole country."[22] In October the president of the Syndicate of Hydroelectric Industries of the state of São Paulo (also a director of the Federation of Industries) made a similar appeal. "Everything is ready for the commencement of power production by Furnas," he stated, "except that small stretch of tie-line." He could not understand, he said, why the BNDE would not concede the financing.[23] In November the Federation of Commerce of the state of São Paulo sent a telegram to the BNDE: "Allow us solicit urgent measures so that BNDE approve financing construction tie-lines Guarulhos region São Paulo, with purpose of greater supply São Paulo and Guanabara."[24]

In December the bank made its decision: the tie-lines would be constructed by Furnas. The company would receive a loan of Cr$2,000 million (about US$4.2 million), with an advance payment of Cr$600 million (about US$1.3 million) so that work could be started immediately.[25] "The creation by the

20. "Rio ameaçado de racionamento de energia elétrica em 1963," *Jornal do Brasil,* Aug. 31, 1962.
21. President of Furnas to President of BNDE, Aug. 15, 1962, BNDE Files.
22. "Colapso de energia ameaça à Guanabara," *Jornal do Comércio,* Sept. 20, 1962.
23. "Furnas: Assunto de debates na FIESP," *Estado de São Paulo,* Oct. 5, 1962.
24. Federação de Comércio do Estado de São Paulo to President of BNDE, Nov. 12, 1962, BNDE Files.
25. Decisão da Diretoria #314/62, Dec. 3, 1962, and Decisão do Conselho Administrativo #216/62, Dec. 11, 1962, BNDE Files.

federal government of the Commission for the Nationalization of Public Utilities [Comissão de Nacionalização das Emprêsas de Serviço Público—CONESP] . . ." wrote the president of the bank in justifying the decision," reveals without a shadow of doubt the interest of the state in nationalizing the foreign-owned utilities shortly. It would not be logical, at such a moment, for a state-sponsored organ such as the BNDE—in deciding between two technically feasible solutions—to pass over a mixed company under government control [i.e., Furnas] in preference for a foreign firm which undoubtedly will be nationalized at any moment." [26]

That the solution was technically feasible, of course, did not mean that it was technically desirable or financially efficient. Despite its cumbersomeness, the Furnas solution was accepted because it was the most politically efficient way of breaking the impasse. When the first generating unit of Furnas went into operation, the tie-lines were completed.

The outcry over the Furnas tie-line with São Paulo Light arose over the fact that a small patch of work would have remained unfinished when the plant was ready to go into operation. This would have meant complete and, what was worse, utterly stupid failure for an otherwise successfully terminated project of monumental proportions. It was the impending crisis of a completed but unusable Furnas Plant that put the São Paulo Light tie-lines in place. Although the matter became considerably involved, it was resolved under the threat of crisis within a period of almost one year.

The story of the Furnas tie-lines illustrates an important characteristic of transmission and distribution. The lackluster popular character of these two, in contrast to generation, was somewhat compensated for by a sequence of events that threatened crisis. The financing for the plant itself had been taken care of several years previous to the tie-line problem, largely owing to the political magnetism of the project. Because dis-

26. Voto do Presidente, Nov. 20, 1962, BNDE Files. (Cruzeiro figures converted to dollars at the unified rate of Cr$475.00, which prevailed at the end of 1962.)

tribution and transmission plans had been left until dangerously close to the end of the plant's construction period, their
execution became infused with a compelling urgency: if
financing were not obtained for subtransmission, the completed
Furnas Plant would not be able to transmit its power.

It might be said that distribution, subtransmission, and
transmission have a "derived appeal," which is a direct function of the stage of execution of the hydro plant whose power
these lines will transmit. The closer the plant is to completion,
the more dramatic becomes the absence of adequate transmission and distribution facilities. The case of the Furnas
tie-lines illustrates the strength that hydro's near-completion
imparts to the cause of transmission and distribution: at that
point the effort required to build the line is absolutely dwarfed
by the dormant kilowatt potential of the almost-completed
plant and the enormity of the electric power loss to be suffered
on the receiving end if the new power can not be transmitted.

The tie-line story shows how the near-completion of a hydro
plant provided a strong lever for mobilizing action in a sector
with a chronic inability to attract resources on its own. The
Furnas tie-lines also illustrate an unusual form of unbalanced
growth, by way of "forward linkage" from generation to distribution.[27] This unbalanced growth sequence might not be
immediately recognizable as such, because the excess that
creates pressure for an increase in the supply of distribution
facilities—that is, in the supply of the "lagging sector"—is
threatened rather than real. Furthermore, it is customary to
think of the pressures of unbalanced growth as being transmitted from one sector to another rather than within a single
sector.

A generalization to be drawn from the specific case of the
Furnas tie-lines is that a surfeit of generating capacity may
spur the correction of the lag in distribution. This was an

27. For the theory of unbalanced growth, and the concept of backward and forward linkages, see Albert O. Hirschman, *The Strategy of
Economic Development* (New Haven: Yale University Press, 1958),
pp. 62–75.

important justification, for example, offered by the Light in its application to AID for financing to expand its distribution and transmission systems. The feasibility study listed the seven major expansions in generation that were under construction in the south-central region in 1965, pointing out that four of these projects were already receiving AID financing. "The plans required for the *distribution* of power generated and transmitted by the above projects," the study maintained, "have not been considered for financing *until now* . . . By eliminating a bottleneck at the distribution level, the project will allow proper and prompt utilization of generation and transmission facilities now in the design stage or already under construction . . . The project should be implemented immediately in order not to jeopardize the benefits expected from the already financed generation and transmission projects in the region." [28]

This breed of unbalanced growth seems even more efficient than the mechanism that requires for its functioning the prior presence of shortage or excess.[29] Because of the shorter con-

28. International Engineering Company, Inc., "São Paulo Light, Rio Light: Transmission and Distribution Expansion, 1965–1970—Economic and Technical Soundness Analysis" (processed, Rio de Janeiro, 1965), pp. 11–85—cited hereafter as International Engineering. Italics mine. The expansions financed in part by AID were the Peixoto Plant (six units, totaling 360 mw), Três Marias Plant (two units, totaling 130 mw), Santa Cruz Thermal Plant (two units, totaling 150 mw), and transmission trunk lines (345 kv) and related receiver stations to transport Furnas power to São Paulo and Rio.

29. In a recent work Hirschman describes similar growth sequences via threatened, rather than real, shortage or excess: "With some types of projects, it is possible for well informed and eager would-be users of the new facility to 'jump the gun,' to act and invest as though the facility were already available: caught short they will then have a considerable stake in rapid completion and can be relied on to exert pressures in this direction . . . When inertia or opposing interests slow the pace of a project's construction and organization, the project authorities will some times foment this kind of pressure from the outside, on the part of the project's prospective users; by thus bringing highly visible pressure on themselves they can be more convincing in making their case for the financial, legal or other support they are being denied." Albert O. Hirschman, *Development Projects Observed* (Washington, D.C.: Brookings Institution, 1967), pp. 99–100.

struction period for distribution, the excess in generation *need not even come into existence* in order to work its effect on distribution. This was the case with the Furnas tie-lines: the imminence of unusable capacity was enough to bring about action to correct the deficiency in the distribution net. The same reaction to imminent excess can be seen in AID's own studies of the power situation in south-central Brazil. "There is the possibility," warned an AID review of developments in power, "of over-expansion of the more spectacular elements such as large power plants, at the expense of municipal distribution systems, rural electrification and organization and management." [30] In an earlier AID loan paper regarding financing of the Furnas-Guanabara line, an important justification had been that, "To date, capital has been concentrated principally on expanding generating capacity, but now attention and funds must also be devoted to the expansion and reinforcement of transmission and distribution systems." [31]

AID, in short, first contributed to imbalance in the power sector by lending for generation and then, pressed by the consequent excess in this branch, started to lend for distribution. The force of the pressure is nicely illustrated by the fact that AID never before committed sums for distribution as significant as the $40 million loan to the Light in 1965. Because Brazil already manufactured a complete range of distribution equipment, and because protective legislation made difficult the importation of such equipment into Brazil, any AID loan for distribution would not have been able to meet the "Buy American" conditions of United States economic assistance.[32] In the case of the Light distribution loan study, however, the AID Mission in Rio bent over backwards to justify the financing, painstakingly tracing the expenditures to be made for

30. AID, "Brazil—Sector and Program Review: Power," File Document (processed), May 13, 1965, p. 10.

31. AID, "Brazil—Furnas Transmission to São Paulo—Guanabara," Capital Assistance Paper: Proposal and Recommendations for the Review of the Development Loan Committee, Document #AID/P6/1215 (mimeo, Rio de Janeiro, 1963), p. 22.

32. Official of AID to the author.

local equipment and trying to show that a major share of them would ultimately end up in the United States.[33]

This story demonstrates how the pressures of the generation excess to which AID was contributing were strong enough to evoke a correction in the agency's power lending. The same pressures impelled AID to seek a way to overcome one of the major limiting conditions on its financing operations—the necessity to finance projects with high direct import components.

In connection with these creators and correctors of excess in power, it is appropriate to refer to a study by the World Bank. "At the present time," reported the bank, "there is a decided imbalance between the program of expansion of generation-transmission facilities being carried out by the publicly-owned utilities, and the program of expansion required to put the distribution systems in shape to distribute the additional power which will become available."[34] The bank itself had made a notable contribution to this imbalance by lending heavily in Brazil for the construction of generation

33. "Of the $122 million to be expended (by the Light) on the project, approximately $95 million represents equipment orders. The remainder represents the cost of labor and professional services. Of the $95 million of equipment procurement, approximately $25 million represents direct dollar costs to be financed by the AID loan by procurement within the U.S. . . . Of the remaining $70 million of equipment, approximately $7 million represents additional imported components which it is not practicable to finance directly with the AID loan but which nevertheless represent a direct foreign exchange cost of the equipment to be manufactured in Brazil . . . This leaves $8 million of the AID loan unaccounted for . . . The expenditure of $97 million of local currency equivalent in Brazil . . . will undoubtedly create general pressure for additional imports. It seems reasonable to conclude that the indirect impact on the [U.S.] balance of payments will at least be equal to the approximately 8 percent of local costs to be financed through dollar conversion by this $8 million of the AID loan." AID, "Brazil—Rio Light S/A and São Paulo Light S/A," Capital Assistance Paper: Proposal and Recommendations for the Review of the Development Loan Committee, Document #AID-DLC/P-338 (mimeo, Rio de Janeiro 1965), pp. 3–4.

34. IBRD, *Current Economic Position and Prospects of Brazil,* vol. III: *Electric Power,* May 1965, quoted in AID, "Sector and Program Review," p. 15.

facilities. Of the $264.1 million of bank funds committed to Brazil's power sector (see Table 7.1), not one loan was for the purpose of distribution. It seems fitting, therefore, according to my version of unbalanced growth in power, that the bank itself commented on the "decided imbalance" between distribution and generation expansion programs.

The history of the Furnas transmission lines reveals that there are crises other than the imminent completion of a hydro plant from which transmission and distribution can benefit. Basic to the growth-promoting aspect of threatened crisis is the existence of unused generating capacity at one point, to which transmission lines can be built or connected from another point where power shortage occurs, as illustrated by the story of Furnas transmission to Belo Horizonte and Guanabara.

One of the major justifications of the Furnas Plant was its approximate equidistance from the three centers of Belo Horizonte, Rio de Janeiro, and São Paulo. The connection with Rio, however, initially served propaganda purposes only, for the company's statutes divided Furnas power fifty-fifty between São Paulo and Minas. Furnas itself admitted, "The initial planning of the Furnas transmission system did not foresee interconnection with Rio Light." [35]

There was also doubt as to the connection with Belo Horizonte in Minas—despite, once again, the image of equidistance. Whereas the fifty-fifty division between Minas and São Paulo showed that the envisaged Rio connection was a good part propaganda, the Furnas agreement to sell almost all its power to São Paulo Light meant that the fifty-fifty provision, in turn, was also initially visionary. The only transmission link of the Furnas Plant that was planned and financed from the start was the line to São Paulo. It was the only transmission link, moreover, included in the $73 million loan granted by the World Bank for construction of Furnas.

35. Central Elétrica de Furnas, S.A., "Plano de desenvolvimento do Rio Grande; segundo estágio: Projeto de Estreito, sistema de transmissão, Furnas unidades 7 & 8," File document (processed), August 1962, p. 12.

Table 7.1. International Bank for Reconstruction and
Development: loans to Brazil, 1952–1963.

Sector	Amount ($1,000,000)	Year
Railroads	$ 12.5	1952
Roads	3.0	1953
Railroads	12.5	1953
Electric power	264.1	1949–1962
The Light	75.0	1949
The Light	15.0	1951
The Light	18.8	1954
The Light	11.6	1959
CHESF[a]	15.0	1950
CEEE[b]	25.0[c]	1952
CEMIG	7.3	1953
USELPA	10.0	1953
USELPA	13.4	1958
Furnas	73.0	1958
Grand total	292.1	

		Percent of power loans	*Percent of total loans*
Total to electric power	264.1	100.0	90.0
Total to the Light	120.4	45.0	41.0

Source: Information from IBRD, *Eighteenth Annual Report,
1962–1963*, pp. 57–58.

a. Companhia Hidrelétrica do São Francisco.
b. Comissão Estadual de Energia Elétrica do Rio Grande do Sul.
c. Subsequently canceled.

In 1959—still four years before completion of Furnas—the
company's propaganda started to come true. The forces that
turned the project's image into a reality came from outside
the company itself. In the spring of 1959, Belo Horizonte
started to undergo a severe shortage of electric power, precip-
itated by the worst dry season in thirty years. Although
rationing was imposed from June to October, the generating
facilities supplying the area had already demonstrated a growing inadequacy, so that it was clear that the coming rains
would not resolve the problem of power supply.

The Furnas Plant would not be ready in time for a Furnas–
Belo Horizonte line to alleviate the immediate crisis. Electric
power for Furnas construction needs, however, was being
taken from the Peixoto Plant, 100 kilometers downstream
from Furnas (see Figure 7.2). Peixoto power was being

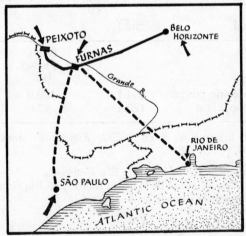

Figure 7.2. Transmission lines to Furnas:
Peixoto–Furnas–Belo Horizonte, Furnas–
Rio de Janeiro, and Furnas–São Paulo.
Source: Brasil, Ministério das Minas e
Energia, "O suprimento de energia elét-
rica à região centro-sul do Brasil no
período 1962/1970," *Relatório do Grupo
de Trabalho,* printed in *Engenharia* (São
Paulo, April and May 1962).

delivered to the Furnas construction site via a 138-kv, 105-kilometer line, built also with a view toward future interconnected operation of the two plants. The Peixoto Plant could spare some more of its capacity, and the Peixoto-Furnas line was already in existence. It was decided, therefore, that the most rapid and economic solution of the Belo Horizonte crisis would be to construct the projected Furnas-Belo Horizonte link before its time, so the Peixoto power could be transmitted to the Minas capital via Furnas. Construction began in September 1959, and the 345-kv, 265-kilometer line was inaugurated thirteen months later—setting a construction record of twenty kilometers a month.[36] The Furnas-Belo Horizonte link was put into place long before it had been envisaged and even before construction had commenced on the line to São Paulo, the only link planned and financed from the start.

The connection with Rio had a similar history. In July 1961 the federal government outlined a plan of emergency measures for power supply to Rio, in anticipation of an extremely dry period that was forecast to occur in the early years of the decade.[37] The major emergency measure recommended was 50-cycle assistance to be provided from the Cubatão Plant of São Paulo Light. Even by 1961, in other words, the Furnas-Rio link was still highly unplanned. Furnas was scheduled to go into operation by early 1963 when, according to power forecasters, the Rio system would be entering full crisis. A Furnas-Rio link would therefore seem to have been a natural resolution of the problem, rather than Cubatão assistance: Cubatão supply to Rio would both involve extra transmission construction by Furnas and function only temporarily.

Two years later, however, another forecasted crisis turned the Furnas-Rio line into a reality. In August 1963 the Ministry of Mines and Energy directed ELETROBRÁS to plan a Peixoto-Furnas-Guanabara line, to be completed by 1965; ELETROBRÁS delegated execution of the line to Furnas. This most visionary of the plant's three transmission links was

36. AID, "Furnas Transmission to São Paulo—Guanabara," p. 8.
37. Plano de Emergência, Federal Decree No. 51,058, July 27, 1961.

already under way before the completion of the project itself, financed by a loan from AID.

The two "propaganda" transmission lines of the Furnas project to Rio and Belo Horizonte were thus put up long before planned. What got them into place was a threatened power crisis in the two centers they were to supply. It is now clear how the history of Furnas' transmission lines relates to the chronic complaints about neglect of distribution and transmission. In view of the alleged fund-raising difficulties of these less spectacular activities, the Furnas transmission story is remarkable. Two transmission lines were put up before planned, and the power companies involved did not even campaign for their construction. The interest of the potential consumer had spurred the action, rather than any promotional efforts of the enterprise that would sell power from these lines. In the language of linkages, one could say that the Rio and Belo Horizonte lines of Furnas were cases of backward linkage (final consumer ⟶ transmission). The Furnas-São Paulo Light tie-line, in contrast, was a case of forward linkage (generation ⟶ distribution).

A hydro project like Furnas has great popular appeal. But in comparison to transmission and distribution, it may be too grand in dimension, cost, and period of execution to lead any specific interest group to feel that it can influence the course of the project, or even that it needs to in the first place. The transmission and distribution line task, in contrast, breaks up the project into smaller parts, each appealing directly to a certain segment of its future consumers. Hence, transmission and distribution presents a power project in a way that mobilizes and channels specific pressures in favor of completion of both plant and lines. During the construction of Furnas and its transmission lines, the newspapers were filled with the following "if's": if the Guarulhos-São José dos Campos extensions of the Furnas São Paulo line were not completed, the Rio-São Paulo line would continue being used to supply the São José area with power from Cubatão, which would leave no room on that line for 50-cycle assistance from Cubatão to

Rio. If the Anhanguera-Guarulhos-Terminal Norte lines tying
São Paulo Light into Furnas were not built in time, São Paulo
would not be able to receive Furnas power. If construction of
the Furnas-Belo Horizonte line were anticipated, the crisis in
the Minas capital could be resolved. And if construction of the
Furnas-Rio link were moved ahead, Rio could avoid imminent crisis.

The focusing on specific interests achieved by transmission
and distribution—premised on the existence or imminence of
excess generating capacity—is illustrated by incidents concerning the Paulo Affonso Plant in the Northeast, constructed by
the federally sponsored CHESF company. "Municipalities,
mayors, councilmen, and journalists strongly berated the management of CHESF, because upon the inauguration of Paulo
Affonso, its power had not yet arrived at the doors of their
houses, at the entrances to their small sugar mills, or at the
gates of their little farms." [38]

The effect that such dissatisfaction could have was demonstrated by subsequent events. The Paulo Affonso Plant generated power at 60 cycles; the city of Recife, one of its major
consuming markets, was based on a 50-cycle system. In order
to transmit its 60-cycle power to Recife, CHESF installed
20,000 kva of frequency-converting capacity. A few months
after the inauguration of the Paulo Affonso supply to Recife,
however, this frequency-converting capacity had been used up
because of the intervening rapid growth in demand. According to a power official, "There was again a lack of power in
Recife and excess capacity at Paulo Affonso. Observers had
estimated that it would take eight to ten years to convert the
city from 50- to 60-cycle operation. With excess power at
Paulo Affonso, however, it took only three years to convert,
and it cost much less than had been anticipated." Based on
the behavior of special interests in this case of Recife, the
official suggested that the same approach be used to promote

38. João Monteiro Filho of Rio Light, quoted in Instituto de Engenharia, *Semana de debates sôbre energia elétrica* (São Paulo: Imprensa
Oficial do Estado, 1956), p. 258.

frequency conversion in Rio, which was long overdue and
would be necessary if the city were to benefit from the future
power development on the Rio Grande. "It is even probable,"
he said, "that the industrial power consumers [in Rio] might
become interested in the [frequency conversion] problem, if
it were made clear that with the change to 60 cycles, harmful
rationing could be avoided. Knowing this, they might not mind
taking on some of the expenses involved. This suggestion may
not seem feasible, but it is directly tied to the interests of the
industrialists themselves. They might be willing to accept such
a financial burden, if they received a guarantee that with the
change of frequency, their supply of power would be normal-
ized." [39]

It is not only the transmission lines that receive support from
localized interests. Prompt completion of the hydro plant itself
takes on critical importance for these groups because of the
specific way in which it is presented by transmission and
distribution. The lines serve to transmit crisis impulses to the
plant at a stage in its construction when enthusiastic support
may have waned considerably. Hydro, after all, is less able
than distribution and transmission to benefit from crisis as a
way of mobilizing action in favor of construction. The completion of a hydro plant is so far removed in time that the
promise to alleviate a current or immediately impending power
shortage can not be of great effect in the campaign for the
plant's construction.[40] Hydro is simply ill-equipped to receive
the impulses of unbalanced growth by the process of backward linkage. Via transmission and distribution, however, it

39. Amaury Alves Menezes, "Análise sucinta do problema da unifi-
cacão," *Revista do Clube de Engenharia*, XXV (July 1962), 199.
40. I have argued elsewhere that this may be a blessing in disguise. A power system may end up in deficit conditions if the technology
is conducive to short-run additions to capacity—as is the case in thermal
generation, for example. Being able to rely so completely on crisis to
push through the necessary expansions in generating capacity, the thermal
system may eventually be deprived of the long-range planning that is
more crucial in the power industry than in others. Tendler, "Technology
and Economic Development: The Case of Hydro vs. Thermal Power,"
Political Science Quarterly, 80:236–253 (June 1965).

can overcome somewhat its insensitivity to the growth pressures of irate electric power customers. Transmission and distribution *reintroduce* crisis, at a more propitious moment, to the execution of a hydro plant.

What is most important about the Rio and Belo Horizonte links with Furnas is that they were emergency solutions that did *not* deviate from long-range programs in the power sector. They fit in perfectly with these plans, and even sped up their realization. In contrast to Governor Lacerda's thermal solution, for example, the crisis-placed Furnas lines were the most rapid and the most rational choice in terms of long-range planning.[41] Because the crisis in hydro transmission comes *after* the long-range planning and construction is under way, it touches only those aspects of power that can be planned and executed over shorter ranges of time. It can be utilized for the system's growth only *after* action on long-range decisions is safely under way. In a thermal system, on the contrary, short-run expansion can be made in generation as well as distribution. Reliance on crisis may therefore undermine the long-range planning necessary for generation.[42]

In conclusion, what transmission and distribution lack in

41. In its loan justification for the Furnas-Guanabara line, AID stated, "The proposed transmission line represents the quickest and most economical means to bring power in these power-short areas. Further, these circuits are shown as being required in the long-range planning for the area's power supply." AID, "Furnas Transmission to São Paulo—Guanabara," p. 9.

42. This factor seems to have contributed to the chronic power problems of metropolitan Buenos Aires, which is completely dependent on thermal supplies (see Tendler, "Technology and Economic Development"). The importance of distinguishing between the various action-mobilizing aspects of crisis was suggested to me by a passage in Henry C. Hart, *Administrative Aspects of River Valley Development* (Bombay, New York: Asia Publishing House, 1961), p. 43: "[Very] costly, in the long run, is the possibility that a nation bent on doing something quickly about floods may alter its basic water development policies in ways that deny it full utilization or a fair sharing of burdens for years to come. Precisely this last has occurred in the U.S. It is possible to correlate quite closely the major departures [i.e., deviations] in national water development policy with the incidence of catastrophic floods, and to show that many of the departures were themselves ephemeral or even without practical result."

intrinsic appeal, they compensate for in the "crisis appeal" derived from near-completion of the hydro plant. Although hydro's attractions may be more majestic, those of distribution and transmission have their own effectiveness in finance-raising terms: the divisibility of the appeal of distribution and transmission allows a more direct contact with those who will benefit from the facilities to be provided. It breaks down a cooperative effort for the public good into distinct segments, which appeal directly to the interests of specific groups and promise immediate benefits.

Excess Generation and the Rate Situation

It is sometimes argued that consumers or public opinion in general will accept the rate increases of a state company more readily than those of a foreign utility—even though the experience with state-owned railroads in Latin America does not inspire much confidence in this claim. According to this view, the only way to solve power shortages caused by frozen rates is to replace foreign with state power. The primary example is the case of Mexico, where power was nationalized, ironically enough, in order to meet the requirements of international lending institutions. These institutions had pressed for a rational rate policy in Mexico, as a condition for lending to the country's partially foreign-owned power industry. The Mexican government decided that the only way to meet their conditions was to grant the rate increases to itself, that is, to take over the power system from the foreign company. The maneuver was successful: resistance of the consumer and the international banker were overcome, and the newly nationalized industry got rate increases and foreign financing.

A possible disadvantage of the Brazilian approach, which assigns the state to generation and the foreign company to distribution, could be that it misses this opportunity to achieve a rational rate policy. Rate-making must be imposed on the public at the distribution end of the business. If the state's avoidance of distribution resulted in a prolongation of the rate problem, state construction would represent only a temporary alleviation of the problems of power supply. The state's electric power services would become deficit-ridden and a drain on government budgets—as happens often with state-run services in any country. Private capital would continue to avoid the industry, or commit itself too tenuously for the long-range growth of power supply. Contrary to this logic, however, the institutional arangement of the power industry in south-central Brazil may actually have facilitated the state's eventual acceptance in 1964 of a more rational rate-making policy.

Basic rate reform, the most direct solution of the rate problem and power shortage, was also the most politically difficult. The construction of generating facilities by the state was politically easier as a short-range solution than the achievement of consensus on reform of existing rate legislation. State entry into generation, moreover, eased the specter of rate reform by introducing less antipathetic groups into the power sector alongside the foreign company. Even if the state companies were not out front fighting for rate reform in distribution, any increase won by the foreign distributor would redound to their benefit. Because of the introduction of the state companies in generation, in other words, rate reform ceased to be exclusively a rewarding of enemies.

There is no doubt that public resistance to state-imposed rate increases is not as strong as resistance to increases sought by a foreign utility. But this is only half the story. As the history of state enterprise shows, it is just as important to know whether the state company will actively *seek* adequate rates. State companies, in contrast to private, have the alternative of falling back on subsidy if rates do not bring in sufficient earnings; more often than not, they have done so. When the ten Brazilian subsidiaries of AMFORP were consolidated under ELETROBRÁS, for example, two had already been operated by state authorities for some time—The Pernambuco Tramways and Power Company, Ltd., and the Companhia Energia Elétrica Rio Grandense. In contrast to most of the south-central region's state power firms, these two were vertically integrated, having charge of both generation and distribution. Yet of the ten AMFORP subsidiaries, the two state-operated ones were in the worst rate situation and had obtained the least number of increases in the immediately preceding years.

Here was a case where the state had taken over a foreign company in distribution as well as generation, but the rate situation had not improved. Necessary rate increases did not follow from introducing a situation designed to make it easier to impose them on the public. That the eight foreign-owned utilities had a better record on rate increases than the two state-operated ones may in fact suggest that the interest of the utility itself in pursuing adequate rates is more important than the degree of public resistance to such rates. In regard to the Mexican solution, therefore, the more interesting phenomenon is not that the state was able to impose rate increases on the public, but that it pursued those increases in the first place.

It has already been suggested that some lessening of public resistance to rate increases in Brazil resulted from the state's move into generation. What is more important is that the new structure of the power industry may also have facilitated the emergence of state enterprises likely to prefer adequate rates to subsidies, and likely to fight for them. The propensity of state enterprise to rely on subsidy is not necessarily a result of administrative irresponsibility and incompetence. In an industry where price changes are controlled, as in power distribution, the task of arriving at a proper rate requires exhaustive financial studies as well as the specialized personnel to conduct them. The company must then stand up to consumer resistance when a rate increase is in order. A more effortless alternative for the state company, as a way of earning money, is subsidy. The company may settle for subsidy partly because it is not capable of or interested in making the effort necessary to earn its income through rates. This could be especially true in power generation, where construction is in itself an interesting task and quite distinct from the money-making aspects of the business. In short, the weakness of government enterprise for subsidy in electric power arises from the fact that the alternative—adequate rates—requires considerable effort and brings great unpopularity.

In a country with a continuous and substantial rate of inflation, the pursuit of the proper rate is even more "costly." With inflation, rational rate-making means continual requests for rate increases. This repetitiveness of the necessary rate increase makes earning via rates very costly for state companies. In a country like the United States, where secular inflation during the last half-century was not substantial enough to outrun the significant productivity gains that have occurred in the power industry, rate increases consumed a much smaller share of rate-making activities. In such a non-inflationary country, moreover, an adequate rate might often mean a decreased rate. In that case the initiative and effort to find and impose the proper rate would more often than not be undertaken by the government regulatory agency rather than by the company itself.[43] Inflation, then, by multiplying the costs of rate-seeking, makes it even more difficult to implant rate-making practices in state companies.

Subsidy is often a perfectly acceptable source of financing for state enterprise—for example, in cases where important indirect benefits are involved. Reliance on subsidy in single-purpose power enterprises, however, is less defensible, because of the facility of allocating and charging the cost of the service to the individual user. In cases where customer charges are preferable to subsidy, the latter is often the path by which political interference, nepotism, and general inefficiency enter the state company. In order to change such companies from subsidy-seeking to rate-seeking enterprises, either the cost of rate-seeking must be reduced, or its desirability increased. Having the private company in distribution and the state in generation may facilitate this change in "relative costs."

The generating company has an easier time than the distribu-

43. A truly efficient company, of course, engineers its own rate decreases as well as increases. In an inflationary economy, however, the state utility's failure to pursue a rate decrease would represent a less significant reinforcement of the propensity toward subsidy than would its failure to pursue a rate increase.

tion company in formulating and presenting the case for rate increases. Costs are less complex in generation and easier to ascertain, principally because the generator has only a few large customers taking power at the same voltage. The price increases of the generator, moreover, are automatically included in the rate charged by the distributor, so that they make their first public appearance in the bill sent out monthly by the distributing company. It is the distributor who pays the cost in unpopularity for the generating company's wholesale rate increases. The generator, after winning his increase, passes on to the distributor the "popularity cost" of imposing it.

This cost-passing is important because unpopular actions may, after all, be more difficult for a state enterprise than for a private firm—despite the Mexican case. The foreign company is "specialized" in unpopularity; its mere existence elicits popular resistance. It is geared to living in a hostile environment and has little to lose by taking one more unpopular step. Its endemic unpopularity, is a kind of insulation against pressures from the outside to soften its insistence on increased rates. The state company, in contrast, does not stand in chronic opposition to the public and will be more sensitive to public sentiment. It may be defenseless, for example, against important power-users who exert pressures not to increase rates through the public officeholders on whom the utility must rely for at least tacit support. Just as effective as actual opposition in undermining vigorous rate-seeking policies is the state company's fear that unpopular rate increases will make difficult its coexistence with the sponsoring government.

As the pursuit of rate increases moves from the private to the state sphere, two opposite changes occur in the rate atmosphere. The state firm's rate increases provoke less opposition from public opinion than do those of the foreign utility, as exemplified by the Mexican case. But general opposition to any rate increases at all is more effective in subverting the pursuit of rates because the marginal cost of taking unpopular measures is so much greater for the state company.

If generation and distribution are divided between two

companies, the burden of the rate struggle falls on the distributor. With the state company in generation only, therefore, the relative cost of earning revenue via rates rather than subsidy is reduced. Because the distributor is a private company, the burden of rate-seeking falls on the enterprise most able and likely to carry on the struggle. Whether the private utility expends the effort to carry on a continuous campaign for adequate rates is not a choice between two ways of gaining revenue, as it is for state enterprise. For the private utility, the pursuit of adequate revenue is an unquestioned expense of carrying on its business.

The division that assigns the private sector to distribution and the state sector to generation is a specialization with its own logic of comparative advantage. The money-making function is performed by the company most adept at it, and the construction function is carried on by the company most apt to pursue it vigorously. What is essential is that the technology guarantees "trade," that is, an exchange of benefits between the two branches. The money passes from distribution to generation, and construction eventually passes from generation to distribution because of the overloading of distribution facilities caused by the new injection of wholesale power. Were the private company the owner of one generation-distribution system, and the state company of another—as in the case of the AMFORP subsidiaries—there would be no such exploitation of comparative advantage, no forced passing on of benefits.

It was earlier suggested that the private company in distribution served as a "buffer state," keeping antagonistic state companies apart. In the case now under discussion, the private company also serves to keep two interests apart—the state company and the state—by channeling the rate, on its way to the state company, through the private distributor. In the earlier argument the private buffer state prevented harmful conflict between state companies. In this case, it helps to prevent harmful "collusion" (i.e., subsidy) between state company and sponsoring government.

Up to this point the relationship between state generation,

private distribution, and rates has been discussed without reference to the relative capacities in the two branches of the industry. If there is excess capacity in generation, this simply reinforces the tendencies toward rate-seeking. The foreign company's "extortionate" position, implying that it will not undertake major expansion in distribution without a previous rate increase, turns out to be a crucial factor in setting the rate-seeking mechanism in motion. For if the distributing company makes expansion contingent upon satisfactory rate increases, as the Light did, then the possibility of excess generation capacity in relation to distribution facilities is an effective way of getting the state companies on the side of increased rates. Even if these companies are existing partially on subsidy and are not themselves urgently interested in adequate rates, they still will not be able to sell their power if the distributor does not have the capacity to buy. In these circumstances the state companies are likely to become active supporters of a rational rate policy. Their support is important, for it tempers considerably the popular impression that rate reform is a "sell-out" to the foreign company.

The president of Furnas was a major participant in the campaign leading to the rate decrees in 1964. When Furnas brought its first units into service in September 1963, the distribution facilities of its major current and future customers (Rio and São Paulo Lights) were in an extremely deteriorated state. The Light was conditioning any updating and expansion of its distribution facilities on reform of the rate situation. Without a change in rate legislation, in other words, the earning power of Furnas would be directly threatened by the inadequate capacity of its major customer. "The inadequacy of *generating* facilities has already been removed for the time being," declared CANAMBRA in 1966, "with the completion of the 990 megawatt Furnas Hydroelectric Plant, and power supplies are now commensurate with demand over almost all the South-Central Region. Unfortunately, the restraint on demand brought about by inadequacy of distribution facilities is far from being overcome. In fact the situation has probably deteriorated still further during the past year." [44] To see the Furnas president favoring rate increases was not surprising: he had always supported rate reform, even before assuming the presidency of the company. But that he would play a major role in the campaign must have had something to do with the fact that, without rate reform, his company would have had difficulty selling as much power as it wanted to its major customer, the Light.

It is now clear that, although the rate decrees of November 1964 had a somewhat arbitrary history, the existence of new state generating companies with imminent excess capacity was important in preparing the atmosphere for those rate changes. Up to 1965 the price of power was not high enough to call forth, of itself, adequate expansion in power facilities. Because of the institutional barriers to rate increases, however, acute shortage was not effective in bringing about a price change of the magnitude necessary to regularize the supply of power. What happened instead was that the power industry expanded lopsidedly, outside of the system of price incentives: the state went into the generation business without waiting for price signals to change.[45] But the inevitable lopsidedness

44. CANAMBRA, "Power Market: Projected Requirements (Section 3)" (mimeo), June 1966, pp. 3–11. Italics mine.

45. Price was not necessarily a disincentive to new investment in power. The ten percent return allowed in electric power was not considered inadequate, but rather, the inflation-eroded capital base on which that return was calculated. At any point in time a perfectly adequate return could be earned in electric power by a new firm with a capital base not yet devalued by inflation. The new state generating companies, therefore, did not represent a complete disregard of price signals. Of course, in order to say that the state's entrance into power was not in absolute disobedience of these signals, one must assume entrepreneurial ignorance about future inflation, or that future expectations do not bear on the potential firm's decision to enter the industry. Needless to say, a company will not invest in fixed capital if it knows that today's attractive return will be unattractive tomorrow. The assumption of ignorance, however, may not be so fantastic. If the potential entrepreneur thinks that, once within the power sector, he will be influential enough to change the institutional barriers to raising price, this can be just as effective in neutralizing his pessimism about the future as a change in the barriers themselves. Since the potential entrepreneur being discussed is the state, it would not be unreasonable to assume such expectations.

caused by this price-ignoring expansion in one branch of power supply was crucial in facilitating the price change that finally did occur. It created influential organizations whose earnings would be threatened without eventual price change and, just as important, contributed toward lowering resistances to such change. Instead of the normal sequence in which an increase in price calls forth an increase in supply, the exact opposite happened: an increase in supply was to some extent a *prior* condition for bringing about the increase in price.

The development of state power companies in Brazil may seem an unnecessarily tortuous route for bringing about a change in the price of power. However, a somewhat analogous sequence occurred in the history of power rates and state power production in the United States. In the American case, moreover, a change in price was one of the deliberate aims of public policy in its sponsorship of state power enterprise.

Long after the concept of federal regulation of electric power rates was accepted in the United States, the question of rate decreases presented considerable problems. The private utilities argued that if the federal government enforced a rate decrease, the difference between the original and the decreased rate represented government expropriation of private property without due process of law—that is, without compensation. As long as this interpretation was supported in the courts, the Federal Power Commission could declare a power rate unjust but had no authority to enforce its decision.[46]

Had this question arisen in Brazil, it would have been purely academic. Inflation made rate increase, not decrease, the important issue for price change in the power sector. In the United States, however, productivity increases were not swamped by inflation; moreover, a good part of the rate controversy occurred during the 1930's when deflation was the prevailing phenomenon. Decreases in rates, therefore, were

46. Joseph Sirera Ransmeier, *The Tennessee Valley Authority: A Case Study in the Economics of Multiple Purpose Stream Planning* (Nashville: Vanderbilt University Press, 1942), pp. 30–32.

at least as important as increases for policy-making in the American electric power industry.

Because the legal question of how to enforce price decreases was of difficult resolution—and probably seemed hopeless to government officials in view of the influence of the privately owned utilities in the courts—proponents of fair prices in power, anxious for immediate results, searched for other ways to bring down prices in the power sector. Their solution was public competition, as a way to get back to competitive rates and to avoid the legal impasse.[47] Hence, one justification for introducing state production in the American power industry was that it would indirectly bring about a change in the price of power. The sequence was surprisingly analogous to what happened in Brazil—and more deliberate.

An interesting aspect of the comparison between the United States and Brazil is that both cases occurred under exactly opposite conditions, although they involved the same phenomenon: an increase in supply that precedes and facilitates a change in price. In both cases, interested parties wanted to stimulate a price change that would have occurred if the market had been competitive. In both cases, the price change was difficult because of institutional and legal resistances. And in both cases, the problem of price change was approached indirectly: it was solved by an autonomous increase in supply, which in the short run met the supply problem by circumventing institutional resistance to price change, and in the long run tended to weaken these resistances and thus solve the

47. "An important incidental purpose of the inclusion of power at many recent public projects has been to fashion a competitive instrument to supplement commission regulation for control of privately owned power utilities . . . Unless company property (in the sense of capitalized "excess" profits) can be taken without compensation [i.e., through enforced rate decreases], the power of rate control is quite without meaning.

"Thus, the principles of the courts led to a logical impasse in the field of rate regulation. Because of the difficulties under which regulation has been forced to operate, the view has become increasingly general that it should be supplemented by other forms of control (of which the most frequently suggested has been public competition)." Ransmeier, *The TVA*, pp. 30–31.

price problem itself. The American case, in short, demonstrates that the Brazilian experience of an increase in power supply preceding a change in price was not an unusual, or unreasonable, sequence.

The difference between the two cases is even more interesting, for its brings out once again the importance of inflation in the history of events in the Brazilian power industry. In the United States, power rates were declining, or at least stable. In Brazil, the tendency was upward, owing to the predominant influence of inflation. This meant that the advocate of rate change (decrease) in the United States was the government; in Brazil, that role fell to the private utility. In the United States, the private utility was on the defensive, while in Brazil, this reactive role fell to the government. The direction of price change, in other words, determined who, in a regulated industry, would initiate "aggression" in the private enterprise-government conflict. If price tendencies were upward, the private utility would mount campaigns against the government, constantly demanding rate increases. If cost tendencies were downward, the government would initiate action against the private utilities, attempting to enforce rate decreases. In an upward-price country such as Brazil, the government's position *vis-à-vis* the private utility was therefore more passive. It did not have to initiate attack on the private utility to carry out its regulatory function, as it had to in the United States. It could discharge its duties by reacting to the "offenses"—the campaigns for rate increases—of the private utility.

This price-changed-determined relation of each government to its private utilities is illustrated by the different way state-sponsored power production was introduced in the two countries. In the United States the state commenced power production in order, among other things, to compete with private enterprise: it would enforce acquiescence on rates by underselling the private utilities in the market. In Brazil, on the contrary, state-sponsored power was introduced with the intention of cooperating or "colluding" with private enterprise.

It would supplement the supply of privately owned facilities, as well as operate in functional interdependence with private enterprises.

The chronic pampering of generation in Brazil may have been self-correcting, in that distribution eventually had to receive some attention, if only to allow generation to come into operation. The power sector contained within it, in short, a rather unusual mechanism of unbalanced growth. Through the deintegration of the industry, two "sectors" were created. Distribution and generation were able to expand separately up to a certain point, at which excess capacity in the state's generating plants was threatened. When that point was approached, the catching-up of distribution became crucial to the existence of generation. Those who contributed to excess in generation pressed for expansion in distribution. Furnas became champion of the Light's distribution expansion, and the international lending institutions who had concentrated on generation started to caution against neglect of distribution.

Having the government move into power generation can be seen as an interesting way of economizing on growth promotion. The power sector, both distribution and generation, is badly in need of expansion. The state enters into generation alone, for its activities in this sector will create pressures that will take care of distribution. A passage in a report of Juscelino Kubitschek's economic policy-making council suggests the operation of this mechanism. "Because of a lack of resources for a program of investment in both generation and distribution, the government and the state power enterprises have to decide on one or the other. They will be pressured by industrial development to give priority to generation. This contributes to a greater aggravation of the problem of distribution." [48]

48. "Relatório do Conselho de Desenvolvimento (1958)," quoted by Alexandre Henriques Leal, "O problema do suprimento de energia elétrica ao estado da Guanabara e regiões vizinhas," in Clube de Engenharia, "Semana de debates sôbre o problema de energia elétrica no estado da Guanabara; relatórios parciais," (processed, Rio de Janeiro, 1962), p. 19.

This sequence of unbalanced growth is likely to be one-directional. Overexpansion in distribution is improbable because of the built-in conservative bias of distribution expansion. In other words, the sequence can start out only by excess in generation, or the threat of it. There is a good chance that this excess, relative to distribution, will occur, for generation, especially when severed from distribution, is richly endowed for the purposes of attracting competent talent, financial backing, and political support. The overemphasis on generation, therefore, does not necessarily perpetuate the problems of rate stalemate and distribution neglect. It may simply initiate the sequence by which these problems are eventually resolved.

Bibliography   Index

Bibliography

Official and Semiofficial Documents—Brazil

Banco Nacional de Desenvolvimento Econômico [BNDE]. Project files of the BNDE. 1953–1965.

————. *XIII exposição sôbre o programa de reaparelhamento economico—exercício de 1964.* Rio de Janeiro: Processed, 1964.

Brasil. Conselho de Ministros. *Programa de Govêrno: Bases.* Brasília: Departamento da Imprensa Nacional, 1961.

Brasil. Congresso. Câmara dos Deputados. *Anais da Câmara dos Deputados.* 1946–1952.

Brasil. Conselho de Ministros. *Programa de govêrno: Bases.* Brasília: Departamento da Imprensa Nacional, 1961.

Brasil. Conselho Nacional de Águas e Energia Elétrica [CNAEE]. Coordenação do Racionamento de Energia Elétrica [CREE]. Files of the CREE, Rationing of 1963–1964.

Brasil. Ministério da Agricultura. Departamento Nacional de Produção Mineral. Divisão de Águas. *Código de Águas e leis subseqüentes.* Rio de Janeiro: Ministério da Agricultura, 1958.

————. *Relatório dos delegados do Brasil à 3ª Conferência Mundial de Energia.* Rio de Janeiro: Serviço de Publicidade Agrícola, 1939.

————. *Utilização de energia elétrica no Brasil.* Rio de Janeiro: Papelaria Mendes, 1935.

Brasil. Ministério das Minas e Energia. "O suprimento de energia elétrica à região centro-sul do Brasil no período 1962/1970." *Relatório do Grupo de Trabalho,* printed in *Engenharia* (São Paulo, April and May, 1962).

Brasil. Presidência da República. *Plano nacional de eletrificação e Centrais Elétricas Brasileiras, S.A.* Rio de Janeiro: Departamento da Imprensa Nacional, 1954.

――――. *Plano trienal de desenvolvimento econômico e social, 1963–1965.* Rio de Janeiro: Departamento da Imprensa Nacional, 1963.

Brasil. Presidência da República. Conselho do Desenvolvimento. *Plano de desenvolvimento econômico,* 1957, vol. II: *Meta de energia elétrica.* Rio de Janeiro: [Departamento da Imprensa Nacional], 1957.

――――. "Relatório do Grupo de Trabalho encarregado da revisão da legislação sôbre energia elétrica." Document No. 7. Mimeographed, September 1956.

Brasil. Presidência da República. Ministério de Planejamento e Coordenação Econômica. *Programa de ação econômica do Govêrno, 1964–1966 (Síntese).* Documentos EPEA No. 1. Rio de Janeiro: Serviço Gráfico do IBGE [Instituto Brasileiro de Geografia e Estatística], 1964.

Clube de Engenharia. "Semana de debates sôbre o problema de energia elétrica no estado da Guanabara; relatórios parciais." Rio de Janeiro: Processed, 1962.

Companhia Brasileira de Engenharia. "Plano de eletrificação do estado de São Paulo." 8 vols. Mimeographed, 1965.

Federação das Indústrias do Estado da Guanabara—Centro Industrial do Rio de Janeiro. "Pesquisa industrial para o Relatório, 1964." Handwritten questionnaires.

Guanabara. IV Reunião de Governadores. "Relatório do Sub-grupo de Trabalho encarregado de estudar problemas de suprimento de energia elétrica à Guanabara." Rio de Janeiro: Mimeographed, June 1961.

Instituto de Engenharia. *Reuniões de estudos e debates sôbre problemas do Vale do Paraíba.* São Paulo: Imprensa Oficial do Estado, 1958.

――――. *Semana de debates sôbre energia elétrica.* São Paulo: Imprensa Oficial do Estado, 1956.

São Paulo. Secretaria da Viação e Óbras Públicas. Departamento de Águas e Energia Elétrica [DAEE]. "Complementação térmica do sistema elétrico de São Paulo." *Relatório elaborado pelo Grupo de Trabalho.* 2 vols. São Paulo: Mimeographed, 1964.

———. "Plano de eletrificação de estado de São Paulo." *Mensagem encaminhada à Assembléia Legislativa do Estado em 7 de novembro de 1955.* São Paulo: Processed, 1955.

São Paulo. Secretaria da Viação e Óbras Públicas. Departamento de Águas e Energia Elétrica. Conselho Estadual de Energia Elétrica [CEEE]. "Atas do Conselho Estadual de Energia Elétrica." Typewritten, 1952–1958.

International Lending Institutions

CANAMBRA Engineering Consultants, Ltd. "Final Report on the Power Study of South-central Brazil." 7 vols. Processed, December 1966.

———. "Interim Report on Relief of Power Shortage in the Guanabara-Niterói Area." Mimeographed, June 7, 1963.

———. "Methodology for Long-term Power Market Forecasting, and Application to South-central Brazil." Typewritten paper submitted through the Brazilian National Committee to the World Power Conference Sectional Meetings, Tokyo, October 1966, by Antônio Dias Leite, Stefan H. Robock, and Leonid Hassilev.

———. "Power market: Projected Requirements (Section 3)." Mimeographed, June 1966.

———. "Power Study of South-central Brazil." 5 vols. Processed, December 1963.

———. "Revised Forecast of the Market for Power through 1970." Mimeographed, May 1964.

———. "Supplementary Power Studies: Memo submitted by Stefan H. Robock." Mimeographed, July 1964.

International Bank for Reconstruction and Development [IBRD]. *Eighteenth Annual Report, 1962–1963.*

———. "Extract from: Cost of Capital in the Choice between Hydro and Thermal Power." By Robert Sadove; Document No. IBRD EC-53. Washington, D.C.: Mimeographed, December 15, 1963.

———. "$49 Million Power Loan in Brazil." Press Release No. 66/7. Washington, D.C.: Mimeographed, March 9, 1966.

Joint Brazil-U.S. Economic Development Commission (Comissão Mista Brasil-Estados Unidos para Desenvolvimento

Econômico.) *The Development of Brazil.* 17 vols. Washington, D.C.: Institute of Inter-American Affairs, 1954.

———. *Projetos: Energia,* vols. X-XIII of Portuguese version. Rio de Janeiro, 1954.

———. "A Usina Termoelétrica de Piratininga (São Paulo Light & Power Company, Ltd.)." Annex I. Rio de Janeiro: Mimeographed, November 7, 1952.

Joint Brazil-U.S. Technical Commission [Abbink Mission]. "Report of the Joint Brazil-U.S. Technical Commission." Rio de Janeiro: Mimeographed, February 7, 1949.

United States. Department of State. Agency for International Development [AID]. Rio Mission. "Brazil—Furnas transmission to São Paulo—Guanabara." Capital Assistance Paper: Proposal and Recommendations for the Review of the Development Loan Committee. Document #AID/P6/1215. Rio de Janeiro: Mimeographed, [1963].

———. "Brazil—Peixoto Power Plant Expansion." Capital Assistance Paper: Proposal and Recommendations for the Review of the Development Loan Committee. Document #AID/DLC/P-263. Rio de Janeiro: Mimeographed, June 17, 1964.

———. "Brazil—Rio Light S/A and São Paulo Light S/A." Capital Assistance Paper: Proposal and Recommendations for the Review of the Development Loan Committee. Document #AID/DLC/P-338. Rio de Janeiro: Mimeographed, June 9, 1965.

———. "Brazil—Santa Cruz Thermal Plant (CHEVAP)." Capital Assistance Paper: Proposal and Recommendations for the Review of the Development Loan Committee. Document #AID/DLC/P-138. Rio de Janeiro: Mimeographed, April 29, 1963.

———. "Brazil—Sector and Program Review: Power." File document. Rio de Janeiro: Processed, May 13, 1965.

———. "Brazil—USELPA (Chavantes) Power." Capital Assistance Paper: Proposal and Recommendations for the Review of the Development Loan Committee. Document #AID/DLC/P-255. Rio de Janeiro: Mimeographed, June 9, 1964.

United States. Department of State. American Embassy, Rio de Janeiro. "Airgram." Processed, 1963–1965.

Power Companies

American and Foreign Power Company, Inc. [AMFORP]. *Annual Report*. 1962–1964.

——. Files of AMFORP: Companhia Paulista de Fôrça e Luz [CPFL—subsidiary in São Paulo]. 1954–1960.

Brazilian Traction, Light and Power Company, Ltd. *Annual Report*. 1945–1965.

Brazilian Traction, Light and Power Company, Ltd. COBAST [Companhia Brasileira Administradora de Serviços Técnicos]. "A Review of the Past Load Growth Trends and of the Future Loads in the Rio and São Paulo Systems." Document #MHM-610. Mimeographed, November 27, 1959.

Brazilian Traction, Light and Power Company, Ltd. Rio Light S.A. —Serviços de Eletricidade. *Relatório da Diretoria*. 1964–1965.

Brazilian Traction, Light and Power Company, Ltd. São Paulo Light S.A.—Serviços de Eletricidade. *Relatório Anual*. 1958–1964.

Centrais Elétricas Brasileiras, S.A. [ELETROBRÁS]. "Entrevistas a que se referem fls. 4, 5 e 6 do 'Relatório do Grupo de Trabalho da ELETROBRÁS.'" File document. Rio de Janeiro: Typewritten, 1961.

——. *Relatório Geral*. 1962–1964.

Centrais Elétricas de Minas Gerais, S.A. [CEMIG]. "A CEMIG e a usina de Estreito no Rio Grande." File document. Processed, January 1963.

——. "Estudo do mercado energético da Companhia Fôrça e Luz de Minas Gerais: Evolução histórica—perspectivas futuras." 2 vols. Belo Horizonte: Mimeographed, 1964.

——. *Relatório Anual de 1964*.

——. "Survey of Tendencies of the Electric Power Market in the South-central Region of the State of Minas Gerais." File document. Mimeographed, May 1957.

Centrais Elétricas de Urubupungá, S. A. [CELUSA]. "O que é a CELUSA." Public relations brochure.

Central Elétrica de Furnas, S.A. "Plano de desenvolvimento do Rio Grande; segundo estágio: Projeto de Estreito, sistema de transmissão, Furnas unidades 7 & 8." File document. Processed, August 1962.

————. "Power Development of the Rio Grande." File document. Processed, August 1962.

————. *Relatório da Diretoria.* 1960–1964.

————. "A usina de Furnas." Public relations brochure.

Companhia Hidrelétrica do Vale do Paraíba, S. A. [CHEVAP]. *Relatório de 1963.*

International Engineering Company, Inc. "Cia. Auxiliar de Emprêsas Elétricas Brasileiras: Report on the Expansion of Eleven Power Distribution Systems in Brazil." Rio de Janeiro: Processed, 1965.

————. "São Paulo Light, Rio Light; Transmission and Distribution Expansion, 1965–1970—Economic and Technical Soundness Analysis." Rio de Janeiro: Processed, 1965.

Books

Ackerman, Adolph J. [*Asa W.*] *Billings and Water Power in Brazil.* Madison, Wisconsin: by the author and The American Society of Civil Engineers, 1953.

Bonbright, James C. *Principles of Public Utility Rates.* New York: Columbia University Press, 1961.

Cardoso, Fernando Henrique. *Empresário industrial e desenvolvimento econômico.* São Paulo: Difusão Européia do Livro, 1963.

Cavers, David F., and James R. Nelson. *Electric Power Regulation in Latin America.* Baltimore: Johns Hopkins Press, 1959.

Fishlow, Albert. *American Railroads and the Transformation of the Antebellum Economy.* Cambridge: Harvard University Press, 1965.

Furtado, Celso. *Desenvolvimento e subdesenvolvimento.* Rio de Janeiro: Fundo de Cultura, 1961.

Hart, Henry C. *Administrative Aspects of River Valley Development.* Bombay, New York: Asia Publishing House, 1961.

Hirschman, Albert O. *Development Projects Observed.* Washington, D.C.: Brookings Institution, 1967.

————. *The Strategy of Economic Development.* New Haven: Yale University Press, 1958.

Ransmeier, Joseph Sirera. *The Tennessee Valley Authority: A Case Study in the Economics of Multiple Purpose Stream Planning.* Nashville: Vanderbilt University Press, 1942.

Richers, Bouzan, Machline, Carvalho, Bariani. *Impacto da ação do govêrno sôbre as emprêsas brasileiras.* Rio de Janeiro: Fundação Getúlio Vargas, 1963.

Robock, Stefan H. *Nuclear Power and Economic Development in Brazil.* Washington, D.C.: National Planning Association, 1957.

United Nations. Economic Commission for Latin America. *Energy Development in Latin America.* E/CN.12/384/Rev.1. Geneva, 1957.

World Power Conference. *Survey of Energy Resources, 1962.* London: The Central Office, World Power Conference, 1962.

Articles

Andrade, Henrique. "A atual crise de energia em São Paulo," *Engenharia* (São Paulo), 11: 1–13 (April 1953).

"A barragem de Três Marias assinala um programa do govêrno," *Eletricidade* (Lisbon), July-September 1960, pp. 259–260.

Brasil. Conselho Nacional de Águas e Energia Elétrica [CNAEE]. *Águas e Energia Elétrica* (Rio de Janeiro), 1949–1964.

"O Brasil não pode parar: Furnas," *Manchete* (Rio de Janeiro), April 12, 1960.

Centrais Elétricas Brasileiras, S.A. [ELETROBRÁS]. *Revista Brasileira de Energia Elétrica* (Rio de Janeiro), 1963–1965.

Clube de Engenharia. *Revista do Clube de Engenharia* (Rio de Janeiro), 1950–1964.

Correio da Manhã (Rio de Janeiro), 1957–1964.

Cotrim, John. "O problema da energia elétrica no Brasil," *Revista do Conselho Nacional de Economia* (Rio de Janeiro), 9:99–116 (May-June 1960).

———. "Solução para um problema crucial," *O Observador Econômico e Financeiro* (Rio de Janeiro), 20:78–88 (October 1955).

Diário de Notícias (Rio de Janeiro), 1957-1964.

Dias Leite, Antônio. "Problema financeiro dos serviços de eletricidade da Guanabara." File document of the Federação das Indústrias do Estado da Guanabara. Mimeographed, November 1962.

"Fifteen Years of Economic Policy in Brazil," *Economic Bulletin for Latin America*, 9:153–214 (November 1964).

Fundação Getúlio Vargas. *Conjuntura Econômica* (Rio de Janeiro), 1952–1966.

————. *Revista Brasileira de Economia* (Rio de Janeiro). 1962–1965.

"Furnas: Ação substituiu palavras," *O Cruzeiro* (Rio de Janeiro), April 16, 1960.

O Globo (Rio de Janeiro), 1957–1964.

O Jornal (Rio de Janeiro), 1957–1964.

Jornal Carioca (Rio de Janeiro), 1957–1964.

Jornal do Brasil (Rio de Janeiro), 1957–1965.

Jornal do Comércio (Rio de Janeiro), 1957–1964.

Lindblom, Charles E. "Decision-making in Taxation and Expenditure," in *Public Finances: Needs, Sources, and Utilization*. A Conference of the Universities-National Bureau Committee for Economic Research. Princeton: Princeton University Press, 1961. Pp. 295–336.

Lopes, Lucas. "Electric Energy in Brazil," in Joint Brazil-U.S. Economic Development Commission, *Brazilian Technical Studies*. Washington, D.C.: Institute of Inter-American Affairs, 1954. Pp. 273–308.

Meek, Ronald L. "The Allocation of Expenditures in the Electricity Supply Industry: Some Methodological Problems," in *Public Expenditure: Appraisal and Control*. Edited by Alan T. Peacock and D. J. Robertson. Edinburgh and London: Oliver & Boyd, 1963. Chapter II.

"Portions of F.P.C. Report on Northeastern Blackout Nov. 9," *New York Times*, December 7, 1965.

Simonsen, Mário Henrique. "Tensões em países subdesenvolvidos: O papel da economia nos setores público e privado e as tensões surgidas da administração de uma economia mista," *Desenvolvimento e Conjuntura* (Rio de Janeiro, October 1962).

Tendler, Judith D. "Technology and Economic Development: The Case of Hydro vs. Thermal Power," *Political Science Quarterly*, 80:236–253 (June 1965).

Tribuna da Imprensa (Rio de Janeiro), 1957–1964.

Última Hora (Rio de Janeiro), 1957–1964.

Wionczek, Miguel S. "Electric Power: The Uneasy Partnership," in *Public Policy and Private Enterprise in Mexico.* Edited by Raymond Vernon. Cambridge: Harvard University Press, 1964. Pp. 19–110.

Interviews

The author interviewed sixty persons. Because of the frequently political nature of the questions discussed, the names of those interviewed are not cited. Written sources are used as evidence wherever possible. Interviews were conducted with current or ex-officials of the Banco Nacional de Desenvolvimento Econômico, the Ministério das Minas e Energia, the Conselho Nacional de Águas e Energia Elétrica, the Comissão Nacional de Energia Nuclear, the Missão Brasileira Junto às Nações Unidas, and the Departamento de Águas e Energia Elétrica of the state of São Paulo; the Brazilian Traction, Light and Power Company, ELETROBRÁS, Furnas, CHEVAP, CHERP, USELPA, CELUSA, CEMIG, and AMFORP; the World Bank, CANAMBRA, the Inter-American Development Bank, the International Engineering Company, and the U.S. Agency for International Development.

Index

Abbink Mission, 14n, 43, 45
Abbink Report, 45
Accommodation: additionals, 46; foreign exchange, 71
Accounts collection, 182
Ackerman, Adolph A., 106n
Additionals, 46, 50, 69–70; foreign exchange, 51; foreign exchange cost increase compensated, 65; purchased power cost increase compensated, 66; codified, 70; consumer nonacceptance, 76; and foreign exchange accommodations, 76–79
AID, 39, 89, 91, 95n, 142, 180, 223–225; urges generating industry to contract work, 180–181; notes weak financial management in generation, 183
ALCOMINAS, 120n
Aluminum industry, 119
American and Foreign Power Company. See AMFORP
AMFORP, 26, 110, 112, 120; Goulart and Kennedy, 85–86; overloading and neglect, 86–87; and purchase of foreign utility company, 87; resistance to Furnas, 198
Anhanguera Station, 214
Aparecida, 33
Aswan Dam, 126

Banco Nacional de Desenvolvimento Econômico. See National Development Bank
Bariri Plant, 35
Barra Bonita Plant, 35

Barros, Adhemar de, 147
Basic rate: increase politically difficult to solve expansion in power sector, 46; no procedure for increase of, 48; increase in 1955–1956, 76
Belo Horizonte, 37, 110; power shortage, 228
Bhering, Mário, 29n, 175n
BNDE, 60, 62, 74, 127, 142, 215–218; seeks equity participation to escape effects of inflation, 57; Light equity participation, 216
Bonright, James C., 68n
Brasília, 108
Brazilian Traction, Light and Power Company. See Light
Brazil-United States Technical Commission, 14
Brevity of construction period, 88–90

CANAMBRA, 21, 25, 40–42, 114, 240; generation overexpansion, 211–212
CANAMBRA Engineering Consultants, Ltd., 7n, 41
Capacity, installed, 1948–1965, 12–13; economic growth and, 17
Capital expenditure and net revenue, Light, 47
Caraguatatuba Plant, 113–114, 117
Castelo Branco, Humberto, 204n
CEEE, 17n
CELUSA, 35–36, 110, 115, 126
CEMIG, 36–37, 110, 118, 120–122, 175–176, 179–181, 188; generation and distribution, 27,